A PRAGMATIST RECONSTRUCTION

HABITS OF WHITENESS

TERRANCE MACMULLAN

Indiana University Press
Bloomington & Indianapolis

This book is a publication of

Indiana University Press
601 North Morton Street
Bloomington, IN 47404-3797 USA

http://iupress.indiana.edu

Telephone orders	800-842-6796
Fax orders	812-855-7931
Orders by e-mail	iuporder@indiana.edu

The paper used in this publication meets the minimum requirements of American National Standard for Information Sciences—Permanence of Paper for Printed Library Materials, ANSI Z39.48-1984.

Manufactured in the United States of America

Library of Congress Cataloging-in-Publication Data

MacMullan, Terrance.
  Habits of whiteness : a pragmatist reconstruction / Terrance MacMullan.
     p. cm.— (American philosophy)
  Includes bibliographical references and index.
  ISBN 978-0-253-31813-8 (cloth : alk. paper) — ISBN 978-0-253-22071-4 (pbk. : alk. paper)
  1. Whites—Race identity—United States—History. 2. Race awareness—United States—History.
I. Title.
  E184.A1M146 2009
  305.800973—dc22

                    2008050145

                              1 2 3 4 5 14 13 12 11 10 09

For Becca, Sylvia, and Liam

Contents

Acknowledgments

While the shortcomings in this work are mine, whatever insights it might hold grow from conversations I've held with people far wiser than myself. I would like to offer them my thanks.

The people at the University of Oregon deserve my deep appreciation for letting me be part of such a genuine scholarly community. I thank my fellow Oregon grads, especially Alex Stotts, Kim Garchar, John Shuford, Maurice Hamington, Greg Johnson, Don Morse, Ken Pendleton, and Lorraine Brundige. I owe great thanks to my professors, including Nancy Tuana, Mark Johnson, John Lysaker, Cheney Ryan, and Naomi Zack. My friend and mentor Scott Pratt has my eternal gratitude for showing me such patience and respect and making possible my life as an academic.

This work would have been impossible without the Society for the Advancement of American Philosophy, whose members exemplify the very best of the pragmatist spirit. I extend my thanks to all the people who make SAAP such a welcoming environment, and especially to Paul Taylor, Eddie Glaude, Judith Green, Shannon Sullivan, Colin Koopman, Lee McBride, Erin McKenna, Leonard Harris, Michael Sullivan, and David McClean.

Good fortune brought me to Eastern Washington University, where I befriended many people who've helped immensely with this work. I thank my students for indulging my idiosyncrasies and offer special thanks and encouragement to Caleb Woodrow, Jeff Ewing, Richard Devenport, Chris Phipps,

Rommel Watson, Jordan Biltof, Natasha Vanderlinden, and Evan Buelt. I thank my wonderful colleagues at Eastern, including Tracy McHenry, Dana Elder, Scott Finnie, Wayne Kraft, Steve Scott, Garry Kenney, Nancy Nelson, Lynn Briggs, Gary Krug, and Pam Schierman. I thank Ruth Galm at the Office of Grant and Research Development and Helen Bergland from the Teaching and Learning Center for their help in securing vital research grants. Most of all, I acknowledge the love and support I've received from two outstanding people: Mimi Marinucci, whose trust in me made real my dream of being a teacher, and Kevin Decker, whose humor, intelligence, and passion embody the ideal of the Deweyan public intellectual.

Two dear friends, Leif Solem and Basem Aly, receive my thanks for reading and improving early drafts of this work. I had the pleasure of working with many great professionals at Indiana University Press. I offer great thanks to Dee Mortensen and John Stuhr for their patient advice at every step of the process. I also thank Carol Kennedy for her attentive and insightful copyediting.

Everything good in my life rests on my family's love and support. I thank my parents, Ed and Joan, for their constant love and confidence. I thank Ed, Heather, Lissa, Gary, Peter, Gail, Sue, and Michael, my brothers, sisters, and their spouses, for their generosity and care. Most of all I thank the love of my life, Becca, for her patience, affection, and inspiration. Finally, I thank my two wonderful children, Sylvia and Liam, for reminding me that love is the most important gift in life.

Some passages in this book were published previously. Brief passages scattered across many chapters (4, 5, 6, 8, 9, 10, and the conclusion) were previously published in "Is There a White Gift?: Pragmatist Responses to the Problem of Whiteness," *Transactions of the Charles S. Peirce Society* 41, no. 4 (2005). Also, much of my discussion on contemporary debates on whiteness in chapter 7 was previously published in "Beyond the Pale: A Pragmatist Approach to Whiteness Studies," *Philosophy and Social Criticism* 31, no. 3 (2005).

Habits of Whiteness

Introduction
"¡¿Que Haces Gringuito?!"

Race remains a divisive issue in the United States, and racism still festers as a poorly understood problem. However, an array of signs indicates that we live in a moment of special opportunity during which we might yet grow true communities and heal the wounds of racism. The maturation of a generation of thinkers born after the civil rights movement, the success of dynamic political leaders of color such as President Barack Obama at rallying multiracial citizen-coalitions, widespread disaffection with self-interested and mercenary notions of citizenship and identity, and the ebbing of white demographic majority all hearten us to finally realize the long-deferred promise of healing and community.

This work contends that our problems concerning race still deny us fully fair and democratic communities largely because of the failure of white people—that is, people like me who live and are seen as white—to recognize, understand, and reconstruct our habits of race. While I am mindful of critics who are concerned that discussions about whiteness might themselves perpetuate the privileging of white experiences and points of view, I argue that we have more to gain in terms of racial healing by having white folk in this country talk and think seriously about race than by continuing the status quo, where white folk by and large studiously ignore the subject.

My ultimate hope is that white folk, through the reconstruction of our racial habits, might help achieve the kinds of just, healthy, and diverse communities that the great majority of us, of all ethnic and racial backgrounds, want. However, we can't get there by pretending that we are somehow "post-race" or that the civil rights movement washed away once and for all the miasma of racism. For example, a recent poll showed that race still powerfully influences how we see the world and our progress toward a racially fair state of affairs:

> Nearly 60 percent of black respondents said race relations were generally bad, compared with 34 percent of whites. Four in 10 blacks say that there has been no progress in recent years in eliminating racial discrimination; fewer than 2 in 10 whites say the same thing. And about one-quarter of white respondents said they thought that too much had been made of racial barriers facing black people, while one-half of black respondents said not enough had been made of racial impediments faced by blacks.[1]

We can renew our democratic community only when we work through and not around the particular histories and situations that condition our individual lived experiences. In this book I will offer an analysis of how our particular and inherited ideas and habits regarding race have impoverished our society. It is a work that rests on the shoulders of many better thinkers. For example, this book hopes for the savvier, more pluralistic version of the Deweyan Great Community that Eddie Glaude Jr. describes in his visionary work *In a Shade of Blue:* "I argue for a conception of a great community colored a deep shade of blue, a view of community and democracy that takes seriously the complexity of racialized experiences in the United States and instantiates new forms of communication aimed at producing democratic dispositions capable of addressing the challenges of our current moment."[2] One of my premises is that many white folks won't be on board with a deep blue analysis of American democracy because they fail to see the extent to which unnoticed habits (which I call habits of whiteness) condition their actions in ways that perpetuate long-established systems of racism and prevent them from being the sorts of friends, neighbors, and citizens they ought and generally want to be. This is why I share Glaude's commitment to taking race seriously and worry about using colorblindness as a solution to our racial problems. I worry that we might well get people to stop using race talk without affecting in the slightest the more subtle and habituated features of racism that still adversely affect the lives of millions of people and deny us all the fruits of true community. Further, I will argue that these habits of whiteness also perpetuate a cultural numbness or emptiness that prevents white people from enjoying the rich and meaningful cultural experiences all people need.

This book analyzes the current problems of racial whiteness through a pragmatist analysis drawn primarily from the works of two of the greatest American intellectuals of the twentieth century: John Dewey and W. E. B. Du Bois. It argues that the intractability of current philosophical and political arguments regarding race stems largely from misunderstandings about the nature of race and racism that can best be clarified through pragmatist models of inquiry and habit. This work is also driven by a sense of urgency; although scholarship of race is a crucial tool for solving the problem of racism, the problem itself is hardly just academic. My hope is that we can extend these thoughtful conversations about whiteness and race beyond academic circles to engage the broadest possible audience in order to foster community-based solutions to these long-standing problems before the problems of racism become even more acute and violent. Many white Americans still zealously defend their racial privileges, and the ugly resurgence of nativism in the twenty-first century portends that many white Americans will defend their privileges in even more disturbing and violent ways as we pass inevitably from a majority group to a plurality and ultimately a minority in the next half century.[3] I agree, therefore, with Ian Haney López, a foremost scholar on the relationship between racial identity, law, and violence, when he counsels that the immanent demographic decline of whites in America is cause for both hope and concern because "the declining percentage of whites in America imperils continued white dominance. This may sound like good news to those otherwise dedicated to ending racial hierarchy. But for those comfortable with the status quo, and to those who recognize that change often brings conflict, there's cause to worry."[4] I worry too that we, as a nation, are in danger of sliding back to a very ugly place in terms of race unless more of the intellectuals who work on race fully engage the broader public to reasonably discuss and resolve our problems. I am also hopeful because I think that many of our problems regarding race are not rooted in conscious racial hatred, but in unexamined behaviors and impulses that lead people to say and do things that are at odds with the ideals of equality and humanity that almost all people hold.

Another premise of this work is that practices, habits, and assumptions that stem from the concept of whiteness as a superior and pure group within the human family still survive. These holdovers from our long era of legalized white supremacism in America continue to degrade the experiences of people of color and deny us all the full promise of a truly democratic community. Most white folks nowadays readily, and I think honestly, condemn the *idea* of white supremacism; we tell ourselves that it is a long-gone relic of the past that is currently espoused only by fringe groups such as the neo-Nazis and skinheads. If we are not from there, we might point to the South and say that white folks *there* are the only laggards on this point. I argue instead that, contrary to this comforting bromide, white supremacism (like sexism, homophobia, and ableism) still operates in the mainstream and influences the behaviors of even the most well-meaning people, from every region, whether liberal, moderate, or conservative. This disconnect between ideas and habits not only is disturbing on its own terms, but should also elicit concern for what it signifies about our ability to address and solve real problems as a public body. It is a sign, as Dewey might say, that we need a new public using new language to imaginatively and intelligently address a problem that does not fit old solutions or old language.

As I said before, I think there is cause for cautious hope that the time is right for a new public to redefine the way we talk about and handle race. At a crucial point in his campaign to win the Democratic nomination for president, Senator Barack Obama gave an address on race. He used the address, in part, to counter-spin controversial comments by Rev. Jeremiah Wright Jr. that had been placed on an endless loop on cable news. The mainstream press framed the speech largely as a mere political move: an attempt to staunch the bleeding caused by the comments of Senator Obama's longtime pastor. Most commentators sadly missed the fact that this speech was a bellwether moment in the history of presidential campaign rhetoric about race, which before this speech consisted almost entirely of carefully calibrated platitudes designed to comfort the listener. Instead of playing it safe by denouncing Rev. Wright as a crank, reassuring the white majority that we don't have problems with race anymore, and saying something like "I don't even *see* race," Senator Obama paid his audience the compliment of speaking about race in a nuanced way that acknowledged both the reality of racism and the progress we've made against it. It was a speech for which he knew he would have to pay a political price. I mention this speech here because he spoke of why he was able to disagree with what Rev. Wright said and did without disowning him or loving him less. At a crucial moment he used an apt example that highlights the complicated role of habits in our racial politics.

> I can no more disown him than I can disown the black community. I can no more disown him than I can my white grandmother—a woman who helped raise me, a woman who sacrificed again and again for me, a woman who loves me as much as she loves anything in this world, but a woman who once confessed her fear of black men who passed by her on the street, and who on more than one occasion has uttered racial or ethnic stereotypes that made me cringe. These people are a part of me. And they are a part of America, this country that I love.[5]

The distance that Senator Obama sees between his grandmother's love for him on the one hand and her fear of black men and her willingness to make racist comments on the other is the distance that I see between the *conscious* good intentions and desire for justice that I think the overwhelming majority of white people hold in their hearts and the *unconscious habits* that are bred into to the bones of these very same people, that lead many of them to do and say things that are at loggerheads with their commitment to principles of justice and fairness. She is not *"a racist"* for having a fear of black men, nor is she off the hook in terms of racism simply by having a mixed-race grandson. She is *both* loving kin to people of color *and* a vessel for racist habits. Senator Obama made it clear that his grandmother loves him so much that she would gladly walk through fire for him, but at the same time would rather not walk on the same side of the street as a man who looked just like him. I think he used this example because just about every white person has relatives that they know are good and loving people who nonetheless have some pretty old and even ugly habits regarding race. Maybe he was hoping we'd go the next step and see that it is not just our grandparents and parents who fit that bill; maybe he was hoping we'd each see ourselves, no matter how many friends of color we might have, as being like his grandmother to a certain extent. This book is an attempt to engage the habits that are the root of this incongruity and reconstruct them with imagination and intelligence into new ones that will foster community.

To be clear, even though I had an unusual upbringing for a white kid from New Jersey and have spent many years consciously studying the subject, I believe I am myself very much still the vessel for habits of thought and action that are racist. But this book is not about chest beating, liberal guilt, or utterly counterproductive self-hatred. Indeed, I will argue in chapters 9 and 10 that white, liberal guilt is actually one of these problematic habits we need to reconstruct. This work is my attempt to use the tools drawn from pragmatist philosophy to find a constructive way of handling a very real and slippery problem. I think that the best way I can both show that whiteness continues to degrade our communities *and* to actually progress toward a solution is to understand our current racial problems through a pragmatist model of habit. More specifically, this book uses John Dewey's conceptions of inquiry and habit and W. E. B. Du Bois's critiques of whiteness and racial conservationism to develop a pragmatist model that describes race generally and whiteness specifically as habits. Using a pragmatist conception of categories and habits, this work frames whiteness as an interactive phenomenon over which white Americans have a great amount of control, and argues that white Americans have an obligation to identify and uproot habits of whiteness. Finally, it opens the possibility that people who currently identify as white might develop new identities that are more amenable to fostering democratic community than the idea of whiteness and more compatible within America's increasingly multicultural composition.

A pragmatist understanding of race as a set of interrelated habits facilitates the kind of honest and constructive discussions about the problems of racism that might, I hope, avoid the quagmire of pointless and recriminating accusations about good or bad intentions regarding race. For many white people, a racist is just a person who burns crosses or hurls racist epithets. When we say, "I'm not a racist," it usually buttressed with other statements like, "I have black friends" or "I voted for Barack."[6] I think that many white folk are quick to decry racism so that we can then get onto saying something to the effect of "I don't really see race." I will argue here that while we must obviously treat all human beings as having equal worth and dignity, it is not the case that a commitment to human dignity and worth requires me to ignore people's particular situations in terms of race, gender, class, age, sexuality, or health. Indeed, acting as if we can ignore each other's particular situations is often counterproductive to the task of achieving universal fairness and dignity. I think this is what Cornel West means when he says that "[a] color-blind society is a false hope."[7] While dangerous and *overtly* white-supremacist movements such as Christian Identity, neo-Nazism, and the Ku Klux Klan still exist and need to be swept into the dustbin of history, I argue that the problem of white racism is not located primarily with people who *consciously* discriminate against other people or *explicitly* argue in favor of white supremacism. Using the works of Du Bois, Dewey, and contemporary race theorists, I argue that racism, like many other complex behavior patterns, goes deeper than our intentional mind into the realm of habit. While I have great respect for the many theorists who argue that we should ultimately strive for a post-race society, I worry that holding up such a colorblind ideal will both undermine our ability to address the bulk of the problem and deny us the gifts of race.

To point to a simple and more comfortable example, think of the distance between the intentions and habits of a person who is trying to lose weight. A dieter can have the best of all intentions when it comes to health and eating; these intentions are completely besides the point, however, if the person caps off each day of careful calorie counting by absent-mindedly munching snacks before bed. When we reduce the issue of the separation between habits and intentions to a simple example like this, it might seem that no reasonable sane person could have one part of self so unhitched and out of sync with another part. Yet I know I've caught myself, more than once, acting on unhealthy habits that are at odds with my healthy intentions. I'd even be willing to bet that every reader has caught herself or himself in the same kind of disconnect. To move from the snack cupboard back to the issue of racism, I will argue that white folk, by and large, do not notice the extent to which our habits regarding race are at odds, often drastically, with our intentions regarding how we would like to be in terms of race. A pragmatist model of habit is very useful for addressing this problem because it shows that an individual might have the best of all intentions when it comes to race even as he or she acts on learned and inherited habits that originate from our nation's long and brutal era of legalized white supremacism that formally ended only within the last fifty years. Looking at the problem of racism through a pragmatist model of habit acknowledges that most white people speak truthfully when they say, "I have no racist intents and I think of myself as no better or worse than anyone," even as it forces us to see how racist habits continue to direct our actions and thus force us to account for our actions and examine our habits. It shows us that we are not at all in the post-racist society many white folk would like to pretend we are in. We are instead in a precarious limbo. Behind us we see the cruel times before the civil rights movement, when crowds of white Americans would publicly, brazenly, and brutally resist legalized racial equality or even the mere *idea* of racial equality. But we have not yet reached that dreamt-of place and time where racial equality, healing, and community are *lived realities acknowledged by all.* I think that Du Bois, Dewey, and the many other wise folk I mention here can help us make good progress to that place and time, in which I very much want to live and raise my kids.

So I will argue that a pragmatist model of habit gives us a practical method for how to reconstruct these unethical and undesirable racist habits into more felicitous ones that match the non-racist ideals espoused by most people. The other, perhaps more controversial, assumption driving this work is that white people will remain largely hostile or apathetic toward the project of establishing a pluralistic and culturally diverse society until we address the potentially explosive topic of cultural pride among people of European descent. Put simply, I think that in order to fully realize the deep cultural and behavioral transformation that are preconditions to a fully pluralistic democratic community we have to answer the question, "What should white people bring to the multicultural table?" Even as we fully excavate and reconstruct these long-operative habits of white privilege and racism, we need to identify how white people might be able to participate in the Du Boisian exchange of the gifts of race in a non-racist way.

The critical study of race and racism has been a bitter, if sorely needed, tonic for the relatively few liberal and educated whites who've tasted it. Anyone who has taught race issues to white students is familiar with the balking, denial, and recalcitrance this subject elicits from a white audience. This desire to reject the entire topic is hardly limited to white students, and the colorblind response has been adopted so zealously by so many white folk precisely because most of us would rather the whole conversation just die. Again, since we too often frame ethical issues in terms of intent, many white folks say to themselves something like, "Why do I need to hear about white racism when I've never even considered being a skinhead?" This work argues that white people need to get over this negative response to race talk in order to identify and dismantle habituated systems of white privilege. However, it also argues that this first task of seeing and reconstructing the deleterious habits of whiteness will be more successful if white folks also recover the cultural treasures that Du Bois and other contemporary thinkers such as Lucius Outlaw Jr. see as intimately connected to race. Du Bois and his intellectual descendents urge us to build diverse human communities *through* race, not in spite of it. As he famously wrote, "race groups are striving, each in its own way, to develope [*sic*] for civilization its particular message, its particular ideal, which shall help to guide the world nearer and nearer that perfection of human life for which we all long."[8] We need to balance both sides—the need for white folks to see and uproot systems of racism that give them unfair privileges with the need to rediscover and reconnect with meaningful and life-sustaining cultural traditions—in order to effect a meaningful resolution to this problems.

Underneath our uncomfortable and generally unproductive conversations about race in America in the last several decades lies a dormant and unused resource. White folks have convinced themselves to see racial justice for people of color as a net loss for white people. This is why so many politicians ever since the Republican Southern Strategy of the 1960s have been able to score such easy political points by rallying poor and working-class whites to oppose measures such as affirmative action. I will argue that these politicians have it exactly backward: everyone, including white folk, has *much more to gain than to lose* through a full conversation about race and white racism and the reconstruction of our racial habits. Even though Du Bois railed passionately and eloquently against the evils of whiteness, his work on the gifts of race holds great and healing promise for Americans raised as and seen as white. When our ancestors or grandparents adopted the habits of whiteness in order to reap economic and social benefits reserved for white folks they were making a Faustian bargain. They gained worldly wealth and power, but to do so they had to trade away their cultural souls. The first half of the bargain has certainly come to pass: think of the staggering distance between the generally comfortable standard of living enjoyed by most white Americans and the grinding poverty from which most of us descend. Unfortunately, the second part of the bargain has come to pass as well, as seen in our unsustainable and unhappy lifestyles that are oriented far more around tasks and commodities than around life, community, or culture. White folks will stop being impediments to or passive spectators of the journey to true racial healing when they see that every step we take together moves us away from the cultural alienation many of us feel and toward long-lost cultural treasures that are incomparably more precious than gold.

The key to this reconstruction of the habits of whiteness is to analyze the relationship between the habits of whiteness and the impulses behind them. Disagreeing somewhat with the only other book-length treatment of whiteness as habit, Shannon Sullivan's *Revealing Whiteness,* this book advances the claim that these problematic habits *can* be reconstructed into patterns more compatible with diversity and democracy by organizing the impulses beneath them into new habits.[9] This pragmatist reconstruction, which includes a fuller and more charitable account of Dewey's work on habit formation and reconstruction, hopes that people who currently identify as white might develop new identities that are more amenable to fostering democratic community than the idea of whiteness and more compatible within America's increasingly multicultural composition.

While everything in my past in some way or another leads into this book, it mostly emerges from three sets of experiences that led me to philosophize about race and whiteness. The first set of experiences started when my father's work moved me and my parents away from my four siblings in Edison, New Jersey, to Miramar, Puerto Rico, in 1976. I was three years old, and we knew no one in our new community. While the move was originally intended to be a short-term affair, I ultimately lived in Puerto Rico for the next eleven years. Among the uncountable things for which I am indebted to my parents is their decision to *not* put me in Saint John's School, which at the time was the de facto *gringo* school for Anglo-Americans living in Puerto Rico, but instead enroll me in the Catholic parochial school down the block, *Academia del Perpetuo Socorro*, which translates into English as that most Catholic-sounding of all school names, "The Academy of our Lady of Perpetual Succor." There is nothing at all wrong with St. John's: it is a fine and well-regarded school. It's just that at the time it was more or less a stateside, English-speaking school transplanted into San Juan. If I had gone there, I think I would not have had the full experience of Puerto Rican culture I received at Perpetuo.

Despite the lachrymose name, I had a great time at Perpetuo. The teachers and students were very hospitable to the new kid in the small community, and the school was well run. However, this did not change the fact that I was one of only three *anglo* kids in the entire K–12 school, and I was always the only *gringo* in my classroom. Add to this my natural tendency toward geekiness, and I was very much the outsider. Since all my classes were taught in Spanish, I picked up the language fairly quickly. However, we spoke only English at home, so my Spanish was never as good as that of my classmates. More significant, however, was the fact that I was often reminded of the fact that I was the *gringo* of my class, and did not fully belong. One grade-school teacher, the only one who was anything less than wonderful to me, used to enjoy perking the class up by calling on me as "*gringuito*" or mocking my mispronunciations for cheap laughs.

Gringo is a hard, if not impossible, word to translate into English. It is definitely not nice, though. It is not the same thing as "white" in the States; arguably there is no real concept of "white" in Puerto Rico. My friend Hugo, for example, had parents who were from Spain and France; in the States he would be seen as white. Nonetheless, since he was born in Puerto Rico, he was *boricua* (the indigenous people of Puerto Rico were the Taino, and they called the island *Borinquen* and its inhabitants *boricua*). An immigrant to Puerto Rico from, say, Ireland or England would not be called "*gringo*" but instead by their nationality. In my experience with the word, it was just Euro-American, English-speakers from the States who were *gringos* because the concept is rooted more in the history of colonialism than a biological taxonomy of race.

What was more disturbing than being called "*gringo*" by my teacher was the frequent experience of walking around my neighborhood to a friend's house or the *mercado*, only to have an adult stop me and try to help me back to the tourist hotel from which I must have wandered. "Are you lost? Are your parents staying at the Caribe Hilton?" They would look confused and startled when I responded, "*Gracias, pero no estoy perdido. Vivo aquí mismo en Miramar.*" ("Thanks, but I'm not lost. I live right here in Miramar.") For my entire childhood I associated my pale skin, light hair, and European features with being odd and not quite belonging. While I would not learn the word for many years, my *anglo* features and accent alienated me from my surrounding world. This alienation was compounded by the fact that I was alienated *from* something that was indescribably rich and beloved by my friends and neighbors: the culture of the Puerto Rican people. This is why I would never say I was a victim of racism (though, to be sure, the fact that the school-yard bullies targeted me before all others was pretty overwhelming). To be immersed in *lo puertorriqueño* was a joy I can still scarcely put into words. It is something I would have missed if I had just known the tourist Puerto Rico.

Our literature classes covered not only the classics of the Spanish literature, but also masterpieces by writers such as Alejandro Tapia y Rivera and Julia de Burgos drawn from Puerto Rico's own five-hundred-year-old literary tradition. Our social studies classes covered the works of liberatory thinkers such as the great "Citizen of the Americas," Eugenio María de Hostos. We all loved playing instruments in the *aguinaldo* Masses celebrated at dawn in the days leading up to Christmas. Our music classes involved traditional Caribbean songs and dances at a level of performance that frankly blew away that of later classes I had in high school. If you didn't know the difference between Dominican *merengue* and Cuban *salsa* by the time you were in third grade, you were in *trouble!* My music teacher's favorites were the *danzas* of Juan Morel Campos, especially his infectious *"Felices Días."* We took field trips to visit the Art Museum of Ponce where we saw *El Velorio,* a classic paining by Francisco Oller depicting in riotous color a toddler's wake (*velorio*) in the humble home of a peasant, or *jíbaro*. I'll never forget seeing tears well up in my teacher's eyes as she talked about the work since it was my first encounter with the transformative power of art. The hands-down favorite, though, was when we would go to Old San Juan to visit four-hundred-year-old forts like El Morro, which bore the scars of victorious stands against warships from every European empire. From a very early age I was deeply affected by the beauty of Puerto Rican culture, but saddened that I was always one step removed. I did not fully understand these experiences until many years later when I read the opening chapter of *The Souls of Black Folk,* where Du Bois recounted looking at the white world through a veil. However, I was looking not at the white world, but at Borinquen, through a veil.

This all changed when I was fourteen and my parents sent me to Georgetown Preparatory School in Rockville, Maryland, where I had the second set of experiences that motivate my interest in race and whiteness. Again, I was very fortunate and privileged to attend a great school staffed with excellent educators. However, it was only during my first year in the continental U.S. that my experiences in Puerto Rico came into resolution. When I left the campus to walk around Rockville or to take the Metro to D.C., I became socially invisible for the first time in my life. It was a profoundly weird experience to walk around without people looking at me. No one stared at me because I looked like a *gringo* from the Hilton who was for some reason walking along Avenida Miramar. No one tried to shepherd me back to the beach resort or singled me out because I was not one of them. I blended in with all the white people on the Metro going in to the city for work. In even ethnically diverse communities of Maryland, my whiteness became my ticket to privileged access to any place I chose to investigate. While I learned that this sort of invisibility was the norm for most white Americans, it felt very odd to me for a long time.

The difference between these two sets of experiences was most stark when I thought about the different treatment I received in each place when I engaged in typical adolescent mischief. In my final months in Puerto Rico, I wandered away from a party with a few friends, all of them Puerto Rican. We alleviated our boredom by doodling with our fingers in the grime of an unwashed car. After less than a minute, the owner of the car came charging out of his house brandishing a broom; he must have thought we were trying to steal his car or his radio. What I'll never forget was that he was shouting "¡¿Que haces gringuito?!" ("What are you doing, little gringo?!") Even though there were four of us, he homed in on me and ignored my fellow graffitists. I ran down the block and dove into some bushes while my friends rounded a corner and nonchalantly came back a few minutes later as if nothing had happened. He was still yelling at me to come out, pacing up and down the street, while my accomplices walked right past him on the sidewalk. The man took no notice of them.

A few years later in Rockville, a few friends and I (all of us white) were looking to alleviate the boredom of suburbia on a Saturday night, so we paid a couple of college students to buy us a case of cheap beer. We took it to a parking garage that was closed for repairs, and began swilling our cut-rate brew. We were not there for more than a few minutes when a cop pulled into the parking lot, shined his floodlight on us, and ordered us to onto the ground. We, of course, ran like hell. Most of us got out of his line of sight quickly, but he spotted one of my friends and chased him as he ran onto our campus. We each snuck back into our rooms by well-rehearsed routes, covered our breath with mouthwash, and snuck back to the top of the stairs to see if we'd made a clean getaway.

Down in the foyer, we could hear the cop talking to the priest who was the prefect on duty. The officer was telling our prefect that he saw four kids drinking in a garage and he spotted one of them running back to our campus. The Jesuit in charge of the dorms that night immediately took a stern tone with the officer and dismissed his concerns, saying that no "Prep-man" would do such a thing and that the culprits were most likely from another school and were probably hiding on our campus. He said something to the effect of "Why don't you do your job and find those trespassers and stop harassing my boys?" The police officer patiently assured the prefect that one of them entered the dorm and that he would like to talk to the students in the dorm. The prefect at that point told the officer he needed to leave the campus. I will never forget the bewilderment I felt as I watched an elderly priest grab a police officer by the elbow and lead him out the door, all the while chastising him like *he* was the errant child. Our whiteness, along with our class, functioned literally like a shield that protected us from the consequences of our actions. Even then I felt deeply ambivalent; I was relieved that we were not going to get caught and I would not face expulsion, but felt disturbed by the event and complicit in a lie, even though I hadn't said a word.

In addition to living whiteness as a privilege instead of as a marker of difference, the other thing that struck me about life in Maryland was that I missed the culture that nurtured me for eleven years. I'll never forget the look of total bafflement I put on a priest's face when I asked him where the percussion instruments were kept in the chapel. I myself was stunned when I learned that we were supposed to *sit* during music class, that it was *not* okay to dance while we sang as all normal people did, and that no one sang *bomba* or danced *salsa* or even knew what the heck a *güiro* was. In Puerto Rico boys and girls would dance close, cheek to cheek, starting in the third grade: at my first high-school mixer I almost got slapped when I went to put my arm around my first dance partner's waist. No one told me you were supposed to pretend your dance partner was emitting a dangerous level of radiation by keeping your torso as far away as possible, with your arms rigidly extended.

Since it was a Jesuit school, we received a very strenuous and excellent education in the classics, theology, and literature of the Western Canon. Most of our teachers were excellent and many of the classes were great (including junior-year music). Most rewarding was the fact that every educator reinforced the need to work for social justice as summarized by the motto *unum utraque,* or "be one for others." However, the material still felt very distant me. It was nothing like the intimacy I felt reading Julia de Burgos's poem "*El Rio Grande de Loíza*" while actually *sitting* on the banks of the Loíza River during one field trip, or the excitement of hearing my teacher read aloud María Bibiana Benítez's poem about the valiant defense of the island against seventeenth century Dutch invaders—"*La Cruz del Morro*"—while she pointed out over the bay to show exactly where the battle took place! No one handed out pieces of *lechón* (traditional pit-roasted pig) from the barbeque pits in front of their apartment buildings, and the entire town did not turn out for an all-night, candlelit musical procession involving a huge and majestic statue of *La Virgen* (the Virgin Mary) around the town before Easter. While I learned that I would never get in trouble unless I was very stupid and got caught red-handed, it seemed a pretty poor trade-off for losing contact with an amazingly vibrant and living culture.

Only much later did I discover the deep pockets of marvelous cultural traditions in Maryland. However, to find them I had to look past the ubiquitous strip malls, homogeneous corporate eateries, and gated communities that flanked the major roads and Metro stops. I probably would have wasted a lot less time getting buzzed like many American teenagers if I had know about, for example, the jousting competitions that have been held in Maryland for over three hundred years and are the state's official sport or the annual rituals of communities around the Chesapeake Bay that stem from their fishing, crabbing, and clamming traditions. This is all to say nothing of the macabre festivals and creepy remembrances for Edgar Allen Poe that happen in Baltimore every year! This cultural vacuity that I, like most teenagers, felt at the time was exacerbated most by the fact that I lived in a school far from any family members, which left me with no connection to the family traditions and histories that I now hold dear. Reflecting back on this period makes another part of Du Bois's work resonate very deeply for me, namely his emphasis on the fact that races, as he calls them, contain within themselves gifts of culture that we must nurture and share in order to live happy and fulfilled lives. In Puerto Rico, I had a very palpable and keen feeling of these gifts. In Maryland and in my later life, I had little sense of what these gifts might be for me. I argue that one key to finding alternatives to whiteness is for white people to look past the often false and nostalgic histories with which we are presented to recover more complex, often painful, histories that not only give us access to these cultural gifts, but also concretize the reality of white racism in ways that help us see white privilege and racism now. In my case, the search to recover these cultural gifts led me to explore the turbulent, troubling, and uplifting histories of my Irish, Italian, and German forebearers, which help me see not only how hard they had to work for me to have my currently privileged life, but also how their ascent to the middle class was made possible only by a system that tipped the field in their favor and denied justice to people of color who had often been here for much longer than my ancestors. It is my continued reconnection to these lost histories that lead me to ally myself now with immigrants, Native peoples, and people of color who face many of the same, and much worse, troubles that my ancestors faced.

The third set of experiences came much later, when I started teaching philosophy at Eastern Washington University in the small rural community of Cheney. I really enjoy teaching at this small state school of around ten thousand students, especially since many of them are first-generation college students and returning or "non-traditional" students. While we are making strides in terms of diversifying the student body and faculty, the majority (about 80%) of the student body is white. Fortunately, our institution has engaged in a vigorous campaign to make Eastern's intellectual and social culture more diverse and hospitable, not just along lines of race and ethnicity, but also gender, age, sexuality, and religious affiliation.

One day during the 2006 spring term, I was writing announcements on the board before a lecture on Du Bois, including one for a campus-wide diversity workshop that I was moderating on behalf of the President's Advisory Committee on Diversity.[10] I wasn't even done writing the announcement when two white students, who are both bright and rambunctious, asked in a very combative tone, "So, do they let white crackers like us come to these meetings?"

I was immediately very angry, but was luckily facing the board so I had time to compose myself. My first reaction was to rebuke them forcefully for what I thought was a very ignorant and inappropriate statement. I instead tried to use it as a teaching moment. I turned to them and said, "Well, I'm moderating the session, and I'm a white Mick, so what do you think?!" After I got a laugh from the class, I asked them, "Do you honestly think that there would be a problem if you went?" They reiterated the canard, woefully common in our country, that these kinds of diversity workshops were about "white male–bashing." One of my students then said something remarkable that crystallized for me a dimension to the problem of whiteness I had been struggling to put into words. She said, "It is just hard as a white person to have to see all this diversity and affirmative action stuff and not feel offended and excluded." I asked them if they could point to a single instance during which any people of color had excluded them, and, after much evasion, they replied that they could not. I asked how she could be excluded when white women are the largest single demographic on the campus and the student body president was also a white woman. I then asked them that if they felt excluded while actually being part of a huge white majority, how might a student of color feel being in an extremely outnumbered minority. They did not answer, but seemed to be thinking about the issue differently.

While these two students came around to a certain point, I needed more time than I had to get them to really start engaging white privilege and racism. Luckily, we have had time to revisit the issue many times in office hours and off campus. It is worth noting that both of these students see themselves as very committed to principles of procedural fairness and justice. Both are straight, but very active in Queer Pride activities on the campus, and each has publicly confronted evangelical ministers who used to come frequently to campus with large banners announcing the sinfulness of homosexuality (along with feminism, socialism, and, for some reason, Catholicism and the I.R.S.). What I learned from them is just how easy it is for white folk, especially ones that live in very homogeneously white communities, to be painfully blind to their own privilege and the realities of race in America. I also got a greater sense of the "town and gown" divide that alienates many poor, rural white communities from universities and higher learning in general.

Later that very same day, I was visited in my office by another white male student from the class, who had looked very attentive and out-of-sorts during the lecture on Du Bois. He said that he wanted to review the lecture with me, especially Du Bois's idea that races, as he defines them, entail a cultural gift. The student said he was fascinated by the idea but that he felt Du Bois was not at all speaking to him as a white person. When I asked him why, the student instead answered with a question. He prefaced his question by saying that he knew he had benefited his whole life from a series of privileges he didn't deserve and that he had no right to complain about anything, and Du Bois had no reason to write to or for him as white: nonetheless, he told me that he felt perennially lost and guilty, and that as far as he could tell, it had something to do with being white. I couldn't help but laugh when he asked, "What is my gift?" When he looked confused and hurt by my reaction, I apologized and explained to him that I had been wrestling with that very question for a long time and that it was at the heart of a book I was working on. In speaking to him I realized that his question and the other student's combative stance were, to use Deweyan language, two different ways of organizing the same impulse. They were all trying to make sense of their feeling of unease regarding what role they, as white people, should play in projects of cultural diversity. They helped me see that in order to eliminate systemic racism and achieve a more fully democratic community we need to address this issue of cultural pride and the need for all people to be active and caring participants in projects of cultural diversity.

One of the main reasons that white people are generally dismissive of or antagonistic toward projects of cultural diversity is that they can't see how they might connect with these projects. White people committed to righting the countless wrongs of white supremacism absolutely must be race traitors in the sense that they must draw attention to the habits of whiteness, resist its privileges, and dismantle systems of oppression.[11] However, while all people who pass for white are white in the sense that they garner certain unjust privileges by virtue of matching a certain phenotype, all people of European descent are also more than, or capable of one day *being* more than, just white. Our justice system says that any person who commits a crime must pay a price to society for their offense and meditate on what they have done. Nonetheless, no one is really rehabilitated until they can move on and find something positive in themselves to share with their community, until they have something to give. White people still have a lot of work to do to fully divest themselves from white privilege, but if we want this sort of liberatory work to extend beyond the currently small group of white people who see white racism as a problem, we need to follow the primary task of uprooting the weeds of racism with the equally important task of sowing the seeds of new crops. Right now we still have a lot more brambles to uproot, but we've little more than barren furrows where we've stopped racism's growth. Without positive alternatives to the habits of whiteness, people who currently live as white won't have access to the cultural gifts that Du Bois and others say must be cultivated and exchanged for the sake of health and peace. Worse yet, the progress we've made won't be sustainable and will likely be lost as economic pressures and demographic changes stoke the embers of racial animosity.

By way of analogy, let me point out how a vocal minority of Christians in America have spent the last twenty years arguing that the only way to be a Christian is to oppose reproductive choice, equal rights for gay people, and social welfare and to support American imperialism, tax breaks for the rich, and corporate control of society.[12] Nonetheless, Christians much more in line with the Gospel's actual message of forgiveness and humility—Christians such as Jimmy Carter and Jim Wallis—have in recent years rejected this corporate and imperialist version of Christianity in favor of a Christianity that fosters humility, charity, and responsible environmental stewardship.[13] In order to fully make white people participants in a fully multicultural society, we need to find a way to work a similar redescription. We need to redefine *pride* for white people just as Christians of conscience have sought to redefine what it means to be a Christian.

Now "White Pride" is about as scary an idea as you can find in American politics and history; it is often used as a rallying cry for the small but growing number of overt white supremacists who yearn for a RaHoWa (Racial Holy War) they hope will come. It stands for the idea that white people need to be proud of an inherent racial superiority and be willing to defend it violently. While I salute the Christians who try to redefine Christianity to be more fully humble and inclusive, the idea of "White Pride" is obviously a morally and intellectually bankrupt idea that is too cruel, divisive, and stupid to warrant rehabilitation or redefinition. One of the things that I hope this work, especially the section on the history of whiteness, will show is that there is simply nothing in or about *whiteness* per se that is worthy of pride. Nonetheless, white people—again people who fit the long-used category of whiteness—need to identify and foster the gifts of race in the Du Boisian sense in order to fill the cultural void now occupied by little more than commercialism. We need to find the cultural resources that all people need to be healthy and happy. We need to find them in our histories and our communities. We need to find cultural gifts about which we can be proud beyond the old and empty pride in whiteness.

While this book strives to be a work of scholarly philosophy, it is more an attempt to resolve these experiences using tools found in pragmatist philosophy. It won't read like a normal philosophy text in that it does not make any pretensions to universal ideas of Truth, Beauty, or Justice. Instead, it is a minor text in the growing and living canon of work that tries to recover philosophy's relevance by addressing the real problems that affect the lives of real people. John Dewey summarized what I am trying to do here when he wrote: "Philosophy recovers itself when it ceases to be a device for dealing with the problems of philosophers and becomes a method, cultivated by philosophers, for dealing with the problems of men."[14] It strives to pose and answer questions about the intersection of race and philosophy that were posed far better by past thinkers like Du Bois and contemporary ones like Lucius Outlaw. I write this book in the hope that, even though I write from a position of class, gender, ableist, and sexual privilege, I might help advance the liberatory struggle Outlaw described in *On Race and Philosophy* when he wrote:

> The struggle of our people continues to be that of seeking progressive liberation at a level capable of being shared by many given the level of development of the cul-

ture as a whole. It is too a continuing struggle for many who are non-black, including many whites. It is, overall, the struggle to harness and direct the capabilities of the society as a whole in the maximum utilization of resources with minimal waste and environmental destruction toward the satisfaction of essential human needs with minimum exploitation and oppression—that is, toward the achievement of forms of life based increasingly on reasonableness democratically envisioned and realized.[15]

It is also a work of philosophy very much in the spirit of Robert Bernasconi in his essay "Waking Up White in Memphis," where he describes (again, far better than I could) how his new experiences as a "white" (in opposed to "English") man in the American South led to a "rebirth of his philosophical life."[16] He goes on to write:

> Insofar as I conceive philosophy as the quest for illumination set off by the experience of something bewildering, addressing my comprehension of my new surroundings gave me a partial resolution of a problem of how to live as a white philosopher in the United States. It was only a partial resolution because I could see for myself that racism was not primarily about individual comments or intentions. That is only an epiphenomenon of the underlying racism, which we try to gesture at with the phrase *institutional racism*. Furthermore, insofar as racism is a system that reproduces itself—through the cycle of poverty, for example—then only a major reorganization of society will address it, not simply a revision of personal attitudes where everything else remains the same. Personal attitudes are not the main source of the problems and they cannot provide the solution.[17]

This work is an attempt to better understand the habits of whiteness that I argue are crucial and misunderstood elements of the institutional racism Bernasconi mentions, and to reach a more complete solution that extends beyond the issue of personal attitudes. It is also an effort to develop a better answer for my future students when they ask, "What is my gift?" and to find a better response when they challenge the legitimacy of work that strives to foster cultural diversity. It is above all an attempt to engage a problem that, while not discussed enough in North American society, cries out for resolution before it violently thrusts itself onto the center of our political stage.

Further, this work has a limited scope: it analyzes the history and workings of whiteness so to suggest a reconstruction of particular problematic habits. Due to this focus, this work will not engage many other important issues involving race and politics that might be of interest to an engaged reader, such as the effect of recent immigration from Africa in revising notions of blackness in America, or calls for a legal recognition of mixed-race identity, or interactions between Latino, black, Asian, and Native communities. By omitting these topics I am not indicating that I think they are unimportant, only that the other topics that I do address are more relevant to a discussion of a pragmatist reconstruction of the habits of whiteness. A better writer might be able to blend all these threads into one cohesive tapestry. I am encouraged by the fact that many such writers are hard at work on texts that address a wider range of considerations about race and politics.

The problem of whiteness, and the best way to correct it, is the focus of this work. By "the problem of whiteness" I mean the practices, habits, and assumptions that impede human flourishing and democracy and that stem from the concept of whiteness as a superior and pure group within the human family. The problem of whiteness has three facets (which will first be explored in part 2 through the work of Du Bois, and then fleshed out further in part 3). The first is white privilege: the special advantages (political, social, psychological, and economic) that people who are perceived as white enjoy over and against people perceived as non-white. The second is prejudice against people of color: the acts of violence and oppression still weathered by people who are not seen as white. The third is cultural vacuity: the cultural loss for many people who identify as white that started when whiteness as a cultural identity supplanted older, more particular cultural identities based on ethnicity and place that offered richer, more life-affirming cultural traditions and practices. These three facets of the problem of whiteness are compounded by what many theorists (whom we will encounter in part 3) term the invisibility of whiteness: the inability of most white folk to perceive the ways in which their whiteness offers them advantages and imposes disadvantages on people of color. However, in this pragmatist analysis, I reframe the invisibility of whiteness as the habitual dimension of whiteness: the aspects of the concept of whiteness that have become so embedded in our thoughts, behaviors, and perceptions that they are no longer apparent, even as they continue to impact behavior.

This work proposes a solution using tools drawn from the works of W. E. B. Du Bois and John Dewey. It is therefore written in the same pragmatist spirit that motivated Bill Lawson and Donald Koch to edit their anthology *Pragmatism and the Problem of Race* and say, "[C]ontemporary pragmatists must ask themselves whether they are content to restate the old ideas of the founders of the movement or use these ideas to work out the reconstruction of pragmatism to deal with contemporary problems and issues."[18] Part 1 offers a selective history of whiteness in North America that dedicates a chapter to each of two uniquely illustrative historical moments in the evolution of whiteness: Bacon's Rebellion of 1675 and the Draft Riots of 1863. This first section advances three claims regarding whiteness. First, it is a social construct that varies over time and place. Second, whiteness nonetheless appears in each age to be a natural kind. Third, whiteness is defined more through the exclusion of those who are defined as non-white than according to a positive definition of whiteness. The features of whiteness revealed in these historical events will guide the inquiry into the current problem of whiteness by giving us a clearer sense of what is problematic about whiteness. These two historically oriented chapters show not only how we can understand the formation of the habits of whiteness using Dewey's model of habit, but also the crucial point that whiteness has always been defined negatively through violence against the people of color.

Part 2 moves the focus of the work away from the topic of whiteness per se in order to present pragmatist resources essential to the critique. Chapter 3 presents the interactionist model of inquiry that Dewey advanced as an alternative to the dominant Western epistemological model, which Dewey called the spectator theory of knowledge. It also examines his claim that inquiry is best understood as a response to a pressing, existential problematic situation. This model of inquiry, which conceives of knowledge as the product of a relationship between knower and known instead of a conception of knowledge as the passive observation of an independent reality, will result in an understanding of whiteness that accepts its social construction, even as it counsels against its outright elimination. The fourth chapter links Dewey's theory of inquiry to his extensive analysis of habit to show how we might reconstruct the habits of whiteness once we understand the mutually reinforcing relationship between concepts, impulses, and habits. This chapter details how a careful application of Dewey's model of habit formation shows that destructive habits such as those of whiteness can neither be ignored nor approached solely through environmental changes, but must be reconstructed by identifying the impulses that motivate the habit and redirecting them into new habits that place the individual in better relationship with their environment. Dewey's model of habit is a particularly apt tool for addressing the problem of white racism because it shifts discussions of race and racial injustice away from particular, intentional acts of racial conflict and toward systemic, habituated patterns of racial thinking and acting that are out of place in a democratic and multicultural society.

The concept of race and critique of whiteness found in the work of W. E. B. Du Bois makes up the subject matter of chapters 5 and 6. Chapter 5 defends a pragmatist reading of Du Bois in light of competing interpretations that place him outside the American tradition. It also shows why race for Du Bois was a phenomenon too complicated to be reduced to a biologically based taxonomy of humanity and too valuable to be eliminated from our lives. A race, as he describes it, is a group of people rooted in a common past and sharing a common disposition toward the future based upon a shared past. While their common past has to do somewhat with shared morphological features, it is culture, not biology, that most defines a race and imbues it with normative weight. This analysis of Du Bois's work pays particular attention to an aspect of his work insufficiently studied in scholarly literature: his use of religious metaphor to explain race and whiteness. It argues that such a deployment, far from being a facile rhetorical ploy, issues from Du Bois's recognition of the fact that since race in America emerged from a Christian context, American racism could be opposed only through a reconstruction of this very same religious language.

The final chapter of part 2 presents Du Bois's crucial distinction between the idea of whiteness, which he sees as a thoroughly flawed category, and white people, who he sees as having a legacy far older and more humane than mere whiteness. This distinction, along with his conception of race, and Dewey's notion of habit, shows us how whiteness is a phenomenon that is both socially real and detrimental, but also habitual and revisable.

Part 3 carries the Deweyan tools and Du Boisian analysis into contemporary philosophical debates on race and whiteness. It makes the case that whiteness has changed since the beginning of the civil rights movement in ways that require us to attend to the apparent normalcy of whiteness. White folk defended their privilege in earlier years through explicit appeals to scientific and religious authorities that treated the white race as superior. However, the civil rights movement effectively salted the earth where such blunt claims took root. Using Dewey's idea of the reciprocal relationship between concept and habit and Du Bois's insight that white privilege exists beneath the notice of most white folks, the first chapter of this section, chapter 7, shows how white privilege still persists because of the nature of habits that escape conscious attention but still impact thought and behavior. Feminist and Native American analyses of race and whiteness support this critique and show how whiteness as a collection of habits still forestalls racial justice, even in a context where the egalitarian message of the civil rights movement is widely extolled.

Chapter 8 surveys the prominent scholarly approaches to whiteness, including various *eliminative* responses that seek to purge race and whiteness altogether, as well as *critical conservationist* responses that try to conserve the idea of race while removing its problematic elements. This survey of scholarly literature on whiteness serves two purposes. First, it orients the pragmatist approach developed here within the range of different perspectives now current in the literature and highlights the differences between my reconstructive approach and Sullivan's psychoanalytic-pragmatist approach. Second, the survey demonstrates the practical value of a pragmatist approach to the problem of whiteness that makes full use of Dewey's work on the interaction between concepts, impulses, and habits.

The fourth and final section proposes a solution to the problem of whiteness by reconstructing current habits of whiteness into ones that are more democratic and pluralistic. It describes the current problem of whiteness as having primarily to do with a set of habits that were established in the eras of legalized white supremacism but still persist today beneath the notice of most white folk. In chapter 9 I lay out a Deweyan approach to the problem of white habit that reconstructs the current problematic habits of whiteness by identifying the underlying impulses and directing them into new habits. This chapter lays out the first step of this reconstruction by identifying the three primary problematic habits of whiteness: *habitual antipathy to what is strange, habits of entitlement, and habits of guilt.* It explains why the problems outlined in chapter 8 stem from these habits and how we might reconstruct them. This conception of habituation is important because it offers a useful framework for actually solving the problem of white racism. Seeing whiteness as a set of habits moves the discussion of racism away from fruitless talk about bad or good intentions and instead establishes a model for understanding racism that holds that the racism can be habitual and live in the deeds of even the most well-intentioned individual. Furthermore, a Deweyan model of habit helps us see how and why the habits of whiteness need to be reconstructed into new habits that are more in line with the spirit of a fair and democratic community.

Chapter 10 shows how we can reconstruct problematic habits of whiteness into patterns more compatible with diversity and democracy by organizing the impulses beneath them into new habits: *habits of compassion, shame, and remembrance.* These new habits emerge from a pragmatist inquiry into the problems of whiteness that takes the "given" impulses at the root of older, problematic habits of whiteness and combines them with new concepts about the meaning of whiteness and race to yield new habits that further the twin goals of identifying and dismantling systems of white racism and recovering and fostering the cultural gifts that were largely forgotten when European Americans adopted habits of whiteness.

I conclude the book by returning to my personal relationship to the habits of whiteness that I discussed earlier in this introduction. Using examples drawn largely from my own family history, I show how these new habits can cause white Americans to better see and therefore dismantle systems of unwarranted white privilege. Further, I show how a pragmatist reconstruction of whiteness leads white people to look before and around whiteness to recover the sorts of cultural gifts that Du Bois and others counsel are necessary for healthy and prosperous interaction in a culturally diverse world. The result is a better understanding of whiteness that reveals both how white people still benefit unjustly from whiteness and a path toward a healthier relationship to history and culture that would encourage white people to participate in instead of oppose projects of cultural diversity.

HISTORY

Bacon's Rebellion and the Advent of Whiteness

Before the White Race

While the many interlocutors engaged in the discussions of whiteness disagree on various points, one thing is clear from all perspectives: the category of whiteness, along with the conceptual and embodied habits it engendered, has dramatically influenced the lives of people living in this part of the world for the last three hundred years.[1] The history of whiteness has been so rewardingly chronicled by such a great number of historians that it would be superfluous to do so again here. Instead, in this part I examine two illustrative moments in this history: Bacon's Rebellion in colonial Virginia in 1676 and the Draft Riots of 1863 that rocked New York City during the Civil War. An examination of these moments and the periods immediately before and after them provides support for three claims that are important for this work as a whole. First, whiteness is a social construct that varies over time and place (and is not a fixed, irreducible feature of human biology). Second, though whiteness changed from age to age, once it emerged as a legal and social category in the eighteenth century, it was treated as a natural kind in each age. Third, whiteness was established largely in a circular or negative fashion rather than through a clear articulation of who is white; its boundaries were defined primarily through the exclusion of those who were defined as non-white in their current age.

Fortunately, the first two theses are relatively uncontroversial now among people who study race and whiteness. David Ingram succinctly summarizes this point: "Race theorists have conclusively demonstrated that racial categories linking the physical, mental, and behavioral traits of selected individuals to a hidden nature putatively shared by them as a group are without scientific basis."[2] However, they still warrant a brief review in order to shore up the third claim, which does not enjoy the same consensus but is central both to an understanding of the habits of whiteness and to their reconstruction. While this chapter will deal in detail with only two moments in the history of whiteness, it is useful to start with a brief chronology of the evolution of whiteness according to three influential histories of the subject: Theodore Allen's *The Invention of the White Race,* Matthew Frye Jacobson's *Whiteness of a Different Color,* and Kathleen Brown's *Good Wives, Nasty Wenches, and Anxious Patriarchs.*[3]

Jacobson organizes the twisting history of whiteness in the United States into three epochs.[4] The first begins in 1790 with the enshrinement of whiteness within U.S. immigration law. The second begins in the 1840s with the massive influx of Catholic, rural Irish immigrants (which led to a widespread questioning of just who should count as white). The third era begins in the 1920s with the rise of the eugenics movement and its attempts to scientifically draw the boundaries of whiteness. I will adopt Jacobson's divisions but will add two additional stages, one on either side of his three. Using Brown's and Allen's excavation of the historical origins of whiteness, I propose that a full understanding of whiteness requires that we examine a preceding age: the era when whiteness emerged as a meaningful category in the Virginia colonies in the wake of Bacon's Rebellion in 1675–76. Since this work strives to address the *contemporary* problem of whiteness, we must also look at the current era as a fifth age of whiteness that began as a response to the civil rights movements of the 1960s.

Many historians of race in America such as Winthrop Jordan, Edmund Morgan, Theodore Allen, Kathleen Brown, and Matthew Jacobson point to Bacon's Rebellion as the one moment that, more than any other, precipitated the advent of whiteness. This moment was a point of no return for the development of the racial system that was to dominate American society for the next three hundred years. Using the most illustrative surviving documents from the era—the laws and records of the House of Burgesses of Colonial Virginia—we can chart these laws chronologically and look at how they changed immediately after the rebellion. In so doing, we reiterate how whiteness is socially constructed (which is ground very well covered), but more importantly see how white privilege and identity gained their social value predominantly through the *privation and degradation* of people with non-European ancestry instead of through any clear positive definition of whiteness.

Bacon's Rebellion is a crucial moment for the study of race in America because it shows us that there was a time at which people of European, African, and indigenous American descent did not live according to the habits of race that created systems of racial apartheid and hierarchy that would seem natural and unavoidable to generations of subsequent Americans. This is no small point, as it promises that since European Americans once did not think themselves white we might again interact in a way that is not impaired by white supremacist habits and ideas. The rebellion was a movement named after Nathaniel Bacon, a recently arrived Englishman and plantation owner who fought against the forces of the colonial governor, William Berkeley.[5] The conflict originated over differences between the two groups (the "frontier" families represented by Bacon, and the large plantation elite represented by the governor) regarding the colony's "Indian policy." These immigrant groups were in general agreement over the broad details of how the colony should deal with the surrounding Native peoples: both believed in the need for the colony to expand through warfare and assimilation in order to acquire more land for the tobacco monoculture that was the purpose of the colony and the economic lifeblood of the British Empire. Allen points out that this issue became a serious point of contention. He says of this disagreement: "The issue between Berkeley and Bacon was not whether Indians were to be displaced by the advance of the English settlement—they were in fundamental agreement on that—but merely the priority to be given to it at a given time, and thus the rate at which it was to be done."[6] It was in the governor's best interest to maintain a temporary, strategic friendship with the Doeg, Pamunkey, Rappahannock, and Nottoway peoples who lived to the west of the Chesapeake settlements because they were valuable trading partners who sometimes accepted bounties to capture and return escaped European and African bonds-people. They also served as a buffer between the colonies and the Native peoples further west who were less amicable with the settlers. However, the governor's alliance with these Native peoples angered the small planters, who saw the indigenous peoples only as threats to their smaller, more isolated western settlements. As the governor reserved the great majority of the land under his control for tobacco plantations, independent European farmers were forced to expand westward in small groups, thus coming in frequent conflict with indigenous peoples. After a tumultuous power struggle during which Bacon led unauthorized raids against the Pamunkey Indians, got elected to the House of Burgesses on his anti-landowner and anti-Indian policies, was arrested by Governor Berkeley for sedition, and was then freed by a mob of two thousand Virginians, Bacon led a series of assaults on the colonial forces in Jamestown and the indigenous peoples to the west. After nine months of rebel attacks and colonial counterattacks, the rebel forces were routed by Capt. Thomas Grantham's thirty-gun *Concord* near West Point, Virginia.

Despite his military failures, Bacon demonstrated considerable political acumen in tapping the current of discontent among African and European bonds-people, landless laborers, and owners of small land plots toward the tiny elite who controlled the vast majority of the colony's land. While the tobacco monoculture was producing staggering profits for the Crown, it was wreaking extreme hardship on the majority of the population. We see as much when we read Governor Berkeley's lament of "[h]ow miserable that man is that Governes a People where six parts of seven at least are Poore Endebted Discontented and Armed."[7]

The rebellion was also a clear indicator to the colonial rulers that despite their differences in heritage, language, and custom, the laborers from England, Ireland, and Wales were willing to work with the free and enslaved laborers from African civilizations for their mutual benefit. Indeed, Edmund Morgan, in his classic *American Slavery, American Freedom,* argues that European servants and African slaves "initially saw each other as sharing the same predicament."[8] Reinforcing the idea of pan-laborer amicability, Morgan states: "It was common, for example, for servants and slaves to run away together, steal hogs together, get drunk together. It was not uncommon for them to make love together."[9] We see an example of this early amiability between laborers from African and European backgrounds in the 1684 confession of Roger Court Crotosse, a European Virginian indentured to Col. John West. According to his confession, in one year's time Crotosse stole food from his master a total of seven times; his pilfered feasts included hogs, turkeys, potatoes, sheep, and a lamb.[10] What is significant is that when he absconded at night to eat, he was invariably joined by at least one enslaved African Virginian.[11] Other than indicating the sad state of a laborer's life in an agricultural colony where food was in such short supply that laborers risked time added to their indenture and public whipping in order to have a good meal, Crotosse's confession shows us that people of African and European ancestry were willing to enter into covert pacts for mutual support. This bond, across what would later be considered racial lines, is exactly that Bacon fostered by pointing to the possibility of establishing small settlements dedicated to yeoman agriculture instead of tobacco.[12]

Bacon's Rebellion is yet another indication of the fact that whiteness is a social construct that varies over time and place and could be gotten rid of. While it is probable that the English thought of themselves and other Europeans as different from Africans, the composition and behavior of Bacon's forces shows that at this time there was no sense of whiteness as an essentially different and superior category of human being that would make a poor English laborer think of herself or himself as inherently better than and socially superior to an African laborer (as would widely be the case a mere fifty years later).[13] Indeed, it is possible that "white" did not yet even exist as a recognized social category, as it would not be used as a legal designation until 1691.

Claims that a person was "white" or "Negro" served little or no purpose in the inquiries of laborers, who were more concerned with divisions of economic privilege and religion. Since there was no concept of white racial superiority and there *was* a strong sense of solidarity between European and African laborers, Captain Grantham faced "foure hundred English and Negroes in Armes" near West Point, Virginia, one hundred of whom (eighty Africans and twenty Europeans) died standing together rather than accept the captain's offer of manumission and safe passage home.[14] It is this multiethnic (or to use later categories, multiracial), solidarity that leads Allen to argue that "Grantham's testament has a significance that is beyond exaggeration: in Virginia, 128 years before William Lloyd Garrison was born, laboring-class African-Americans and European-Americans fought side by side for the abolition of slavery. In so doing they provided the supreme proof that the white race did not exist."[15]

The solidarity within the rank and file of Bacon's rebel army was a phenomenon that white supremacist ideology and habits would render nearly impossible for another three hundred years. This invidious racism did not manifest because people of European descent subsequently discovered that they were really white all along and therefore better than all Africans and indigenous peoples. Instead, motivated in part by Bacon's Rebellion, the European rulers of the colony began to distinguish European laborers from those of African or indigenous descent in terms of legal, religious, and social privileges. By instantiating "white" as a privileged group within the law, the colonial government fostered a new way for Europeans to think of themselves, their relationships with other people, and their place in the world. This new category, which emerged from older notions of Christian cultural and moral supremacy, reconstructed pre-existing habits of thought and behavior into new ones that in time became so enmeshed in the social fabric of the colonies that the grandchildren of the European servants and farmers among Bacon's ranks would not think themselves the equals of the grandchildren of the African laborers who also fought for freedom.

It is because of the success of these habits of thought and behavior that races generally and whiteness specifically could be seen by subsequent generations as natural kinds. As habits, practices of race division could come to organize interactions with other people without conscious intent and could, on reflection, appear as given rather than taken. In the words of Edmund Morgan, the solution to the problem of populist solidarity in the colony "was racism, to separate free whites from dangerous slave blacks by a screen of racial contempt."[16] It is from this nascent system of privileges and exclusions that whiteness emerged. These previously non-existent habits of racial division were so economically useful, socially gratifying, and psychologically soothing for Europeans and European immigrants to the Americas that they quickly became integral parts of their social, scientific, and political worlds. It *worked* for these European settlers to think of race generally and whiteness specifically as ahistorical natural kinds since they justified why they were entitled to these advantages while others were not.

We can see how the category "white" came into being by looking briefly at some relevant laws that were enacted before and after the rebellion. These laws not only will demonstrate that an individual's classification as "white" came with a myriad of significant privileges, but will support the politically relevant claim about whiteness that it *came into being negatively.* That is, whiteness and white privilege became valuable only to the extent that those considered to be non-white were *deprived* of important rights and privileges that they had previously enjoyed and were essential to living a relatively free and fulfilling life. Recognizing that whiteness was engendered through negation is crucial for this project, as it underlines the exclusionary impulses that Du Bois and others see at the heart of white supremacist racism and that I argue are the most long lasting and damaging features of the habits of whiteness. It is this *definition through negation* that causes subsequent generations of white people both to be unaware of the many unjust privileges attached to whiteness and to be concerned, even obsessed, with protecting the privileges to which they feel entitled.

The Laws of Virginia before Rebellion

When we look at particular laws from before and after this conflict we see that the idea of a white race was like a conceptual quilt stitched together from predominant assumptions about religion, gender, and sexuality. Furthermore, whiteness is also linked historically to issues of class in that concerns about protecting white supremacy were most acute when people considered non-white were either gaining a degree of economic autonomy (such as during the period of Reconstruction) or creating alliances with European American laborers (as in Bacon's Rebellion). All this is to say that while we can (and sometimes need to) look at whiteness as a distinct phenomenon, it is an idea that is deployed in conjunction with a range of other categories including gender, religion, class, and criminality.

The first and perhaps most essential point is that the term "white" was a relative latecomer to Virginia (appearing first in a law enacted April 16, 1691).[17] The terms "salvages" (*sic*—the archaic spelling of "savages") and "Indians" are much older; we see them in the very first orders sent to the original governor of the colony from King James I in 1606: "Wee doe specially ordaine . . . the ministers of said several colonies . . . that the true word, and service of God and Christian faith be preached . . . not only within every of the said several colonies . . . but alsoe as much as they may amongst the salvage people which doe or shall adjoine unto them."[18]

Similarly, the term "negro" was also used long before "white"; in a fashion that is telling of the way that race will later be articulated along lines of sex, gender, and religion, the term first appears in these early court minutes: "September 17th, 1630. Hugh Davis to be soundly whipped before an assembly of Negroes and others for abusing himself to the dishonor of God and shame of Christians, by defiling his body in lying with a negro; which fault he is to acknowledge next Sabbath day."[19] Historians of the era point out that since Hugh Davis is given no ethnic or racial qualifier, while his partner is specifically mentioned as a "negro," we know that Hugh Davis was of European descent.[20] The use of the specific terms "negro" and "savage" as well as the absence of the term "white" from the statutes until fifteen years after the rebellion points toward how whiteness came into being negatively. That is, the term "white" emerged as a particular or specific term for the category of those people who did not belong in the older categories of "negroes" or "Indians." Until 1691 there was no specific referent for the group of people who would later be white: they were simply generic colonists from Europe.

For example, the first act using the term "negro" clearly demonstrates this definition through negation. Because of the constant threats to the small colonies from Dutch traders and indigenous raiders, the burgesses enacted on January 6, 1639 that "ALL persons except negroes to be provided with armes and ammunition or be fined at pleasure of the Governor and Council."[21] Here we see "negro" function as an exclusionary category. Gun ownership, which was a duty for all heads of households—either men, or unmarried or widowed women— was excepted for men and women of African descent. This is not the same as *barring* them from owning guns (that law would come in 1680, and will be discussed shortly), but it indicates that "negroes" were different enough to be excluded from the generic category. The group consisting of European Virginians is marked with the generic "ALL persons."

We see "negro" again function in an exclusionary way in another law that was designed to deny African-descended women what was perhaps the sole female privilege in the colony: the freedom from taxation. On March 2, 1643, the burgesses ordered that "there be tenn pounds of [tobacco] per poll & a bushel of corne per poll paid to the ministers within the severall parishes of the colony for all tithable persons, that is to say, as well for all youths of sixteen years of age as upwards, as also for all negro women at the age of sixteen years."[22] This law denied Virginian women of African descent the slight gender benefit afforded under the dominant English conceptions of femininity, where women were supposedly too delicate to do field work, and thus were incapable at working at the quintessential economic activity of the colony.[23] Since women of African descent were not considered as feminine as their European counterparts by the lawmakers, they were forced to pay a poll (or person) tax that European women did not.

As the seventeenth century progressed, the category of "negro" changed further from one that was denied certain universal and gender-specific rights to one that was seen as essentially different from the European norm. Racial categories further deepened in December 23, 1662, with an act called "An act for mulatto children being bond or free, to serve according to the condition of the mother." It reads in part that "all children borne in this country shalbe held bond or free only according to the condition of the mother, *And* that if any christian shall commit fornication with a Negro man or women, hee or shee soe offending shall pay double the fines imposed by the former act."[24] This legal principle (known later as *partus sequitur ventrem,* or "the part follows its origin") would start the habit of seeing slavery as a hereditary feature of a human being that was passed down from the mother. More generally, it fostered one of the most vicious habits of white supremacist racism: that of determining a person's legal and social worth according to morphological features and heredity. This law, and others like it, is therefore pivotal in developing the habit of seeing race as a politically relevant natural kind. This law was also the precursor to the "one-drop rule" that would define racial groups in this country well into the twentieth century. While this law does not *equate* African descent with slavery, it lays the groundwork for such thinking. As Kathleen Brown says of this law, "If being a slave was something one became at birth, rather than as a consequence of military defeat or indebtedness, certain groups of people could be seen as being inherently suited to slavery. The notion that enslaved women could pass their bound condition on to their children strengthened the appearance that slavery was a natural condition for people of African descent."[25] This act made having a European Virginian mother a privilege, but only relative to the *worsened* status of those people who had mothers of African descent. The legislation did not *give* European American children any goods or rights they did not already have, but it made them a privileged class because they did not have their freedom *taken* from them. This act is also significant for its separation of "christian" from "negro," where "christian" is the same category that would later be called "white." While the law implies that non-European people are not part of the group of normative "Christians," it is still ambiguous.

The Virginia Burgesses clarified this ambiguity five years later, and in so doing continued the process of demarcating the boundaries of race and whiteness. In 1667 they enacted "An act declaring that baptisme of slaves doth not exempt them from [*sic*] bondage." It reads in part:

> WHEREAS some doubts have risen whether children that are slaves by birth, and by the charity and piety of their owners made pertakers of the blessed sacrament of baptisme, should by vertue of their baptisme be made free; *It is enacted and declared by this grand assembly, and the authority thereof,* that the conferring of baptisme doth not alter the condition of the person as to his bondage or freedome.[26]

This law made it so that children born into slavery could not enter the normative category of citizens (i.e., Christians) through the sacramental act that had defined Christianity from its earliest days. Furthermore, since "christian" was historically equated with a right to freedom in English law, this law had the effect of "cutting off an important avenue by which African slaves had demanded release from bondage."[27] In effect, it stated that all Christians were free, *except* those who inherited the slave status from their mothers, all of whom were of

African descent. All Christians were free, *except* virtually all Christians of African descent. A slave could be a *confessed* Christian and hope for life everlasting, but while their life lasted in Virginia it belonged to another Christian. Of course, this still leaves the matter of the very few *free* Africans living in the colony, who at this time *did* inhabit an intermediary realm as both "negro" and "christian."[28] This, however, would change in 1670, when the burgesses held that "all servants not being christians imported into this colony by shipping shalbe [*sic*] slaves for their lives," where "christians" means people from the "christian" countries of Europe.[29]

Kathleen Brown's commentary on these two acts indicates their essential role in the development of racial taxonomy: "With this measure [of 1670] the colony effectively refined its definition of slavery, limiting bondage to imported Africans. Together, the two statutes culminated thirty years of legal measures defining Africans as slaves and excluding them from the family, gender, and religious privileges enjoyed by the English."[30] This 1670 measure was the last act passed before the rebellion that had any significant impact on the idea of race. Before moving on to see some of the laws that passed after the rebellion, it is important to assess the state of racial (or proto-racial) laws and policies, and look briefly at a 1669 law concerning runaways that will offer an instructive point of comparison.

First, laws targeting people of African descent were designed to *deny* them the basic rights of citizenship that accrued to people from "christian" nations. Similarly, we already see a kind of exceptionalism marking people of indigenous and African descent, while a kind of transparency marks people who would later be called white. The status of European Virginians either is not mentioned or is designated by terms that stand for the normative status, such as "christians" or "ALL persons" while African Virginians and Native peoples are denied this status through specific legal fiat. Second, whiteness apparently does not yet exist as a meaningful social, political, or legal category in the colony. We see a proto-white category in the use of the term "christian," but it is a haphazard category that lacks clear definition. Furthermore, it lacks the sort of strict biologism that is the hallmark of racial taxonomies. Third, while they were certainly better off than people of African descent living in the colonies, or the nearby indigenous people facing constant encroachment upon their lands, the European-descended people of the colonies enjoyed no privileges above those of basic citizenship. Of the approximately 34,000 European descendents living in Virginia in the 1670s, over a sixth (6,000) were indentured servants, who were almost exclusively in Virginia against their will, performing grueling and life-threatening labor. The key difference was that these European servants benefited from the assumption that as Europeans, or "christians" in the parlance of the colonies, they could expect to eventually achieve the free status that was normative for Europeans (unless they committed crimes that extended the time of their indenture). Excluding the very small clique that governed the colony, the remaining free European Virginians lived a life marked by food shortages, dour theocracy, and constant physical danger. Their Europeanness exempted them from certain powerful disadvantages faced only by Africans and indigenous peoples, but could not much mitigate the fact that most were still poor and hard-pressed.

This relative aspect of the privileges these European Virginian colonists enjoyed reveals an important feature of white privilege: it gains its currency from the fact that there are others (non-whites) who are denied the basic rights of citizenship, and not because white folk, as a class, are given privileges that elevate them above the basic rights of citizenship (in the way that categories of lordship or peerage did). This aspect of white privilege does not make white supremacist racial hierarchies any less oppressive than feudal or caste hierarchies. On the contrary, the negative nature of white privilege *requires* exclusionary violence in order to maintain or increase the social value of whiteness. If everyone is taken care of, being a poor white person doesn't have any value. There *have* to be people really poorly off for a white person at the bottom of a class or social structure to feel as if there is some value in being white. Further, it is because whiteness evolved out of the normative legal category of citizenship that white folk, then and now, could remain oblivious to their relative, but no less significant and unjust, privileges.

Returning now to the 1670s, we can see just how desperate were the lives of all servants (both indentured and enslaved) when we read a law passed in October 19, 1669, called simply "Against Runaways":

> WHEREAS diverse good lawes have been made to prevent runaway servants which have hitherto in great parte proved ineffectuall, chiefly through the wickednesse of servants . . . : *Be it therefore enacted* that whosoever apprehends any runaways wither servant by indenture, custome, or covenant, not having a legall passe . . . shall have a thousand pounds of tobacco allowed him by the publique.[31]

The law is significant for its breadth; it takes pains to specify that it applies to *all* servants (a term that included both indentured European laborers and lifetime African laborers), whether they are servants because of "indenture, custome, or covenant." It also designates that all servants must carry passes or face punishment. This law is significant because it is more or less raceless: it cares not *why* the escapee is a servant, but only that they be returned. To make an important link ahead in my analysis, this law is consistent with millennia-old habits regarding criminality. When the law effectively tells the authorities, "If someone violates the law [n this case the law that a servant cannot leave without permission] then you need to find and punish them, regardless of who they are," it is following in an ancient tradition of apprehending wrongdoers. It is a habit, that is, it is a pre-reflective cognitive or behavioral practice. It involves looking in hiding places, being on the lookout for people who are out of place or acting suspiciously, that we can see functioning in societies as old as the ancient Israelites or Babylonians.

In 1680 we find another law that, on first glance, appears very similar to the one above. Enacted a mere four years after Bacon's Rebellion, it involved exactly the same legal area (escaped servants) and had very similar language. However, it was different in important ways, and this difference was immensely important in its effect on the evolution of race and whiteness. It reads in part:

> [I]f any negroe or other slave shall absent himself from his masters service and lye hid lurking in obscure places, committing injuries to the inhabitants, and shall resist any person or persons that shalby any lawfull authority be imployed to apprehend and take the said negroe, that then in case of such resistance, it shalbe lawfull for such person or persons to kill the said negroe or slave soe lying out and resisting, and that this law be once every six months published at the respective county courts and parish churches within this colony.[32]

Where the first law shows a concern that all servants be monitored, this later law, and dozens others like, it is conspicuous in its specific targeting of "negroes." This *negative attention* on non-whites was instrumental for the development of white privilege. This type of law initiated new habits by which the colonists organized their experiences of each other. These laws reordered old habits of punishment and justice into new ones that focused first on morphological features that distinguished a person who was a "negro" from a "christian." With habits of this sort established, those not marked for special scrutiny could move more freely, even if they were actually committing a crime. Where the 1669 law maintained old habits of being on the lookout for *anyone* who was acting like or looked like an escapee (Were they lurking far from groups of people? Were they walking alone at night? Were they wearing clothes reserved for servants—in this case rough cotton shirts and pants dyed blue?), the 1680 law helped revise these habits in a way that began to constitute race as we now know it. This is because the 1680 law, by emphasizing "negroes," made *morphology* a powerful and meaningful legal trait. Where previous laws had to do basically with questions of "Is this person *doing* something wrong?" the 1680 initiated the question "Are they the wrong *sort* of person?" where a person's kind is determined by their morphology. Someone with pink skin and straight flaxen hair is not the kind of person about which the 1680 law is concerned. Such a person can be passed over by one of the ad hoc slave patrols. Someone with mahogany skin and curly black hair *is* the sort of person the law, and the posse, is concerned with. They *receive* a degree of concern and suspicion that the other person does not.

The legal requirement of seeing particular morphological features involving skin and hair color as relevant became attached to the evolving habits and categories of race that European scientists and political theorists used to account for certain supposedly innate moral, intellectual, and political differences between different human populations. The new laws in the colonies (as well as the new economic and political realities, like the rise of European slave markets in Africa) revised older habits. These revised habits submerged some aspects of experience (such as creed or class of the enslaved people) and highlighted others (such as the morphological features that most readily identified someone as enslaved or not). The theorists trying to explain experience (such as the enslavement of Africans) report on the experiences in ways that are conditioned by habit (most notably the habit of placing a great deal of emphasis on morphology). Though they are newly habituated to seeing race, the biological dimension (the fact that morphology is determined by ancestry and heredity) makes it seem as if race is antecedent and given, not constructed. While the categories of race defined whiteness as superior and thus led to certain powerful political and cultural privileges, the embodied and subtler habits regarding race (especially those that involved reading other people's morphological features for cues as to how they should be treated) also contributed to white privilege by drawing negative attention to the features defined as non-white. To see how this privilege came into being, we need to look now at how the laws of Virginia changed after Bacon's Rebellion in the years 1675 and 1676.

The Laws of Virginia after Rebellion

The rebellion was a cataclysmic event for the rulers of colonial Virginia. It was a challenge to their authority in a region that was precariously governed, at a time when they still remembered the brutal battles in England between monarchists and supporters of Cromwell. We see the effects of this uprising on their psyches no more clearly than in the laws passed after it. Almost the entirety of the first session after the rebellion (which was called on February 20, 1677) was dedicated to reporting on and responding to the rebellion. Some of the acts passed in that session were designed to specifically redress harms done during the rebellion: "An act for the releife of such loyall persons as have suffered losse by the late rebels"[33] used the colony's coffers to reimburse landowners for any "horses, sloopes, boates, armes, servants, slaves, and other goods" they may have lost during the rebellion, while "An act concerning servants who were out in rebellion" ordered that "all such servants as have joined with or borne armes under Nath. Bacon . . . be punished for the tyme they have beene absent . . . from their masters."[34] However, other laws did not have to do with issues of culpability and redress, but instead instituted a new social order articulated along lines of gender and race. This new order would stabilize the colony by instituting a new logic of race that directed attention away from issues of class inequity and toward ideas of racial and gendered privileges and rights. Brown aptly summarizes the effects of these new post-rebellion laws when she argues that "[d]uring the last quarter of the seventeenth century, white legislatures systematically stripped enslaved men of the trappings of masculinity enjoyed by white men: property ownership, gun possession, and access to white women. In so doing, they transformed the rebellious potential of autonomous white men into a form of domestic patriarchy that reinforced rather than undermined the social order."[35]

The most obvious attempt by the Virginia Burgesses to delineate racial lines came in June 8, 1680, when they called to order the session where they passed "An act for preventing Negroes Insurrections." This act is odd for several reasons. First, Virginia had recently experienced a rebellion lead by a group of *Englishmen* that was so severe that it nearly broke the colony away from the English empire. Further, the colony would not experience an attempted slave revolt until 1687, and the first somewhat successful revolt would not occur until 1730.[36] While people of African descent certainly contributed to the rebellion, the leaders and organizers were landed Englishmen. Thus, while the burgesses had faced a serious challenge from European rebels, and no concerted threat from people of African descent, they passed the colony's most draconian laws against Virginians of African descent, men in particular. This act stated in part that "it shall not be lawfull for any negroe or other slave to carry or arme himselfe with any club, staffe, gunn, sword or any other weapon of defense or offence, nor to goe or depart from of his masters ground without a certificate from his master."[37] It further held that "if any negroe or other slave shall presume to lift up his hand in opposition against any Christian" he would receive "thirty lashes on his bare back well laid on."[38] After the rebellion, the House of Burgesses occupied itself with an almost pathological attention to monitoring African Virginians as a means of maintaining order in the colony. This act did not repeal the 1669 act "Against Runaways," and thus European servants still needed to be hunted down if they tried to escape. However, it does indicate a deepening legal prejudice against non-Europeans. Soon after this period, life-bonded servitude (or slave labor) became more economically viable than indentured servitude, so the problem of fugitives of European descent became a much less pressing issue, leaving almost the full weight of the colonial authority's gaze to fall on people of African descent.

In 1682, the burgesses enacted a law that limited full citizenship to Europeans and relegated *all* non-Europeans to a status beneath citizenship. The act held that "all servants . . . brought or imported into this country, either by sea or land, whether Negroes, Moors, Mollattoes or Indians, who and whose parentage and native country are not christian at the time of their first purchase of such servant by some christian . . . shall be adjudged, deemed and taken to be slaves to all intents and purposes."[39] Thus, slavery was a status limited only to non-Europeans, while Europeans could expect the basic rights of being treated as people who were inherently free (and could lose their freedom only temporarily through indenture). Also, to prevent or minimize the intermixture of these increasingly distinct categories, the burgesses passed a series of laws that criminalized or penalized marriage and sex between "Christians" and non-Europeans.

The first such law was enacted in April 1691, and was called "An act for suppressing outlying Slaves." This law is important not only for continuing the process of racial demarcation, but for being the first law passed in Virginia to make use of the term "white" to describe a category of persons, and is the first such documented use of the term anywhere in Virginia or the English-speaking colonies:[40] "[W]hatsoever English or other white man or woman being free shall intermarry with a negroe, mulatto, or Indian man or woman bond or free shall within three moneths after such marriage be banished and removed from this dominion forever."[41] The act further criminalizes sex between white women and any non-white men when it ordered that "if any English woman being free shall have a bastard child by any Negro or mulatto, she pay the sume of fifteen pounds sterling, within one moneth after such bastard child shall be born . . . , and that such bastard child be bound out as a servant by the said Church wardens until he or she shall attaine the age of thirty yeares."

Not only were non-whites singled out by laws that denied them the basic rights of citizenship, but any intermixture between European Virginian women and men of African descent was penalized. Further, while this law made the paternity of any and all children borne by white women a matter of important legal concern, it made the paternity of any and all children of African Virginian women an unlegislated matter. Thus, the sexuality of white women came under great scrutiny, while the sexuality of black women drew little legal attention. Brown comments on this difference: "Perceived by the courts as the population most likely to blur racial boundaries and incur expenses for masters, white servant women bore the brunt of many of the new regulations. White men, meanwhile, avoided prosecution for interracial sexual misconduct and, increasingly, all sexual misconduct, creating a distinctly skewed grid of prosecution for interracial sexual activity."[42]

It is significant that the first use of "white" occurs in a law that was pivotal in establishing white supremacist racial categories by combining the negative attention on the bodies of African Americans (men in particular) with age-old Christian monitoring of the bodies of women. Controlling the sexual contact between non-European men and European women was crucial to establish the category of whiteness as superlative and "pure." That is, if "white" was to mean free, and "Negro or mulatto" was to mean unfree in a situation where the child followed the status of the *mother,* it became absolutely essential to prevent a situation where a child had a father of African descent (and would thus be mulatto, and thus unfree) and a mother of European descent (and would thus be eligible to be treated as free). Any such child would be a living, breathing contradiction; someone who had to be legally free and unfree simultaneously.

The 1691 legislation finalized the contours of race in Virginia, and would serve as a model for racial categories for the next three centuries. Whites were the only people who had a presumption of freedom and citizenship, and all non-whites—captured in the oft-used phrase "Negroes, Moors, Mollattoes or

Indians"—were presumed to be unfree and non-citizens. A handful of subsequent laws widened the gap between white and non-white. One session called on October 23, 1705, was fateful for the categories of race and whiteness. It enacted legislation that held that all "negroes" had to be tried before "Oyer and Terminer Courts" (which were juryless tribunals that were much harsher than normal trials),[43] that non-whites could not "be witnesses in any cases whatsoever,"[44] and that white colonists received more lenient physical punishment from their masters or the courts.[45] Another session in 1723 held that "no free negro, mulatto, or indian whatsoever, shall have any vote at the election of burgess, or any other election whatsoever."[46] These laws combined to make "whiteness an exclusive category" that was denied to any person with any non-white ancestry.[47] With the exception of *one law* (the one mentioned above that lessened the legal punishments for white servants and criminals), European Virginian colonists did not *gain* anything from this new racial taxonomy. There was no law that lessened their taxes, no law that guaranteed they could receive land, no law that gave them access to any institution to which they did not already have access. Their condition improved relative to those of indigenous and African-descended peoples only because the conditions of non-whites worsened.

Christian religious institutions helped solidify whiteness in the post-rebellion period as a device of social control by disseminating the racial concepts being implemented within the law at the time. Allen states that in Virginia "the laws mandated that parish clerks or church wardens, once each spring and fall at the close of Sunday service, should read . . . these laws in full to the congregants."[48] The ability of the early Protestant church to sanction violence against non-Europeans in the name of God made whiteness itself seem an ordained category, rather than a fabricated one. This way the church, along with the law, initiated a new birthright for people of European ancestry, notified them of their new privileges, and encouraged them to take advantage of them.

This legal distinction, created within a religious context that already supposed a hierarchy whereby Christian Europeans were superior to "heathen" Africans and Native Americans, fostered a false sense of social and psychological superiority, whereby Europeans living in the early colonies soon forgot the times where they saw their lot as thrown in with that of Africans, and instead began to think of themselves as inherently different from, and better than, African and indigenous people. This sense of superiority was further inflated by certain practices that were open only to whites, the oldest and most disturbing of which was the nightly patrolling of the highways and roads for runaway slaves.[49] W. E. B. Du Bois succinctly explains why poor Europeans largely adopted this kind of behavior rather than more contestatory actions in concert with Africans. Though he is writing here about the period of Reconstruction, his description is fully applicable to the earlier situation at the beginning of the seventeenth century:

> Considering the economic rivalry of the black and white worker . . . , it would have seemed natural that the poor white would have refused to police the slaves. But two considerations led him in the opposite direction. First of all, it gave him work and some authority as overseer, slave driver, and member of the patrol system. But above and beyond this, it fed his vanity because he associated him with the masters. . . . [T]he result was that the system was held stable and intact by the poor white.[50]

Sadly, this phenomenon continues little changed in the American Southwest, with vigilante groups such as the Minutemen that are made up almost exclusively of white men who elect themselves to patrol the border between the United States and Mexico.

The practice of poor Europeans policing enslaved Africans was symbiotically related to the concept of whiteness. On the one hand, it was made possible only once some essential (or at least legal) difference was posited between Europeans and Africans. This difference was posited at the level of ideas (or propositions, to use the term that I will develop in chapter 3) through religious, legal, and, later, scientific discourses that took the old wine of Christian exceptionalism (the centuries-old idea that Christians were God's new chosen people and thus better than all non-Christians) and poured it into the new wineskin of racial taxonomies. This difference was posited at the level of behaviors—quite literally "on the street"—through habits of determining how to treat someone according to visible morphological features. Yet, on the other hand, it was a practice that reified the idea of whiteness more than any other at this early stage. This practice, where light-skinned people could and did mete violence, pell-mell, upon dark-skinned people, transferred the concept of whiteness (that is, whiteness as a superlative branch of the human tree) from a fearful idea to a terrifyingly embodied reality. It initiated a habit that was easy to follow. By social status being anchored in morphology, it seemed that the taxonomy of race was ahistorical and given. Since this habit (of reading the morphology of a person to determine their legal, political, and social status) was so immediately politically and socially rewarding for white folk, it did not draw attention to itself, thus seeming all the more natural.

The Relevance of Bacon's Rebellion for Ideas of Race

This first act in the story of whiteness in America already offers support for the three claims regarding the history of whiteness. We see that whiteness is socially constructed in the simple fact that we can locate its historical emergence. It was a concept introduced at a certain historical moment and not a given that was "discovered." It became a concept and habit of thought that exercised drastic social control over the population of the colonies by the beginning of the eighteenth century. The second claim, that whiteness is taken as natural in each age, is not as evident in this age as it will be in subsequent ones because this was the age during which it came into existence. This is the age in which whiteness was naturalized; it went from being something about which people had to be informed to being something taken for granted. We can already find strong negative support for the seeming naturalness of whiteness even at this early stage just by virtue of the fact that we never see any casting about for a definition of whiteness either in the laws, in the discussions of the burgesses, or among religious authorities. When they said, "no white women can marry non-white men," they did not have to attach a list of necessary and sufficient traits: people just knew who was white. To refer forward to Dewey's conception of inquiry, the ideas and intellectual habits of race (the ways of organizing and interacting with the world that relied in part on racial propositions) became naturalized because they *worked* so smoothly and far below the limit of one's selective consciousness in the process of inquiry. The habit of thinking that you comported yourself toward someone in large part according to their heredity and morphology was one that paid dividends.

Finally, the third claim, regarding whiteness being defined via exclusion, is supported by the ways in which the term was put to use. The "first whites" (that is, the first people to be seen and treated by others in the community as white) did not receive any great set of privileges vis-à-vis their previous status. Instead, their white privilege meant that while they were still economically destitute and without any real opportunity to rise in economic or social status, they were *not as poorly off as African and indigenous people.* Whiteness meant that they *could not* be beaten to within a hair's breadth of their life. It meant that their right to vote, testify, marry, and walk freely took on an air of special privilege only once that right was *taken away* from certain people, many of whom had had those rights previously. All the normal things of life—marrying, having a home, having a trade, bringing goods to market, or just walking the road—became privileges only "whites" could enjoy without harassment or worse. Their experience was treated as normative, where Africans and Native Americans were marked as different. Though poor whites were still free to starve to death in the fertile landscape dedicated to the cultivation of an inedible, toxic, but immensely profitable drug, they were free of the slavery and genocide that was reserved for other, non-white groups of people. Even at this early stage of American history we already see many of the disturbing racial dynamics that were prevalent in the twentieth century and still exist today. It is hard to miss the similarities between mobs of poor whites in seventeenth-century Virginia patrolling the roads for escaped slaves and the twenty-first-century Minutemen, who are almost without exception working-class white men, patrolling the deserts for undocumented immigrants. We can see here the inherent connection between this idea of whiteness as a pure category that engenders not only feelings of entitlement and fear of people outside the category but also habits of behavior that are profoundly hostile and antithetical to community.

While whiteness was a powerful legal and social category by the dawn of the eighteenth century, it was still problematically vague. Part of the problem with the category had to do with the powerful relationship between Protestant Christianity and whiteness. As outlined above, the only positive definition of whiteness evolved out of the older term "Christian." However, since the Christians writing the laws in the fledgling colony were survivors of the brutal fighting between royalist Anglicans who saw the king of England as the proper head of the Christian world, traditional "Old English" who accepted the Pope as their spiritual sovereign, and radical Quakers, Anabaptists, and Puritans who accepted neither authority, their view of who counted as a "Christian" was quite particular. As a consequence, the later category of whiteness, though largely synonymous with "European," had a religious valence to it that hampered certain Europeans from being fully "white." For example, the 1705 law that limited the right to testify to "christians" excluded not only the usual list of "negroes, mulattoes, and Indian servants" but also "popish recusants," or Roman Catholics.[51] Thus, in part due to an ancient English prejudice against Gaelic peoples of Europe as well as the more recent wars between Protestants and Catholics, the Irish and Scottish Catholics were viewed with suspicion: they were geographically "white," but politically savage. We will see this same ambiguity regarding the boundaries of whiteness hundreds of miles away and 158 years later during the bloody Draft Riots of 1863 in New York City.

The Draft Riots of 1863 and the Defense of White Privilege

Between Rebellion and Riot

People in America did not accept whiteness as a natural category right away, and people used the category in fairly disparate ways for a long time. It took a while for people to become habituated to the ideas of race and whiteness to the point that they took them as natural features of human biology. While whiteness was a legal designation that required concerted acts of propagation in order for it to take hold in the early colonial period, by the end of the eighteenth century people in America take its reality for granted to the point that it could be used to make significant decisions about citizenship and democratic government. So where the colonial era witnessed the *forging* of whiteness as a racial category, the post-Revolutionary era saw its *deployment* in the creation of the Union. It therefore evolved from a social distinction of dubious value for the mass of poor European laborers to a "natural" way of dividing humanity to a necessary condition for citizenship in the early republic.

In his history of whiteness, Jacobson argues that 1790 was a watershed year for the development of whiteness because that was the year in which the first national Congress passed a unique immigration law that gave an unprecedented significance to being white. It states in part: "that all free white persons who, have, or shall migrate into the United States, and shall give satisfactory proof, before a magistrate, by oath, that they intend to reside therein, and shall take an oath of allegiance, and shall have resided in the United States for one whole year, shall be entitled to the rights of citizenship."[1] This simple law wove tightly into the tapestry of our civic life the idea of whiteness as a superlative and privileged racial group. In one stroke, this law concretized a racial hierarchy that had never been as sharply defined. It extended full citizenship to the poorest immigrant from Europe while casting people of Asian, African, and indigenous descent into a legal limbo where they were unable to represent their interests, regardless of how long they or their family had lived in America. This increase in the political significance of whiteness in the early republic had to do with the connection between whiteness and the idea of "fitness for self-government." That is, citizenship was reserved for "free white persons" because they were the only people deemed "civilized" enough for self-government. Jacobson illustrates the degree to which the very idea of republicanism was determined by the idea of whiteness: "'Fitness for self-government,' a racial attribute whose outer property was whiteness, became encoded in a naturalization law that allowed Europeans' unrestricted immigration and their unhindered (male) civic participation. It is solely because of their race, in other words, that they were permitted entrance."[2] In the early republican era, whiteness became a normative category that, when conjoined with maleness, was equivalent to normative citizenship. Whiteness was just as much about who could participate in the new nation as it was about who couldn't because they were *not* fit for self-government (people of African, Native American, Latino, and Asian descent). However, this simple idea of whiteness came under scrutiny in the nineteenth century because of two interrelated events: the massive influx of Irish immigrants to the United States starting in the 1840s and the New York City Draft Riots of 1863. These two events forced the Yankees of the young republic to redefine the idea of whiteness in order to separate themselves from the mass of European immigrants who were granted entrance into the country as white folk, but were nevertheless distinct from the Anglo-Saxon stock seen as the lifeblood of the United States. As immigration, war, and expansion changed the demographics of the republic, the republic, through laws, sermons, debate, and literature, changed the meaning of whiteness.

The mid-nineteenth century witnessed a dramatic increase in European immigration to the United States. While fewer than 9,000 immigrants came to the United States in the year 1820, nearly a quarter of a million (234,968) immigrants made their way to its shores in 1847.[3] "Black '47," as this year is still known in Ireland, was a pivotal time in the history of whiteness in the United States because it was the first year of the Great Famine, which in five years' time claimed a million lives and forced as many to leave Ireland, ultimately cutting Ireland's population by one-quarter.[4] Most who fled this calamity came to America. Jacobson points out that "by 1860 . . . the foreign born population of the United States was more than 4 million, of whom 1,611,304 had been born in Ireland."[5] As Europeans, these Irish immigrants were legally counted as "white," and were thus allowed entry according to the Immigration Act of 1790. However, since these Irish did not fit the American ideal of a group of people fit for self-government, native-born whites developed an explanation that could account for a group of people who were "biologically" white, yet still suspect as potential citizens.

While America received waves of immigrants from all over the world in the nineteenth century, the Catholic Irish were in a very real sense *the* immigrants of the 1840s and 1850s. While many other immigrant groups attracted little attention and blended easily with American social norms, the Irish were unable to assimilate. Though most Irish women and men spoke English, they did so in their own particular vernacular that was laden with a characteristic brogue. Their pre-industrial, folk customs (from songs to funerals) appeared backward to most native-born Americans. As William Williams says in his history of Irish American music and culture, "[w]ithout the wall of language to hide behind, the peculiarities and archaisms of the Irish folk tradition were very evident for Yankee bemusement and concern."[6] Further, their Roman Catholicism drew the suspicion and ire of native-born Protestants who thought that the Catholics were in America to overthrow democracy on orders from the pontiff in Rome. This threat weighed so heavily on the minds of some American Protestants that myriad political parties emerged, the most famous of which was the Know Nothing Party, that were dedicated solely to combating the perceived threat that Catholic immigrants posed to Anglo-Saxon America.[7] Thus their language, customs, clannish behavior, and above all Catholicism were distorted to form the image of "Paddy" that all Irish men and women would have to confront. Since they stood out so, the Irish received a kind of discriminatory and particular attention that was analogous to that experienced by indigenous and African peoples during the colonial period.

The arrival of immigrants from Ireland, Germany, Italy, and other parts of Europe shifted the focus of racial discourse from issues of white versus non-white to issues regarding the nature of whiteness itself. Jacobson argues, "Whereas the salient feature of whiteness before the 1840's had been its powerful political and cultural contrast to nonwhiteness, now its internal divisions, too, took on a new and pressing significance."[8] Nativists were particularly concerned with the (in)ability of these newly arrived immigrants to live up to the previous assumption that the white race was uniformly "fit for self-government." Furthermore, as there were such wide differences in behavior, experience, and appearance between the nativist whites and the newly arrived immigrants (most of whom had never identified themselves as "white" before they had arrived in the U.S.), there needed to be an explanation to account for the difference between the immigrants and the native whites. The result was yet another change in the definition of whiteness: it was now explained as a vast family of *white races* that could be hierarchically ranked in terms of their innate ability to participate in a republic. Thus, the Paddy and the Yankee were not seen as equally white; where the later could partake of all the advantages of being a white citizen of the republic, the prior was a probationary white person who had to overcome certain biological and cultural defects that impeded his ability to be a white, American citizen.

Comte de Gobineau's work *The Inequality of Human Races* (1855) defined the new racial logic of the time. His work was a caveat to the Anglo-Saxon race that they were in danger of devolving by mixing with "the most degenerate races of olden day Europe. They are the human flotsam of all ages: Irish, cross-bred German and French, and Italians of even more doubtful stock."[9] While de Gobineau himself believed that this racial degeneration was inevitable, his American readers took it upon themselves to prevent this from happening by taking measures against mixing among the white races. The first step in erecting a bulwark between the superior Anglo-Saxons and the degenerate Irish, Italians, Russians, and Germans was to identify the traits of these groups, that they might be avoided and isolated.

The Irish, more than any other group of Europeans, became the objects of these new racial investigations. Jacobson points out that while popular literature of the time discussed the particular traits of Russians, Italians, and Germans, "by far the more powerful language of racial differentiation applied to the Irish."[10]

> Negative assessments of Irishism or Celticism as a fixed set of inherited traits thus became linked at mid-century to a fixed set of observable physical characteristics, such as skin and hair color, facial type, and physique. The Irishman was "low-browed," "brutish," and even "simian" in popular discourse; a *Harper's Weekly* piece in 1851 described the "Celtic physiognomy" as "distinctly marked" by, among other things, "the small and somewhat upturned nose [and] black tint of the skin."[11]

We can see this new logic of ranked white races when we see the frequency with which the Irish were equated to African Americans. This is seen most strikingly in the popular epithets that related the groups to each other; the Irish were frequently referred to as "niggers turned inside out," and blacks were called "smoked Irish."[12] The two groups shared similar depictions in the media: lazy, happy-go-lucky, stupid, childlike, and charmingly incompetent. The final and most insidious commonality between the two has to do with the fact that the hardships that both endured—the manmade famine and attempted genocide from which the Irish fled, and the uniquely horrific Middle Passage and slavery suffered by African Americans—were either trivialized, ignored, or treated as exotic within white-owned and -directed entertainment.[13]

What is most relevant about this new mid-nineteenth-century discourse on the characteristics of the Irish is its relationship to the exceptionalism we saw in the previous discussion of the laws immediately before and after Bacon's Rebellion. Just as the colonial elite talked about, focused on, and legislated the lives and bodies of people who were of African and indigenous descent, Yankee newspaper editors, intellectuals, and politicians in the nineteenth century manifested their suspicions toward the Irish through a discourse that emphasized their difference from an uncommented-upon Anglo-Saxon norm. However, the primary difference between the situations of the Irish on one hand and those of African Americans and Native Americans on the other was that the Irish were probationary whites. As a consequence, many of the Irish in America thought themselves entitled to the freedoms entailed in white privilege. Furthermore, many of the Irish were willing to die and kill to protect their precarious place within the pale of whiteness.

Riot as Ritual Whiteness

The New York City Draft Riots of 1863 were notable not only because they show the disturbing power of the category of whiteness and the depth to which it had penetrated American society, but also because they show us two different groups who both deployed the logic of whiteness. On one hand we see the naturalized Irish and Irish Americans, who rioted in large part because they felt that the Yankees (Protestant European Americans who were born in the U.S. and lived in the Northeast) did not respect the whiteness of the Irish. On the other hand we have the Yankees, who were largely uneasy with the increase of Irish immigrants before the riots, and who saw the riots as raising serious questions about the capabilities of the Irish to function in a democracy. Both groups manifest the traits that Du Bois and later race theorists would associate with whiteness: a preoccupation with making sure that Others (African Americans for the Irish, the Irish for the Yankees) did not cross the boundary to take white privileges undeservedly, coupled with an inability or unwillingness to see their own faults and injustices.

A myriad of causes ushered in these riots, which saw the worst bloodshed in the city until the race riots of 1969.[14] It started on Monday, July 13th, between six and seven in the morning and continued in fits and starts until Union troops, freshly relieved from fending off Confederate General Robert E. Lee's last thrust into Union territory, quelled the violence Friday afternoon. When it was over, between 105 and 119 lives were lost, mostly among the city's African American community.[15] The riots began as a mob action targeted specifically at the perceived injustices of the first federal draft in U.S. history, which had been enacted three months prior with the passage of the Conscription Act. In his definitive history of the riots, *The New York City Draft Riots*, Iver Bernstein shows that resistance to the draft was the galvanizing sentiment for the rioters. "After a brief meeting at Central Park, the crowd broke into two columns and, with 'No Draft' placards held aloft, marched downtown to the Ninth District

Provost Marshal's Office, at Third Avenue and Forty-seventh Street, scene of the draft lottery to be held later that morning.[16]

After dispersing the federal draft agents and setting the building on fire, the anti-draft action quickly degenerated into all-out mayhem, as the mob—which was largely composed of Irish men, women, and children—turned their rage on various constituencies in the city.[17] They attacked people and property connected to the Republican Party, most notably the Spruce St. offices of Horace Greeley's New York *Daily Tribune*. They attacked European Americans who were suspected of or were living, socializing, or working with non-whites: among these were Mary Burke, "a white prostitute who included black men among her clientele"[18] and the household of William and Ann Derrickson, a couple whose house was almost burned down because Mr. Derrickson was black while his wife was white.[19] However, most of their cruelty was wreaked upon the African Americans of New York, including the young inhabitants of the recently built Colored Orphan Asylum, which was burned to the ground in the first day of the riots by a group that numbered in the hundreds or even thousands.[20]

Historians now believe that the rioters, while largely Irish Catholics, were not exclusively so. Bernstein presents evidence that points toward the fact that "some [of the rioters] were German-speaking . . . and some were native born and Protestant."[21] However, while the riots were convulsing the city, the dominant Republican media of the city presented the riots as a purely Irish affair. In an article titled "The Riots" *Harper's Weekly* states it as a "fact that the rioters were uniformly Irish."[22] The article "The Nationality of the Rioters" found in the New York *Times* states that "it is a fact, patent to everyone who has seen anything of the mob, that it is composed almost exclusively of Irishmen and boys."[23] The New York *Daily Tribune* ran an article on "How the Rioters Are Armed" that discusses how an "Officer Bonfield . . . took a sword from a howling Irishman, who was making tremendous threats" and then points out that "of all the arrests made, every one is Irish."[24] Perhaps most telling is that in all of their stories on the riots, the *only* ethnic group singled out by the New York *Times, Harper's Weekly,* or the New York *Daily Tribune* among the rioters is the Irish. Thus, a telling isomorphism holds between the negative exceptionalism toward indigenous and African-descended peoples in the Virginia colonies and the negative exceptionalism toward the Irish in mid-century New York.

This comparison deepens when we look at *how* the Irish are described and depicted in the coverage of the riots. In perhaps the most famous illustration of the riots, Thomas Nast drew a cartoon for the August 1 edition of *Harper's Weekly* that depicts a simian-featured Irishman with the mandatory stovepipe hat and shillelagh rampaging through the city; its caption reads "Gorilla on the Loose."[25] The same periodical tried to make sense of the riots by attributing it to the inherent "impulsiveness of the Celt . . . [that] prompts him to be foremost in every outburst."[26] The most damning image of the rioters is found in a New York *Times* article called "The Spirit of the Mob and Its Promoters." After previously making it clear to its readers that "the mob . . . is composed almost exclusively of Irishmen and boys,"[27] it goes on to explicitly link the Irish to the myth of Indian savagery:

> What most amazes is not the existence of this mob, but its hideousness. There have been other abominations of this sort in America, but nothing that began to be infernal as this. . . . From the very first day, the horde has shown a vileness and depravity of spirit scarcely to be paralleled in any civilized land. . . . It is seen that in spite of our Christian institutions we have thousands of barbarians in our midst, every whit as ferocious in their instincts as the Minnesota savages, and never wanting anything but the opportunity to copy every Indian deed of horror.[28]

Even editorials designed to mitigate anti-Irish sentiments fanned these very flames. A *Daily Tribune* editorial titled simply "The Irish" argues that people should not blame all Irish folk because "*[t]here were no* DECENT *Irish among them* [the rioters]. Irish they all were—every soul of them—but they were the dirty, half-drunken, brutal rowdies, who are the leprosy of that fair-skinned race."[29]

Thus the people who were white beyond a doubt—native-born Protestants of Anglo-Saxon stock—were forced to consider whether they wanted to classify the Irish as white (like them) or more like the Irish had been characterized in Ireland since the Protestant Ascendancy (as sub-civilized savages incapable of self-rule and thus unworthy of legal standing). In "The Spirit of the Mob and Its Promoters" we even see a kind of rhetorical separation fully recognizable to a Virginian colonist from the seventeenth century. To one extreme were the Christian, white, and civilized citizens of New York, who were under attack from the instinctually ferocious, savage, and ultimately uncivilized Irish.

We can contrast the exceptionalism toward the Irish in the above Republican publications with the more general and populist treatment of the riots by Democratic papers such as the New York *Herald*. Where the publications above explicitly or implicitly linked the riots to some flawed character inherent to the Irish, the *Herald* cast the riots very differently, as in its July 14 headlines: "Popular Opposition to the Enforcement of the Conscription" and "Attack on the People by the Provost Guard."[30] Similarly, the democratic and anti-abolitionist paper the *Irish-American* lamented the treatment of the Irish in other periodicals[31] and referred to the rioters only as "the assembled masses" or "the people."[32]

The analysis of the Republican treatments of the Irish above demonstrates how the category of whiteness had changed since its inception in 1691. It shows that the Irish experienced the same sort of negative attention experienced by African Americans immediately after Bacon's Rebellion, though not nearly as severely or systematically. Just as indigenous and African peoples were singled out in the laws of the early colony in a way that gave European Virginians the significant social privilege that came from being relatively nondescript, so the Irish in this era experienced a kind of negative attention because of their Irishness, which led many Yankees to consider them more like "savages" than white folk. However, this chapter illustrates the mercurial and violent nature of whiteness in that it shows that while Yankee whites were questioning the civility and whiteness of the Irish, the Irish themselves were angrily *claiming* their whiteness, and using it as an excuse for the horrors they visited upon their African American neighbors.

To see how the riots were in part an attempt by the Irish to claim and protect their whiteness, we need to look briefly at two incidents that preceded the riots. The first was a fight between a group of Irish American longshoremen and African American longshoremen that took place on April 13, 1863. The Republican *Daily Tribune* described the event this way: "The city was disgraced yesterday by a mob. A few, unoffending colored laborers on the wharves were suddenly attacked by two or three hundred Irishmen."[33] Again we see the exceptionalist treatment of the Irish: to the Yankee Republicans, the Irish were more Irish than white. We can contrast this with the Democratic *Herald*'s description of the attack, which opens: "Quite an excitement occurred yesterday morning . . . occasioned by the old conflict between white and black labor. It appears that about a dozen negroes were engaged in discharging . . . cargo . . . when several hundred white laborers attacked them."[34] The remainder of the article is conspicuous in its lack of condemnation toward the attackers and for its almost humorous tone. Not only did the *Herald* describe the assailants as white, they placed the altercation in the context of labor struggles, in particular the recent increase of African American longshoremen working in an industry that the Irish considered their private bailiwick.[35] The *Tribune* coverage is free of the labor context, but highlights the ethnicity of the attackers, leaving the sense that the attack was largely a matter of incoherent Irish savagery. This story, and the very different coverage it received in these two papers, points to the two different ways that Republican Yankees and Democratic Irish Americans understood and used the idea of whiteness.

The second incident provides an even sharper indication that the draft riots were a violent attempt by the Irish to protect their white privilege from assault. It involved a lynching of an African American man named Robert Mulliner, who allegedly raped a young Irish girl in the town of Newburgh, New York, on June 19, 1863. After the *Daily Tribune* accused two Irish American men, William Cleary and Cornelius McClean, of being responsible for the lynching of Mulliner, the *Irish-American* fired back with an editorial called "Negrophilism and Its Results." Denying the charges of the "Spruce street negrophilist" (Horace Greeley, whose *Tribune* office was located on Spruce Street), the paper goes on to claim that "[t]he real responsibility for the state of feeling to which the summary proceedings of the Newburghers may be traced rests on the heads of those who, like the editors of the *Tribune* and *Independent,* sedulously place the negro, with all his drawbacks of character and condition, in opposition to the white man."[36] In a chilling prophecy of what would happen to the city *in less than two weeks,* the paper closes by saying that "[i]t is these very men who have inflamed the minds of the people, by this ceaseless invitation, to that state in which acts of vengeance, like that inflicted on Mulliner, are only the warnings of the more destructive war which some unforeseen accident may precipitate upon the unfortunate race."[37]

The real problem, according to the Irish editors and rioters alike, was that those who were undeniably white—native-born Yankees—had not fully accepted the whiteness of the Irish. They continued to treat the Irish as if they were on a sort of social probation where they had to prove their whiteness. It is this desire on the part of the Irish to claim and defend white privilege that causes Jacobson to aptly frame the riot, along with other acts of racial violence, as "a racial ritual of civic differentiation," whereby Irish immigrants proved or created their own whiteness through acts of violence against non-whites.[38] Thus, the Irish, who had been equated with African Americans since before their arrival in America, *enacted* their whiteness (or at least their desire to be seen as white) through four days of bloody violence. While purification through violence might seem insane to our eyes now, the Irish mob was actually very much in line with the dominant cultural myth of the time that defined the *ethos* of the white republic. By trying to prove their "whiteness" by attacking a group that was decidedly non-white according to contemporary racial hierarchies, the Irish were simply enacting their own version of what the preeminent cultural historian Richard Slotkin calls the Myth of the Frontier.

Whiteness and the Myth of the Frontier

Slotkin's thesis about the Myth of the Frontier helps explain how the Irish and other immigrants used violence against non-whites and their allies to gain full membership within whiteness. Where whiteness was a relatively simple affair in the eighteenth century, the variety and disparities within whiteness after the 1840s rendered simple legal definitions inadequate. The Myth of the Frontier received its two most persuasive articulations in this era: Jackson Turner's "The Significance of the Frontier in American History" and Theodore Roosevelt's multi-volume *The Winning of the West* (1885–94). The myth accomplished several crucial goals during this uncertain time: it not only justified, but encouraged, the genocide of indigenous peoples and the theft of their land as a necessary part of human progress; it accounted for the gradations within the category of whiteness and articulated how violence committed against indigenous, African, and Latino peoples could serve as an initiation rite for the "probationary" whites to become full members of the white republic.

In his work *Gunfighter Nation*, Slotkin argues that the Myth of the Frontier is the defining myth of the United States: "The original ideological task of the Myth was to explain and justify the establishment of the American colonies; but as the colonies expanded and developed, the Myth was called on to account for our rapid economic growth, our emergence as a powerful nation-state, and our distinctively American approach to the socially and culturally disruptive processes of modernization."[39]

The myth, which stretches back three centuries, establishes violence between "civilized" whites and "savage" non-whites as necessary for the creation of American civilization (which is, at this point in time, conceived of as a white, Christian-dominated America). Within the logic of the Myth, genocidal actions against indigenous peoples and the boldfaced invasion of Mexico not only are blameless endeavors, but are stages in the necessary and unavoidable unfurling of human progress.

The myth begins with a cultural and social transformation: since the "metropolis" (either the cities of Europe in the myth's original form, or the larger cities of the East in its later forms) has become too large and regulated, it has begun to snuff out the vitality of civilization. Therefore, the "true" American (either the pilgrim, the pioneer, or the cowboy) needs to strike out into the "wilderness" in order to preserve his vitality from the stagnating effects of too much civility. Originally, this simply meant starting or joining any of the small colonies, whereas it later meant the westward push of European American expansion. This way, the virile American is able to develop a pure civilization in the "wilderness" that is free of the effete rules of the "metropolis." Thus, the frontier—the crucial boundary between the vitality-draining city and the mettle-testing wilderness—is the arena in which a new civilization is established that blends the order exported from the city with the strength of character forged in the battle against "savages."[40]

In addition to the idea that civilization progresses when it escapes the "metropolis" and recreates itself in "the wilderness," two more related concepts are crucial to the definition of what America was at this time: the "savage war," and "regeneration through violence." As Slotkin states, "[c]onflict with the Indians defined one boundary of American identity: though we were a people of 'the wilderness,' we were *not* savages."[41] Just as Nathaniel Bacon saw no way to survive but to lead attacks against the indigenous peoples of the Chesapeake Bay, America has always defined itself as a people whose survival depends on their victory in a series of "savage wars." These necessary conflicts were premised on the fact that "ineluctable political differences . . . make coexistence between primitive natives and civilized Europeans impossible on any basis other than that of subjugation."[42] Therefore, a total war (one where the object is the complete obliteration of the opponent) was the only means of assuring that "civilization" would progress.

Where the "savage war" was a trope (and later a very real military policy) that looked at the "wilderness" side of the equation, the idea of the "regeneration through violence" looked at the "metropolis" side and what was necessary to purify American culture of its overwrought, European origins. The myth held that the true American spirit—vital, manly, pure—could be achieved only "by playing through a scenario of separation, temporary regression to a more primitive or 'natural' state, and *regeneration through violence.*"[43] Therefore, the various wars with the indigenous peoples living to the West (and later the wars in Cuba, the Philippines, Japan, Europe, and Vietnam) were necessary not only for natural resources and expansion, but as the cauldron in which the American spirit could be tempered of its European weakness. Roosevelt, Turner, and others saw this violence as regenerative to the extent that it cleared away the supposedly savage wilderness to give room for a newly tempered and masculine civilization to take root.

The myth was also used to make sense of various social threats facing the status quo of the young republic. For example, in the chaotic 1870s (which witnessed the Tompkins Square Riot of 1874, the collapse of southern Reconstruction, and Custer's Last Stand) the myth was deployed in various disparate situations. The powerful owners of industry and the national media used "race-war symbolism, drawn from the Myth of the Frontier, to interpret the class warfare of workers and managers."[44] Ku Klux Klan violence against African Americans was also justified, as a necessary defense of white civilization against the animalistic privations of the Negro, while the Sioux War of 1876 "was at once a current event and a symbol of the primal and genetic strife from which the nation was born."[45] Later still, the major conflagrations of the twentieth century were all cast as battles between the forces of good (comprising the U.S. and whoever happened to be on our side) and the forces of evil, who were notable for their inhumanity and barbarism (the German "Huns" in WWI, the Nazis and "Japs" of WWII, the Viet Cong, the Soviet "Evil Empire" of the Cold War, or the Arab "Evil-doers" of the current "War on Terrorism," many of whom were our "freedom-fighter" allies in the *previous* savage war against the Soviet Union in Afghanistan).

So, to return to the riots of 1863, where do the Irish stand in this myth? The answer depends on the context. When the Irish were rioting in the city, engaging in "big boss" politics, or forming the gangs from which the earliest urban fire departments evolved, they were the "white savages" mentioned in the New York *Times*. As Slotkin points out, the prominent Republican politician Charles Francis Adams argued in 1869 that the Irish were one of the "three racially defined 'proletariats'—Celtic in the North, African in the South and Oriental in the Far West," who were incapable of self-rule.[46] However, the Irish were very differently received by Anglo-American society when they donned the uniform of the U.S. Army or Cavalry and fought in the wars that defined the nation ideologically and geographically: the Civil War, the Indian Wars, the Spanish-American War, and later the World Wars of the twentieth century. When they were fighting those who were beyond the pale of whiteness—Lakota, Cheyenne, Apaches, Mexicans, Cubans, and Filipinos—on behalf of the Anglo-Saxon ruling class, they became whitened through violence.

Thus the tragic riot of 1863 seems, though no less inhuman, completely in line with the logic of whiteness. If European Virginians could solidify their economic well-being through laws and policies that denied the rights of people not deemed "white," then the Irish immigrants were simply following suit. Their violence separated them both from the overly civilized (white, wealthy, liberal, Protestant, Republican abolitionists) and those who were not white (their African American neighbors). Just as Roosevelt identified the violent competition of race-like classes as the force that drives civilization upward through its several stages, the Irish in New York were trying to resolve the issue of their whiteness by committing violence against those who, all agreed, were not white. Furthermore, the riots show the extent to which the Irish had adopted habits of whiteness: habits of thought and behavior that assumed that white people were entitled to better treatment than non-whites.

The Yankee concern with the apparent barbarism of their (technically) white brethren fostered a redefinition of whiteness that seems almost comical now in its shallowness and self-serving arrogance. As soon as there are white people who do not fit the mold of Yankee civic ideals, the dominant discourse changes and begins to treat whiteness as ranked, with some whites being whiter than others. As the social and political realities changed, whiteness metamorphosed. The Irish problem did not at all cause dominant Protestant Anglo-Saxons to question the *existence* of whiteness; instead, it caused them to alter the category. Finally, we see that whiteness relied on the exclusion and oppression of others in the writings of a future president and in the mob violence of those at the very bottom of the category. Indeed, Slotkin's work shows us that exclusionary violence against those who are non-white (especially Native Americans) took on a mythic significance for white supremacist, capitalist, patriarchal America.

The era between the influx of immigrants in 1840 and the enshrinement of eugenic science in 1920 was troubling for the nation as a whole and for the category of whiteness. It witnessed a complication of the idea of whiteness from its simple beginnings in the period after Bacon's Rebellion. During this time whiteness became contextual, whereby "an Irish immigrant in 1877 could be a despised Celt in Boston—a threat to the republic—and yet a solid member of The Order of Caucasians for the Extermination of the Chinaman in San Francisco, gallantly defending U.S. shores from an invasion of 'Mongolians.'"[47]

The Lessons of White History

While the folk wisdom of the United States has stated for centuries that "the white race" is a real, received, and antecedent racial group, the discussion here supports the idea that whiteness is a social construct, slowly created through violence, legislation, and other practices of exclusion and privilege. The first moment of whiteness studied in the previous chapter suggests that whiteness had little or no social or political value before the end of the seventeenth century, and it became a legally recognized term only after Bacon's Rebellion. The second moment showed how this supposedly natural kind changed in terms of its definitions and relevance with the influx of poor and largely undesirable European immigrants to the Americas. In both cases we saw not just that whiteness was a social construct, but that it was a particularly cruel and divisive one in that it was defined through acts of legislated or illegal violence.

The second thesis, that whiteness came to be thought of as a natural kind, is supported by the lack of consideration about whether or not the category is real in the first place. After Bacon's Rebellion it is simply introduced in 1691 as a (literally) legitimate category. When the law held that no white women or men could marry people of African or indigenous descent, they did not need to attach an addendum describing who was white. The draft riots and the preceding influx of rural Irish immigrants engendered a degree of reflection about whiteness. However, this was an inquiry designed to account for differences between Yankees and European immigrants, not one that raised any questions about whether or not the white races existed.

Finally, this history of whiteness shows how the boundaries of whiteness were defined primarily through the exclusion of those who were defined as non-white. The newly minted privileges of the poor European laborers in the Virginia colonies (such as freedom from extreme physical punishment or the ability to testify and vote) would not have been privileges but for the fact that these things were denied others (people of African or Native descent). The Irish became white largely by separating themselves from the "lower" races of African Americans or indigenous peoples, by either the biting humor of the minstrel stage, the vicious violence of the 1863 New York riot, or the various military campaigns against Native peoples. To bend Du Bois's famous phrase that "a black man is a person who must ride 'Jim Crow' in Georgia," the history of whiteness shows that a white person is simply a person who *does not* have to ride "Jim Crow" when others do, or a person who *does not* have to suffer chattel slavery when others do, or who conducts, rather than suffers, attacks on Native American homelands.[48]

Recovering the awful history of whiteness is an integral part of the reconstruction of whiteness. Sadly, most white Americans are only vaguely aware, if at all, of the immense suffering and oppression that was justified in the name of protecting white civilization. We need to do much more to come to terms with this real history of whiteness. Seeing the pain caused by whiteness helps us see why and how whiteness is problematic. Seeing how whiteness came into being helps us see how it might be unworked. Finally, seeing that there was a time when European immigrants to this land needed to learn and claim whiteness as an identity shows us that there might be a time when the descendents of Europeans who now live here might one day develop or reclaim identities free of the exclusionary and oppressive dynamics of whiteness. Before turning to the present problem of whiteness, we need to set down the specific topic of race and whiteness, and take up the task of laying out a theoretical framework for approaching whiteness.

PRAGMATIST TOOLS

THREE

JoHN DEWEY ANd INQUIRY

This chapter presents conceptual tools necessary for conducting a pragmatist reconstruction of whiteness directed toward facilitating the resolution of the problem of whiteness in the United States. This analysis will describe race both as a concept and as a set of habits, and therefore proposes a resolution to the current problem through a reconstruction of the concepts and habits of whiteness. Dewey's theory of inquiry holds that concepts emerge from an organism's interactions with its environment. This interactive framework, combined with Dewey's analysis of habits and their role in conduct and thought, directs us to reconstruct concepts involving race and whiteness in order to better change lived experience. By understanding the concept of whiteness that underlies its habits, we are better enabled to reconstruct these concepts and habits, to ultimately ameliorate our lived experiences of race that are coarsened by the problem of whiteness. We need to examine whiteness both as a concept (or more particularly a compound concept comprising kinds and categories) and as a set of habits, because kinds, categories, and habits mutually impact and revise each other, and to fully address the problem of whiteness, we need to understand all three facets of whiteness.

Before I get to the work of explaining why Dewey offers us crucial tools for reconstructing our problems with race, let me say a word about what I mean by "pragmatism." When I make reference to "pragmatism" I do so for two reasons. The first is to situate this work within the tradition of pragmatist philosophers such as Peirce, James, Dewey, Addams, and Du Bois. I do this to acknowledge the thinkers whose works inform my own. The second is to voice my commitment to certain principles that I see at the center of pragmatist philosophy. These include: the rejection of foundationalism or final causes in explaining experience; the acceptance of the belief that philosophy, like all other human endeavors, is marked by incompleteness, failure, and uncertainty and thus needs to be conducted as an ongoing process that requires constant revision and dialogue; the belief that through concerted, communal activity people can improve their lived experiences. Above these general principles that inform my use of the word "pragmatism" is the idea that the purpose of philosophy is to bring a loving wisdom to human communities to abate suffering and encourage human flourishing. To that end, this work, and the pragmatist critique of whiteness at its center, is an attempt to use philosophical tools to analyze and correct the problem of whiteness.

I begin with a sketch of Dewey's interactionist model of inquiry that he designed as an alternative to the dominant Western understanding of how we know, a model that Dewey called the "spectator theory of knowledge."[1] Moving from his critique of traditional models of epistemology and his establishment of an interactionist alternative, I then examine his claim that inquiry is best understood as a response to a pressing, existential problematic situation. From this perspective, categories are established through inquiry in response to felt needs—we can therefore read whiteness and race generally as the products of an ongoing inquiry. At the same time, such an interactionist account of race holds that these concepts, like any concepts, can be revised and reconstructed through inquiry. Just as the concept of whiteness emerged from rudimentary and uncontrolled inquiries in the Enlightenment Era, our reconceptualization of whiteness must also emerge from inquiry, but one that is more reflexive, deliberative, and consciously directed toward improving our experiences of whiteness and race. This model, which conceives of knowledge as the product of a relationship between knower and known instead of a conception of knowledge as the passive observation of an independent reality, will result in an understanding of whiteness that accepts its social construction, even as it counsels against its outright elimination. Dewey's theory of propositions shows how claims about the world frame responses within it. With this theory we can account for the reality of whiteness by looking at it as a concept that responded so well to so many various social, economic, and political needs that it became an operative habit that largely impacted how the colonists, and subsequent generations, understood the world.

Before I continue with my analysis of Dewey's theory of inquiry, I need to say a word about how I see these different theorists relate to each other. In particular, I want to dispel the misconception that since I am using Dewey to describe a general pragmatist theory of inquiry and human psychology and Du Bois to develop an account of race and whiteness, I might also ascribe to the patronizing and Eurocentric formula that Dewey was the more rigorous or even "real" philosopher of the two because Du Bois *just* theorized about race. Instead, I see myself as using the works of these two philosophers in the manner for which they were designed.

Dewey consciously and explicitly engaged in philosophical debates about meaning and human nature. He further worked to show the efficacy of pragmatist theories of inquiry and human nature. Because of his consistent advocacy for pragmatist theories and methods, his collective body of work stands as one of the best elucidations, if not *the* very best, of pragmatism. It is for this reason, as well as his consistent orientation of inquiry as a response to a problematic situation, that this analysis relies on Dewey's work for its theoretical groundwork.

Du Bois was no less a pragmatist or a cosmopolitan thinker than was Dewey. Indeed, he is one of the very few people who sallied into a wider range of studies than Dewey: though Dewey was a political theorist, cultural critic, and educator, in addition to being a philosopher, Du Bois worked and wrote in the fields of economics, history, sociology, literature, criticism, education, and politics, as well as philosophy. However, while Du Bois was a pragmatist philosopher, he did not much bother to talk *about* pragmatism. Instead, he *used* pragmatism in his life-long engagement with the problem that he himself said defined his life more than anything else: the problem of race in America. For this reason, his work does not lend itself to elucidating the basic features of a pragmatic theory as well as Dewey's work, which was largely an attempt to reconstruct philosophical ideas and debates pragmatically. This is not at all because Du Bois was less of a philosopher than Dewey, but because he simply dedicated his life to a different cause. Since he analyzed race so closely, for such a span of time, and through so many lenses, his work is an unparalleled resource for understanding race from a pragmatic perspective.

Eurocentric bias does not lie in saying that Dewey engaged traditional questions of epistemology, ethics, and logic more than did Du Bois. Such a statement would command assent from anyone familiar with both thinkers. Instead, readers within a Eurocentric culture should guard against moving from this comparative and descriptive statement to the wholly unsupported claim that *because* he did not engage in more traditional forms of philosophical dispute, Du Bois was a lesser thinker or philosopher than Dewey. He might have been less traditional than Dewey, but then almost all great thinkers seem odd in their own age. In fact, when we remember that Dewey consistently hoped that philosophy might abandon its ancient and quixotic quest for antecedent certainty through purely rational means detached from practice in favor of an experimental method that rejected the separation of knowing and doing, we can then see Du Bois as *just this new kind of philosopher* who orients his inquiry according to the pressing problems that face humanity.

Spectator Theory of Knowledge

In 1929 John Dewey compiled the notes of the Gifford Lectures that he had presented earlier that year at the University of Edinburgh, and published them as a book titled *The Quest for Certainty*. This work is the clearest articulation of the ramifications that follow from his dissolution of certain fundamental philosophical divisions, such as that between ontology and epistemology, or between *theoria* and *praxis*. Philosophizing in the light of the recent scientific discoveries made by physicists such as Werner Heisenberg, whose findings irrevocably called into question assumptions about the nature of observations that had undergirded science for centuries, Dewey's work similarly rejected a set of philosophical assumptions that he detected beneath almost all of Western philosophy. He called this view the "spectator theory of knowledge."[2]

Dewey starts his critique of the spectator theory of knowledge by pointing out that this basic model of epistemology has been a fundamental part of Western thought for over two millennia.[3] Dewey looks at the debates that have roiled philosophy since the early days of the ancient Greeks, and sees beneath these differences a common feature, namely, that all these different schools, whether they argued for a Parmenedian permanence or a Heraclitan hustle, Cartesian rationalism or Humean empiricism, all held that "what is known is antecedent to the mental act of observation and inquiry, and is totally unaffected by these acts; otherwise it would not be fixed and unchangeable."[4] That is, regardless of how the different philosophies explained the relationship between the knower and the world that made knowledge possible, "the real object is the object so fixed in its regal aloofness that it is a king to any beholding mind that may gaze upon it. A spectator theory of knowledge is the inevitable outcome."[5] In the end, we have a model where "the object of knowledge is a reality fixed and complete in itself, in isolation from an act of inquiry which has in it any element of production of change."[6]

The spectator theory of knowledge has two basic components. The first is that there is a single, fixed reality that is antecedent to our attempts to come to know it. As Dewey says of this theory, "for knowledge to be certain [it] must relate to that which has antecedent existence or essential being."[7] The second relevant aspect of the spectator theory of knowledge is that the known thing is separated from the knower, and is unaffected by the act of knowing itself. This point, which for Dewey is little more than an unsubstantiated article of faith because we cannot know anything that isn't already bound up with a knower, is the assumption upon which the very possibility of certain, unchanging knowledge rests. Once knowledge is assumed to be valuable if and only if it is certain and unchanging knowledge about a permanent reality, then the act of knowing has to be defined in such a way that it reveals the truth about the world *without changing it*. Philosophy in most of the Western tradition strove to grasp the "real."

This second aspect of the spectator theory of knowledge is perhaps the greater of the two when it comes to explaining the prevalence of ocular models in Western philosophy. Touch and taste obviously interact with and potentially change a thing, and our hearing and smell often offer inexact and incomplete reports on the world. However, our vision seems to promise a connection with the world that is both transparent and detached. As we will see later, Dewey and other pragmatists (not to mention phenomenologists and feminists) came to advocate richer models of inquiry that suffused or supplanted ocular models with models of knowing that were variously more embodied, communal, and purposive. This change occurred in large part because people started to see how knowledge is not a pure and antecedent item sitting out in the world, waiting to be beamed into our minds on rays of light. Knowledge is instead produced inside the interactions between acculturated human beings and their environments.[8]

Dewey's Critique of the Spectator Theory of Knowledge

Dewey critiques the traditional hope that certain knowledge of an unchanging reality of the world is achievable by means of inquiry based on ocular models for two reasons. The first stems from the tradition's propensity to elevate theory and deprecate practice. This separation correlates to the two possible ways of responding to an uncertain world: either to "change the self in emotion or idea" or to "change the world through action."[9] The Western tradition long ago settled on the internal/cognitive solution, one that culminated in the quest for certainty through thought. Dewey's first critique of the spectator theory of knowledge rests on an ironic development regarding these two ways of dealing with uncertainty. In trying to achieve a degree of security through a theoretical description of reality, we have ignored the fact that "the thing which concerns all of us as human beings is precisely the greatest attainable security of values in concrete existence."[10] That is, we have let theory, the most useful of all *tools* for the creation of a more secure human existence, become unhitched from the context of human experience. Dewey urges us to abandon the spectator theory of knowledge, arguing that "[t]he notion that thought, apart from action, can warrant complete certitude as to the status of supreme good, makes no contribution to the central problem of development of intelligent methods of regulation. It rather depresses and deadens efforts in that direction. That is the chief indictment to be brought against the classic philosophic tradition."[11] In addition to this chief indictment we find a secondary reason to try to overcome the spectator theory of knowledge. Where the first critique is a negative one—based on the fact that framing knowledge as the act of reckoning an antecedent reality that is unaffected by our inquiries fails to yield the kind of lived and robust certainty we wanted in the first place—this second one is based on the success of an alternate model: the experimental model of the sciences.

Dewey turns to science and its experimental methods of inquiry because it "has completely abandoned in fact the traditional separation of knowing and doing."[12] The scientific method of knowing serves a more appropriate model for understanding the relationship between the knower and the world than the spectator theory of knowledge because it "installs doing as the heart of knowing."[13] While the scientific method clearly played a defining role in Dewey's efforts to correct the spectator theory of knowledge, we need to remember that in suggesting the methods of science Dewey was *not* saying that science has some kind of perfect or even privileged access to reality or truth. Such a claim would not provide a true alternative to the spectator theory of knowledge, but would merely enthrone science as the final arbiter of the antecedent truth of the matter. Instead, Dewey looks to science because of its experimental method. As he says in *The Quest for Certainty:*

> If we frame our conception of knowledge on the experimental model, we find that it is a way of operating upon and with the things of ordinary experience so that we can frame our ideas of them in terms of their interactions with one another, instead of in terms of the qualities they directly present, and that thereby our control of them, our ability to change them and direct their changes as we desire, is indefinitely increased.[14]

Thus, philosophers need to learn from the content of scientific findings, but even more from the ways in which science is conducted. Science is common sense refined and scrutinized. Dewey ends a discussion of intelligence and inquiry in "The Naturalization of Intelligence" by stating:

> There is no kind of inquiry which has a monopoly on the honorable title of knowledge. The engineer, the artist, the historian, the man of affairs attain knowledge in the degree they employ methods that enable them to solve the problems which develop in the subject-matter they are concerned with. As philosophy framed upon the pattern of experimental inquiry does away with all wholesale skepticism, so it eliminates all invidious monopolies of the idea of science. By their fruits we shall know them.[15]

Just as the scientific community has had to relinquish the idea of an unchanging physical reality, philosophy must abandon the quest for certainty or the idea that its purview is to serve as a detached observer of unchanging truth. Dewey, bolstered by the findings of contemporary scientists such as Einstein, Bohr, and Heisenberg, argued that we ought to recognize that the detachment assumed by the spectator theory is, and always has been, illusory. This is because the spectator theory of knowledge fails to recognize that no matter how still we might be, we are always already in an interactive relationship with the world we observe.

The spectator theory of knowledge thus fails for at least two reasons according to Dewey. Insofar as the spectator theory of knowledge strives for a detached and unengaged relationship to the world in order to develop a faithful representation of it, the spectator theory of knowledge forecloses on our attempts to *engage with the world* in order to develop a more secure state of affairs. It asks us to become so still and removed that it prevents us from the kind of engrossment necessary to achieve the security for which inquiry is designed. Secondly, scientific findings of the early twentieth century suggested that the ideal of a completely detached form of observation that has no effect on the object observed is impossible. Try as we might, we will never get at a representation of the world that is free of the impacts of our inquiry. We never observe anything that is outside of the act of observation; we, as inquirers, never leave the knowing relationship. Ralph Barton Perry termed this predicament the "ego-centric predicament" in a 1910 essay of the same name. In the essay he articulates the very problem that Dewey saw at the heart of the spectator theory of knowledge.

> In order to discover if possible exactly how a [thing] is modified by the [knowing] relationship . . . , I look for instances of [the thing] out of this relationship, in order that I may compare them with instances of [the thing] in this relationship. But I can find no such instances, because "finding" is a variety of the very relationship that I am trying to eliminate. Hence I can not make the comparison, nor get an answer to my original question by this means. But I can now conclude that there are no such instances; indeed, I now know that *I should not be able to discover them if there were* [emphasis in original].[16]

Dewey found that this same insight about the impossibility of stepping outside the egocentric perspective in the work of contemporary scientists. In particular, Heisenberg's critique, through his famous principle of indeterminacy, of the Newtonian assumption that the position and velocity of bodies are independent of the act of observation was of great import to Dewey. Dewey was fairly unconcerned with the complex methods used to arrive at this principle, saying "[t]he scientific and the mathematical reasonings which led to his conclusion are technical. But fortunately they do not concern us."[17] What does concern Dewey and his readers is the fact that Heisenberg proved that "if we fix, metrically, the velocity, then there is a range of indeterminateness in the assignment of position, and viceversa. . . . The element of indeterminateness is not connected with defect in the method of observation but is intrinsic. The particle observed does not *have* fixed position or velocity, for it is changing all the time because of interaction."[18]

For Dewey, Heisenberg's conclusions were "the final step in the dislodgement of the old spectator theory of knowledge."[19] It forces us away from the now impossible task of knowing the world as it was before our knowing, and toward a new model where knowing "is a form of doing and is to be judged like other modes by its eventual issue."[20] We therefore know in order to improve our doings and actions in the world. We see this same idea that inquiry is not a description of nature, but a knowing interaction within nature, in Heisenberg's account of how science changed from the Newtonian model after the advent of the Copenhagen interpretation of quantum theory: "Natural science does not simply describe and explain nature; it is a part of the interplay between nature and ourselves; it describes nature as exposed to our method of questioning. This was a possibility of which Descartes could not have thought, but it makes the sharp separation between the world and the I impossible."[21]

The impossibility of the kind of knowledge promised by the spectator theory of knowledge is apparent simply by virtue of the fact that we, as knowers, are not observing a world that is removed from us, but are instead a part of the world that interacts with the world through knowing. This realization leads to a very different understanding of the nature and purpose of knowledge. Dewey asks us to recognize that "[k]nowing is . . . a case of specifically directed activity instead of something isolated from practice. The quest for certainty by means of exact possession in mind of immutable reality is exchanged for search for security by means of active control of the changing course of events. Intelligence in operation, another name for method, becomes the thing most worth winning."[22] By rejecting the spectator theory of knowledge in favor of an inter-actionist model of knowledge Dewey has, depending on how you characterize it, dissolved or evaded traditional ontological concerns in favor of a model of knowing inseparable from our efforts to achieve our ends in the world. Ontology traditionally addressed some form of the question "What *is* over and above what *seems* or *might be?*" It involves a crucial *distinction* between that which the knower brings to the experience (like the particularities of our ocular faculties that make the straight stick submerged in water *seem* bent), and what really is (the fact that the stick *is* straight). Ontology is the quest for certainty about the nature of things beyond or before our imperfect perceptions. However, by collapsing *this very distinction* as we saw above, Dewey's interactionist model remains agnostic about the nature of things beyond the act of knowing.

This refutation of the traditional hunger for an account of things apart from our experience of them is one of the most consistent traits of Dewey's work. We see an early and succinct version of this critique in his 1905 essay "The Postulate of Immediate Empiricism," where he says simply: "Immediate empiricism postulates that things—anything, everything, in the ordinary or non-technical use of the term 'thing'—are what they are experienced as. Hence, if one wishes to describe anything truly, his task is to tell what it is experienced as being."[23]

Such claims only strengthen the point that, for Dewey, the closest thing to an ontological claim that we can safely make (we interact with the world through the act of knowing) is one that forecloses on the possibility of making the sorts of claims with which ontology has concerned itself. Since "knowing is a participant in what is known" we can never know what comes before knowing.[24] If the real is the experienced real, there is no point (or need) to find out what lurks behind our experience. To this extent he leaves aside *traditional* ontological concerns. The world as revealed within a knowing interaction is the one we are stuck with. We therefore need to be honest about the fact that our accounts of reality always assume that they are accounts of reality "as it appears to me now." More importantly, we need to remember that the best sort of knowing is a knowing *for* that does not try to separate the account of the world from the reasons, goals, desires, and problems that motivate the act of inquiry in the first place. As Dewey claims in *The Quest for Certainty,* "the criterion of knowledge lies in the method used to secure consequences and not in metaphysical conceptions of the nature of the real."[25]

Knowing and inquiry are organic, meliorist, and instrumental practices for Dewey; they form one half of an interactive circuit when combined with purposive action in the world. What is real for Dewey is simply the sum of our experiences. Inquiry, either the casual non-systematic sort we engage in every day or the systematic and reflexive sort performed by scientists, does not reveal the "really" real. Instead, it furthers our ability to interact in the world, to stabilize our experiences and achieve our ends. An inquiry into race and whiteness therefore is not an attempt to describe a static and pre-experiential state of affairs, but an attempt to revise and deepen our understanding of our experiences of race and whiteness with an eye on improving our lived experience. This current inquiry into the problem of whiteness is very Deweyan, therefore; he argued that quintessential inquiry is always summoned by a problem.

Inquiry as a Response to a Problematic Situation

The notion that inquiry and the results, ideas, and directed actions that stem from it are responses to a problematic situation is perhaps the most prominent thread across the field of American pragmatists. This unique perspective on inquiry leads us away from attempting to *define* whiteness or race materially or antecedently, and toward the question of how we ought relate to and discuss whiteness in light of the present vicissitudes of the problems of race and racism. In other words, it leads us to not focus on the question "What is whiteness?" where the answer lies in the biological findings regarding people currently defined as white, but instead to try to deal with the more difficult questions: How do we interact with each other in terms of the idea of whiteness? Is this idea, and its associated habits and practices, an adequate response to our present circumstances? Should the idea be reconstructed in light of current problems? The answer to these questions has to do with its history, the values it affirms, and the ways it responds to other values and futures.

Inquiry for Dewey is not a special process reserved for the highly educated few, but a most commonplace event in human experience. Indeed, inquiries "enter into every area of life and into every aspect of every area," and we all "infer and judge as 'naturally' as [we] reap and sow, produce and exchange commodities."[26] This naturalized treatment of inquiry places it on a continuum with the common sense questioning that everyone does every day. This continuity between philosophy, science, and common sense judgments exists because all these kinds of inquiries share the feature that they all respond to problematic experiences. While all fields of human inquiry are linked for Dewey in their ability to solve problems in experience, science is special to a certain extent. As a field of inquiry that is so refined and self-reflexive, its value exceeds its teleological, problem-solving ability (though it does not overshadow this ability). As Dewey says in *Democracy and Education,* "All that we can be sure of educationally is that science should be taught so as to be an end in itself in the lives of students—something worthwhile on account of its own unique intrinsic contribution to the experience of life."[27]

Inquiry starts with the presence of an indeterminate situation; it begins with the recognition that something is amiss. However, it is crucial for Dewey that this indeterminacy does not merely dwell in the mind of the inquirer, but "[i]t is the *situation* that [is doubtful.] *We* are doubtful because the situation is inherently doubtful."[28] He further rejects the idea that an inquiry-generating situation is a subjective affair, saying that "a genuine problem is one set by existential problematic *situations*. In social inquiry, genuine problems are set only by actual social situations which are themselves conflicting and confused."[29] While the inquirer is the one responsible for initiating an inquiry, she does so because some aspect of her environment has fallen into disequilibrium.

For example, imagine the case of a dean at a college who walks down the hall toward her office, as she does every weekday. However, on this day she experiences something new and quite unusual: she finds a group of thirty or so students sitting on the floor directly in front of the door to the administrative offices. This first experience, the one that brings her up short with its oddness, is the moment of indeterminacy. At the very beginning, the dean has nothing to go on: she doesn't even know enough to begin to make sense of the situation. All she knows is that things are not as they should be because her experience is nowhere near her regular pattern. After a few moments of reading the signs the students hold ("DIVERSITY NOW," "Students of Color Need Faculty of Color") and speaking with some of the students, she begins to make sense of the situation: the problem is that these few students claim to represent many others who have grown dissatisfied with a lack of attention on the part of the administration to issues of multiculturalism. She can't get to her office because they are staging a sit-in. At this point, Dewey would say that she has moved from the first stage of inquiry to the second one, from an indeterminate situation to a problematic one.

What is crucial to notice is that the problem is not just "in her head," or a wholly subjective aspect of her experience. She really could not get anywhere near her office to start her day as usual. Similarly, the students are there because of a real conflict, in this case between certain aspects of university traditions and the general mission of institutions of higher learning to be cosmopolitan and broad-minded locations for experimentation and learning. Dewey would call it balderdash to say that this problem was just in her head. Instead, it is a situation made up of various factors: the sense of tradition attached to all institutions of higher learning, the arguments made by feminists, people of color, and queer people for greater diversity in the curriculum and faculty, and the dean's own social position that draws her into this debate (in a way that she would not be if she where the college's registrar or grounds supervisor). Thus, Dewey argues that the indeterminate and, later, problematic experiences that are the catalysts of inquiry are, like in inquiry itself, interactive phenomena: "The indeterminate situation becomes problematic in the very process of being subjected to inquiry. The indeterminate situation comes into existence from existential causes, just as does, say, the organic imbalance of hunger. There is nothing intellectual or cognitive in the existence of such situations, although they are the necessary condition of cognitive operations or inquiry."[30]

We can now look at how Dewey characterizes the sorts of problems that motivate the kind of social inquiry surrounding the issue of racism and whiteness. In the section of *Logic: The Theory of Inquiry* titled "Social Inquiry" he claims first that such problems must "grow out of actual social tensions, needs, [and] 'troubles.'"[31] For example, the problem of child poverty is a pressing problem because a quarter of the children in this country *really do* lack enough food, shelter, and education to grow into healthy adults. This is a problem both for each of these individual children because of the frequency with which they experience cold, hunger, fear, and illness and for our society as a whole, because we need to deal with the immediate shame of hungry children and the future problems of poorly nourished, educated, and socialized adults. Just as inquiry is an activity that is both organic (consisting of certain phenomena that are physical and material) and cultural (having to do with contingent but organizing ideas, categories, and ideals), the problem of child poverty, like virtually all problems, is both organic and cultural. Its organic aspect is fairly obvious: many young people lack the necessary nutrients for adequate development. However, this problem is no less a culturally defined one: cultural constructs such as money, property, custody, and class all play a part in why some children have all they need and much more, while many more have not nearly enough.

Second, a problem that calls for social inquiry must have its "subject-matter determined by the conditions that are material means of bringing about a unified situation."[32] To continue our example, the problem of child poverty is best understood as the problem of insufficient resources (food, shelter, and educational and healthcare facilities) being made available for certain children. This is important because framing the problem this way moves us toward a solution. Instead of being a merely emotive response to a pitiful state of affairs ("It is horrible that so many children go to sleep hungry"), an inquiry focused on the problem of child poverty would organize the subject matter in a way that suggests a resolution ("It is horrible that the richest country in the world doesn't allocate resources so that children don't have to go to sleep hungry"). Of course, the second claim is also powerfully emotional. However, it is different from the first because where the first statement is like a loose sail flapping uselessly in the wind of passion, the second claim, by suggesting a way out of the problem, is more like a sail that has been tied down to catch and harness the emotive gust.

Third, an inquiry-starting problem must be "related to some hypothesis [or] policy for existential resolution of the conflicting social situation."[33] To return to the problem of child hunger, the best statement of the problem of child hunger would be one that suggests a direction toward its resolution: "we can best allocate our society's wealth to end child hunger through an increase in the minimum wage" or some other specific proposal. Even if such a hypothesis failed to result in a resolution, it would yield a richer experiential framework regarding the problem, which would enable a deeper understanding of the problem and a better assessment of potential responses.

Finally, while individuals face various small-scale problems that require individual inquiries, the sorts of broad social problems that interest Dewey in his discussion of social inquiry, Du Bois in much of his work, and us are ones that are defined within "a cultural matrix which is ultimately determined by the nature of social relations."[34] Thus, while certain inquiries might be nearly universal in that they respond to situations that are relatively straightforward and acultural (such as how to pull a splinter from your foot, or how to save yourself from drowning), others are attempts to settle situations that are unique to a particular sociocultural context. For example, the current debate on multiculturalism and the academy entails a series of specific inquiries that would have been articulated very differently, if at all, a mere one hundred years ago.

Attention to the cultural matrix is crucial for an inquiry into the problems attached to racial whiteness primarily because of the particularities of whiteness that we will explore in parts 3 and 4. As a consequence of whiteness's propensity to engender ignorance among whites regarding their privilege it would be ill-advised to try to solve racism without specifically responding to the aspects of the cultural matrix that make white folk reticent to recognize their privilege and prone to want to stop talking about race by urging for a colorblind society.

FOUR

Race as Deweyan Habit

The Conception of Whiteness

This chapter focuses on a work from the middle of Dewey's oeuvre, *Human Nature and Conduct* (1922), to explicate a pragmatist understanding of human nature, instinct, and habit formation. The analysis moves from a discussion of a general pragmatist theory of categorization in the context of inquiry toward a concrete discussion of groups and races. In particular it examines the relationship between key concepts, namely race and whiteness, in the formation of the habits and practices of whiteness. Whiteness operates in American society both as a category that played an overt role in our laws and scientific endeavors and as a set of habits that made the category concrete and framed further inquiry into questions of race. I turn to Dewey's model of habit in the hope that Shannon Sullivan was correct when she wrote that Dewey's "concept of habit can be used to understand the unconscious operations of white privilege."[1]

Framing the current debate regarding racial justice and whiteness within the meliorist conception of inquiry outlined in the previous chapter promises an understanding that charts a course toward racial justice without eliminating the value Du Bois and others see in race. However, in order to pragmatically reconstruct whiteness, we need to explore how the idea at the heart of this book—the idea of whiteness—fits into inquiry. We need to look at whiteness as both a habit and as a concept. Though the civil rights movement removed overt references to the concept of whiteness from the mainstream of our political discourses, whiteness still remains a social problem because of the persistence of habits framed by this concept. Furthermore, since whiteness persists in the form of habitual action, we need to preserve the terminology and discourse of race in order to conduct the necessary inquiry into how to solve the problem of inherited white supremacist habits. It is crucial to integrate both the concept and the habit of whiteness into the inquiry in order to achieve a satisfactory resolution. It is precisely this meliorist and reconstructive dimension of Dewey's work on the interrelation of habits, concepts, and inquiry that was missed in earlier discussions of whiteness as habit, most notably in Sullivan's *Revealing Whiteness*. However, before discussing whiteness as a set of pervasive habits, we need to discuss how the conception of whiteness functions within inquiry.

When we examine the current situation through a Deweyan lens, racial whiteness is a conception that organizes our experience by marking patterns that are relevant to particular inquiries. According to Dewey, there are two sorts of concepts: *kinds* (defined by generic propositions) and *categories* (defined by universal propositions).[2] We can perhaps better grasp Dewey's idea of how concepts function within inquiry by appealing to a metaphor drawn from mythology that will again prove useful in the following chapter when we look at Du Bois's notion of race. Concepts, and their defining propositions, are like the Roman god Janus in that they have two faces: one that looks to the past, and one that looks to the future.

Kinds are the past-looking face of conceptions, in that they are built up from patterns culled from past experiences. Of kinds, Dewey says in *Logic*: "Every proposition that involves the conception of a kind is based upon a set of related traits or characteristics that are the necessary and sufficient conditions of describing a specified kind. These traits are selectively discriminated by observation out of the total perceived field."[3] The conception of a kind is at play when, for example, an inquirer is faced with a singular object that she cannot readily identify.

Take the example of a student cleaning out her dorm room after a year; some unidentified object momentarily perplexes her at the bottom of her closet. She will first take in some of its obvious qualities: long, cord-like, gray, ending in odd-shaped metal and plastic fixtures. Dewey argues that these qualities are vital in determining what kind of thing this particular object is, but says that the kind-ness of the object does not reside *in these qualities*. This is because "[i]mmediate qualities in their immediacy are, as we have seen, unique, non-recurrent."[4] That is, while the inquirer has seen lots of gray, cord-like things very similar to the one in front of her, she has never seen this *exact* shade of gray, or seen something *exactly* this long. This is due not only to the uniqueness of the specific object, but also to the environmental circumstances that impact her inquiry (such as the variations in lighting, atmosphere, tactile sensitivity, etc.). However, this does not stop her from being able to quickly tell what kind of thing this particular thing is because "in spite of [the] existential uniqueness [of the qualities of the object], they are capable, *in the continuum of inquiry,* of becoming distinguishing characteristics which mark off (circumscribe) and identify a *kind* of objects or events."[5] That is, within the continuum of inquiry, she is able to select certain traits (cord-like, and especially the particular shape of the fixtures at the end) and disregard certain others (its particular length and its color) to determine that the thing is a printer cable. She is able to fit it into this kind because her past experience tells her which qualities serve as the defining traits of a printer cable, and which traits of printer cables are accidental (such as color and exact length).

General propositions that define kinds are past-looking because they settle the uncertain aspects of present experience through an appeal to experience that has been (or appears to be) settled. It was her past experience with printer cables that enabled her to make sense of the thing before her. Universal propositions that define categories, on the other hand, are future-looking because they take these settled aspects of past inquiry and use them to guide future inquiry. "Universal propositions are formulations of possible ways or modes of acting or operating. . . . For the universal is stated as a relation of an antecedent *if* content and consequent *then* clause. When its operational application determines existential conditions which agree with the contents of the *then* clause, the hypothesis is *in so far* confirmed."[6]

In this trivial case of the printer cable inquiry, the operational force of the universal proposition regarding printer cables is so obvious it barely merits mention. A generic proposition regarding printer cables might be "All printer cables are cord-like things that have such-and-such shaped ends to them." A universal proposition regarding printer cables would be "If a cable is a printer cable, then one should use it to link a printer to a computer processor." The universal proposition about the thing in front of her would direct the inquirer's actions toward the thing. It would lead her away from trying to fit the cord into the back of her computer monitor say, and would lead her to try to fit it into the printer. Her hypothesis that it is in fact a printer cable would be borne out when and if the cable *did* fit between her printer and the computer, and if the printer managed to work. These would be sufficient conditions to determine that the thing is a printer cable (because only a printer cable can serve such a function) but are not necessary (as the printer cable might not fit, but still be a printer cable designed for another kind of computer or printer).

All of the above bears out the basic shape of Dewey's arguments regarding how generic propositions (that define kinds) organize and give shape to experiences, and universal propositions (that define categories) are prospective and direct how we will test and use present and future experiences. Kinds and categories are concepts that stand between the human past and future. They are links to the past by virtue of the fact that they express certain pertinent patterns of human existence as lived so far. They report on past experience and preserve distinctions that have proven useful. At the same time, they are forward-looking dispositions to the future. Once we have used a kind to define a particular, the associated category tells us how to act toward the thing. Most importantly, however, is that while kinds and categories are stubborn and generally resist elimination, they are flexible enough to change in the face of new experiences that revise our concepts.

When discussing the racial categories that we have inherited and must respond to, we need to start with Europe, as the categories with which we must contend are European in their origin.[7] At the earliest stages of the European arrival on this continent, inquiry of the sort Dewey speaks of was constrained by tradition and theological constructs. It is for this reason that the propositions, both universal and generic, that guided the early colonists did not emerge from open investigations, but from particular interpretations of the Christian Bible and from other folk beliefs of Europe. These ideas imported from Christian Europe largely determined the kinds and categories that the Europeans established here, but in a way that escaped their notice. Dewey explains why when he says:

> [T]he standardized conceptions and rules are for the most part products of habit and tradition. Hence they seem so fixed that they are not themselves open to question or criticism. They operate practically to determine kinds but the grounds or reasons for the kinds that are acknowledged in practice are not investigated or weighed—it is enough that the customary rules are what they are. From the logical standpoint, there is a vicious circle.[8]

The propositions the colonists and others brought with them largely determined how they interpreted their experiences. Such propositions, as Dewey observes, point to perhaps the most challenging aspect of the ideas and habits related to whiteness (as well as the proto-white categories operative in colonial America), namely the *seeming naturalness and obviousness* of not only the generic statements related to whiteness, but also the proscriptive universal statements that established the category of white humans as superlative. Because of the power of religious authority in early eras, the apparent certainty of scientific taxonomies of human kind in later eras, and the immediate value of using these propositions for the colonists, they did not stop to question the appropriateness of the categories and kinds they were imposing.

However, it is not enough to say that the propositions that the early colonists used to categorize the different people of the colony were in place solely because of religious tradition and authority. As Dewey says in the passage above, conceptions are generally the product of tradition as well as *habit.* Habits and concepts mutually impact each other: they form a continuous circuit. From this perspective, kinds and categories are manifestations of habits and dispositions already operating. Kinds capture the past operations of habits, while categories describe dispositions to act in the future in certain ways. As such, they serve to reinforce established habits or, when subjected to inquiry, become a means to reinforce habits and dispositions. If it were the case that racism was only the product of flawed religious or legal decree it would be easy to solve, and would most likely not have survived the intellectual upheavals of the Enlightenment period. Instead, the notions that assumed certain people inherently better than others were more deeply seated than were legal pronouncements. The patterns of thought that we now call racist were intellectual habits as much as they were expressly articulated laws or decrees. It is for this reason that we need to move away from Dewey's notion of inquiry and the roles that propositions play within it in order to look at his analysis of how habits affect our beliefs and behaviors. Only after we have looked at how habits and concepts mutually inform each other and direct human behavior can we return to the specific issue of whiteness.

Dewey's Theory of Habits

It might seem odd to recourse to such a plain idea as "habit" when trying to address the sorts of socially, culturally, and historically thorny questions that are implicated in the problem of whiteness. However, the pragmatic conception of habit—introduced by William James, elaborated by John Dewey, and put to work by Jane Addams and W. E. B. Du Bois—is a crucial conceptual tool for developing an apt response to the continued problem of whiteness.

The habits of whiteness have persisted long after the civil rights movement removed whiteness as a legal category designed to protect white privilege. Reading race through the lens of habit in a fully pragmatic sense, we see that race is not an ahistorical essence that we all carry in our blood, packed with ready-to-use meanings (though this reading does maintain that racial propositions and identities do rely on certain physical traits as markers). At the same time, this method of interpreting race rejects the idea that since the conceptions of race find no direct genetic or biological correlates, the idea of race is merely a cognitive error that can be remedied by purging our lexicons of any terms that lack scientific proof. Instead, this reading characterizes race as a meaningful feature of our experience. It is made up of features that emerge from biology (namely the morphological features that are the signs of the different racial categories) and culture (the inherited but contingent *ways* of reading and responding to these features). On this reading, race is a phenomenon that organizes our behaviors, thoughts, and experiences of the world both consciously and pre-consciously. From a Deweyan perspective, race is "real" though not "given." An analysis of whiteness that pertains to the role of habit suggests that the best path toward a society free of invidious racism leads through a period of *conscious reconstruction of concept and habit through inquiry*.

This use of Deweyan habit differs significantly from Sullivan's recent reading of whiteness as habit, which argues that "[w]hatever significant control over unconscious habits exists is found in the indirect access one has to them via environment."[9] Her analysis focuses on psychoanalytic models that treat habits of whiteness as a murky fen of unconscious feelings of seduction as well as "slippages and phantoms."[10] It is for this reason, she says, that "habits of white privilege are more likely to be changed by indirect, rather than direct, assaults upon them."[11] Instead, by reading Dewey's extensive work on the interrelation of concepts, kinds, and habits, I present the habits of whiteness as no less cruel and problematic, but as part of human interaction that can be changed and improved. It is true, as Sullivan says, that "one cannot completely micromanage the complex transaction of psyche, soma, and world that produces unconscious habit."[12] But this should not stop anyone who takes to heart Dewey's repeated cautions against going on quests for certainty. Pragmatists know that endeavors to solve human problems never come with guarantees. To say that one cannot completely micromanage the problem of white habits does not at all mean one cannot reconstruct them into new patterns that are far better than the previous ones. Habits, being integrated manifestations of the concepts by which we organize our experiences, cannot simply be ignored, wished away, or snuck up on indirectly. They must be treated like any other bad habit that impoverishes human experience. They must be engaged directly to the best of our ability through inquiry and reconstruction.

Emphasizing their fundamental role in our development as organisms, Dewey argues that "habits may be profitably compared to physiological functions, like breathing [or] digesting . . . in requiring the cooperation of organism and environment."[13] As this passage indicates, habit formation not only is a basic human function but also is a function that is inherently interactional. Habits form a connection between our broader biological, cultural, or social environment and us. Thus, since human interaction is widely impacted by cultural forces, habit formation is also a function that enables us to make sense of the world. It is "that kind of human activity which is influenced by prior activity and in that sense acquired; which contains within itself a certain ordering or systematization of minor elements of action; which is projective, dynamic in quality, ready for overt manifestation; and which is operative in some subdued subordinate form even when not obviously dominating activity."[14] Dewey later characterizes the habit as "an acquired predisposition to *ways* or modes of response."[15] Habits are the means through which we make our experiences meaningful, because "the *meaning* of native activities is not native, but acquired."[16]

Habits form because they work; they become sedimented in a person's behavior because they enable him to find equilibrium within the surrounding environment. The longer that a habit functions, the less obvious it becomes. It becomes such a part of an individual organism that it becomes unnoticeable until a problem throws it into relief.

No matter how accidental and irrational the circumstances of its origin, no matter how different the conditions which now exist to those under which the habit was formed, the latter persists until the environment obstinately rejects it. Habits once formed perpetuate themselves, by acting unremittingly upon the native stock of activities. They stimulate, inhibit, intensify, weaken, select, concentrate and organize the latter into their own likeness.[17]

Thus, habits are not only interactional but also conservative: once a habit becomes a part of an organism's response to the environment, it is difficult to notice, let alone remove. Sullivan links this element of habit nicely to the problem of race when she writes that "[a]s an instance of habit, race often functions subconsciously, as a predisposition for acting in the world that is not consciously chosen or planned."[18] In most cases this is fortuitous for the organism because the very fact that the habit has taken hold indicates its likely appropriateness. However, we will see that not all habits are worth keeping.

Habits, which are acquired patterns of responding to and understanding an environment, work by organizing more basic or "native" feelings that Dewey variously calls instinct or impulse.[19] The native activities occur before habits and emerge within each individual organism, but ultimately depend on acquired habit for any meaning.[20] Though an infant responds first to her environment through impulse (as she has learned no habits) any meaning ascribed to her actions depends on her caregiver's habituation. The infant *means* nothing by crying; she merely cries as part of an organic series of interactions. Instead, the baby's father has become habituated (through previous experiences with babies or with people who have had experience with babies) to interpret the crying as indicating a wet diaper, hunger, or some other discomfort. "The inchoate and scattered impulses of an infant do not coordinate into serviceable powers except through social dependencies and companionships. . . . [Her] impulses are merely starting points for assimilation of the knowledge and skill of the more matured beings upon whom [she] depends."[21]

Dewey argues that meaning is therefore a cultural, interactive, and habitual affair. He rejects the idea that we carry innate ideas or even meaningful patterns of behavior, arguing instead that "the *meaning* of native activities is not native; it is acquired. It depends upon interaction with a matured social medium."[22] However, this does not mean that impulses are merely the building blocks of habit. Impulses are also "the pivots upon which the re-organization of activities turn, they are agencies of deviation, for giving new directions to old habits and changing their qualities."[23] An impulse (such as the infant's uncomfortable feeling) might become a trigger or component of a habituated response to an environment (such as crying until receiving the food or attention that dissipates the unpleasant feeling). Similarly, an impulse (such as an acute feeling of pain) might serve as a fulcrum to leverage an organism away from a set behavior (like going for a hard run every day) toward a different one (doing yoga). "Impulse in short brings with itself the possibility but not the assurance of a steady reorganization of habits to meet new elements in new situations. The moral problem in child and adult alike as regards impulse and instinct is to utilize them for formation of new habits, or what is the same thing, the modification of an old habit so that it may be adequately serviceable under novel conditions."[24] Impulses are both inchoate and regulative. They are inchoate in that they lack any original meaning and must thus wait for an acquired habit to make sense of them. At the same time, they challenge and move habit. We see this in impulses that have no ready place within habituated responses. These rogue impulses force an organism to either modify existing habits to make room for these impulses or develop new ones.

The attention to the role of impulse in reconstructing bad habits is, I think, the most significant difference between my analysis of whiteness as habit and Sullivan's. Sullivan is absolutely right to say that white people are incapable of fully removing the epistemological filter that has for centuries made acts of oppression and injustice seem warranted and made the privileges of whiteness seem in line with supposedly race-blind principles of justice. Similarly, an alcoholic can never be entirely sure that he won't fall off the wagon and take another drink. However, it does not at all follow that the alcoholic cannot take some control, even a great deal of control, over his drinking, even though he will still be an alcoholic till the day he dies. Sullivan is certainly right to talk at length about the role of environment in shaping habits, just as any recovering alcoholic knows it is easier to stay sober if you stay away from your old drinking haunts. However, we also need to reflect on problematic behaviors, identify habits that don't work, and start to consciously form new ones as best we can. While I know that I will always see a particular world due to the habits of whiteness, I can start to identify the impulses that have caused me to act our white privilege in the past in the hope that I do so much less, and optimally not at all, in the future.

Habits, and the problems of bad habits, instead of conscious decisions, become the focal point of Dewey's moral philosophy. For him we should not so much worry about our conscious responses to moral dilemmas that are recognized as such, but should instead attend to the habits by which we make thousands of unconscious decisions. In particular, we should examine our bad habits: those that continue to function in our behaviors but have somehow fallen out of harmony with their environment. "A bad habit suggests an inherent tendency to action and also a hold, command over us. It makes us do things we are ashamed of, things which we tell ourselves we prefer not to do. It overrides our formal resolutions, our conscious decisions. When we are honest with ourselves we acknowledge that a habit has this power because it is so intimately part of ourselves. It as a hold on us because we are the habit."[25]

Marx suggested that we adjust the traditional scientific genus categorization of *Homo sapiens* ("the knowing human") to *Homo faber* ("the making human") in order to emphasize that what we make and do defines us more deeply than the thoughts we think. Dewey leaves us a perspective on human nature that indicates we ought to think of ourselves as *Homo habitus* ("the habituated human") because our habits, more than anything else, are what define us. Most basically, "Man is a creature of habit, not of reason nor yet instinct."[26]

Race as Habit and Conception

Having presented the basic components of Dewey's notion of habit, we can now see how it interacts with conceptions. To first discuss their commonalities, both habits and conceptions regulate an organism's ability to find equilibrium in its environment. Both entail a harnessing of past experience to settle present experience and direct future action. In the case of conceptions, past experience guides which traits are relevant qualities for determining the boundaries of conceptions. In the case of habits, past experience is the testing ground that strengthens certain habits and allows them to become sedimented and prevents others from becoming established.

In one sense, habits and concepts form a circuit: a change in a concept can lead to a change in habit, and vice versa. In another sense, habits and concepts impact each other to different degrees. To see how, we need to return briefly to *Human Nature and Conduct* where Dewey argues that

> habits are affections, that all have projectile power, and that a predisposition formed by a number of specific acts is an immensely more intimate and fundamental part of ourselves than are vague, general, conscious choices. All habits are demands for certain kinds of activity; and they constitute the self. . . . They form our effective desires and they furnish us with our working capacities. They rule our thoughts, determining which shall appear strong and which shall pass from light into obscurity.[27]

If it is the case that habits "rule our thoughts," it seems clear that for Dewey habits play a more powerful role in our behavior and experiences than do conceptions. We find more evidence for placing habits above conceptions when we read in his *Logic* that the "formation of ideas as well as their execution depends upon habit."[28] Recall also that Dewey claims in the same work that "the conception of kind [defined by generic propositions] is based upon a set of related traits or characteristics that are the necessary and sufficient conditions of describing a specific kind."[29] Concepts must then rely on habits of thought for their genesis since "[t]o be able to single out a definitive sensory element in any field is evidence of a high degree of previous training, that is, of well-formed habits."[30] Propositions that define concepts are the products of habits of thought that have proven useful in a person's attempt to find harmony in their environment. This recalls Dewey's claim that thought, like all human endeavors, should be directed at achieving a functional equilibrium more than describing a separate and static reality. Propositions, and the concepts they define, survive or fall away according to their useful-ness. While we can talk about concepts without speaking of habits for the sake of clarity or convention (as Dewey does in *Logic*), concepts are nonetheless the products of particularly specialized intellectual habits.

We can now reach back to the historical material from chapters 2 and 3 to make sense of how we can read the conceptions and habits of race through a Dew-eyan lens. First, we need to speak about habits and concepts before and after Ba-con's Rebellion, since this historical event was a watershed in the evolution of race and whiteness. Before the rebellion, we can detect the use of certain concepts that included particular ways of thinking of men and women, children and adults, and nobles and commoners. Of particular note for this study were the propositions regarding laborers and masters, the free and unfree, as well as the different habits of thought concerning "Christians," Negroes, and Mulattoes.

"Christian" (here I mean the geographical sense of the word "Christian" that was distinguished from terms such as "savage," "Indian," and "Negro") as a *kind* (defined by past-looking, descriptive propositions) referred to the group of people who came from Europe (that is, the Christian countries, as the colonists under-stood them). "Christian" as a *category* (defined by future-looking, normative propositions that articulated a disposition toward a thing) distinguished a group of people whom one should treat as free individuals with certain rights. While the intellectual habits regarding Christians were modified according to other impor-tant intellectual habits (such as those related to age, gender, and marital status) we can still see a difference between how the colonists thought one should treat a Christian and how they thought one should treat people who fall within different kinds and categories, most notably Native Americans (or "savages" in their unfor-tunate terminology) and African Americans. We can recall the language of the 1662 law titled "An act for mulatto children being bond or free, to serve according to the condition of the mother" for a clear indication that, even in the pre-rebellion colony, the categories of "christian" and "Negro" were different, as when it reads, "if any christian shall commit fornication with a Negro man or woman, hee or shee soe offending shall pay double fines."[31]

We see very different kinds and categories attached to African colonists. "Negro" as a kind meant simply a person from Africa or of African descent. "Negro" as a category was trickier. On the one hand, we can say that there was a strong leaning on the part of the people who ran the colonies to treat people of African descent as laborers who were generally *not entitled* to the same treat-ment as Christian colonists. We see this in the 1643 law that included African women over the age of sixteen in with all men in terms of their requirement to pay taxes.[32] The same intellectual habit of discrimination against people of Af-rican descent is seen earlier in the 1662 law mentioned above, where it reads "all children borne in this country shalbe held bond or free only according to the condition of the mother" which meant that all children born to life-bonded

African slaves inherited their mother's status, where children born to European women who were indentured for a set amount of time were born free.[33] Yet, despite this marked difference in dispositions toward people of European or African descent, we do not yet see the habit of thinking of *all* African immigrants as laborers who were unfree.

What is most crucial for this discussion is that while the propositions defining Christians and Negroes led to different treatment and status in pre-rebellion Virginia, the more important propositions or habits of thought were the ones associated with "servants" (a term that referred to both indentured and life laborers). The Virginia colony existed to farm tobacco for profit. The majority of the European immigrants were there to work, many against their will. They were there for the same reason that the African laborers were there. It is for this very reason that so many laborers who hailed from different continents were able to see eye-to-eye enough to engage in rebellion. It is for this reason that we read of countless little pacts between "christians" and "Negroes" who worked together to find food, respite, freedom, and physical intimacy with each other. Whether you were a woman or a man, a Christian or a Negro, if you fit into the kind "servant," the rulers of the colony were disposed toward you in more or less the same way. We can say that the category "servant" was defined by propositions such as "if a person is a servant, get them to harvest as much tobacco as possible, regardless of age, gender, or national origin." So, while a person's age, gender, and ethnicity impacted the *sort* of work they did and how they fit into the tobacco plantation labor pool, in the pre-rebellion colony these differences were often less significant than the commonalities that all servants shared. The category of "servant" therefore to an extent trumped the categories involving age, gender, and origin.

Bacon's Rebellion was a cataclysmic change in the social environment that represented a critical problem for the rulers of the colony. In the Deweyan sense, it was a problem that initiated a new inquiry. We can see from the immediate and marked changes in the laws immediately after the rebellion that their solution to the problem of labor discontent was to modify existing concepts and habits. For example, we can read the 1669 law called "Against Runaways" as formalizing habits that rest on particular categories regarding servants.[34] It shows a certain leaning or disposition on the part of masters regarding servants, namely, "if they are not where they are supposed to be, get and punish them." There was a long-standing habit of looking on all servants with a certain degree of suspicion, as people whom one should assume are sneaky and untrustworthy (as when the statue reads that the law was necessary "chiefly through the wickednesse of servants.")[35] After the rebellion, we saw a new law (enacted in 1680) that singled out servants of African descent.[36] The older habit—of keeping an eye on all servants—was modified so that it now meant African laborers required particular attention. The categories regarding Negro and Christian became more significant than those regarding servants. Once the categories (the dispositions) changed, they revised the unconscious habits that determined behavior. This change did not get European Virginian servants completely off the hook, but it did lessen the scrutiny directed at them.

The discernible but undefined habit on the part of Europeans to discriminate against non-Europeans similarly became much more clearly delineated after the rebellion. The habit of patrolling the sexual boundaries between these two groups existed before the rebellion, as seen in the punishment suffered by Hugh Davis in 1630 for "defiling his body in lying with a negro."[37] However, the post-rebellion period witnessed the deepening of this habit. The various laws that meted serious penalties on interracial sex and marriage built upon and extended earlier habits. For example, the 1691 law "An act for suppressing outlying Slaves" not just criminalized non-marital intercourse (as in Hugh Davis's case) but criminalized any union between an "English or other white man or woman" and any "negroe, mulatto, or Indian man or woman bond or free" by holding that any such union would result in exile.[38] These laws in turn changed the propositions that defined the concepts regarding these different sorts of people. Where earlier the categories regarding people of African descent said, "Negroes should *usually* be treated as unfree laborers," the changes in the laws effectively said that "Negroes should, by default, be treated as unfree laborers." While there were free people of African descent in the categories, there were relatively few of them. As chattel slavery from Africa supplanted indentured labor from Europe, the habitual association of the kind of Africans and the categorical disposition toward them as unfree became even tighter. The new habits of racial exclusion did not emerge ex nihilo, but were the product of changes in well-established habits refined by new propositions defining modified categories.

Another change that occurred in the post-rebellion colony had to do with habits attached to morphology. Before the rebellion, the laws held that bailiffs had to hunt down any and all escaped servants, regardless of their age, gender, or ethnicity. What mattered more was an attention to behavioral and sartorial presentation. In particular, most indentured or bonded servants, of all ages, genders, and ethnicities, were forced to wear coarse cotton clothing dyed blue.[39] Further, since the population was sparse, it was possible for the bailiffs in each town to know who belonged there and who did not. This meant that the habits of surveillance were directed at strangers generally, and people in servant's clothing in particular. However, once the laws started to focus more and more on people of African descent, the habits regarding surveillance started to focus on *morphology*. Since a "Negro" was someone with features common to people of Africa, these morphological features became a liability, and a trigger for disproportionate attention. The same can be said for morphological and sartorial appearances associated with Native peoples. Finally, features common to people of predominantly European descent remained unimportant: there was no particular reason to *do* anything to a white person walking on the road. If they looked like they were hiding, or out of place, or wearing clothing that marked them as a servant or a convict, then they drew suspicion. However, European morphological features became the uninvestigated norm against which other, non-European features stood out.

The new kinds and categories regarding people from Europe did not entail a significant improvement for the people referred to by these concepts. One change that did occur was that starting in 1691 the propositions were attached more frequently to the term "white" than the older term "christian." Another change in the category of whiteness (which was more or less equivalent to the term "christian" in the specific geopolitical sense, but not the broader religious sense) had to do with purity and exclusion. In pre-rebellion Virginia, we see many examples of voluntary mixing, both social and sexual, between people who hailed from Europe and Africa. Bacon's Rebellion itself was a notable instance of such mixing. However, the new laws that were inaugurated in the post-rebellion colony took pre-existing habits of thought that differentiated these two groups and deepened them. The new laws changed the propositions that defined the concepts regarding these groups. Where there was previously no law against the marriage between a free "Negro" and a free "christian," the 1691 law, and others like it, encouraged the intellectual habit of thinking that "christians" or "white men and women" should be separate from non-whites. There was a new valence to the category of (or disposition toward) whiteness. It now assumed a much stronger attitude of exclusivity. Add to this the fact that other laws worsened the status of non-whites, and whiteness became not just an exclusive group, but one socially superior to non-whites. This in turn deepened a noticeable but undefined Eurocentric ethnocentrism on the part of European colonists into the kind of clearly delineated white-supremacist racism of later ages.

Sadly, this effort on the part of the burgesses to stabilize their social environment through a change in the propositions, concepts, and habits of race worked. This country would not witness the sort of large-scale solidarity between laborers of European and African descent seen in Bacon's Rebellion until the Underground Railroad almost 150 years later. Changes in Europe and African made it so that indentured labor from Europe became much less feasible than slave labor from Africa. This in turn deepened the association of whiteness with freedom and blackness with enslavement. White workers became much more concerned with protecting their rights as white than with improving their lots as laborers. We see the power of the propositions regarding whiteness in the New York Draft Riots of 1863, where Irish immigrants were incensed at what they perceived to be a violation of their rights as white workers. Even though many were not born in this country, the category of whiteness (which effectively said "treat all white people as free individuals" as well as "treat all white people better than all black people") was so strong that they read the draft as a violation of the freedom that was assumed within kind and category of whiteness.

Dewey's notion of habit enables us to see that racialized habits (habits that entail responding to people and things according to ideas of race) continue to impact our behaviors and would continue to do so even after we have stopped using racial terminology. White supremacist habits (those that entail a proclivity toward people and things that fall within the parameters of whiteness, and a disdain, sometimes violent, for things and people considered outside the pale of whiteness) were incubated within the boundaries of white supremacist concepts. These included the laws that preserved Euro-Americans from indignities meted upon non-whites, scientific theories that placed people of European descent at the top of human taxonomies, and cultural standards that held that all things beautiful, civilized, and refined emerged from European cultures.

Without the modified propositions that defined new kinds and categories regarding race, the habit of responding favorably and ethically to someone with pinkish skin while responding cruelly and dismissively toward anyone with a different hue might never have come into existence. However, even though we have largely dismissed the literal equation of whiteness with civilization from our laws, scientific texts, and artistic institutions, we still operate according to habits that bear the marks of these ideas. It is for this reason that Dewey's notion of habit is apt for addressing the problem of whiteness. It redirects our discussions of race and racial injustice away from particular, intentional acts of racial conflict and toward systemic, habituated patterns of racial thinking and acting that are at odds with each other or out of place in a democratic and multicultural society. It helps account for how racist practices are perpetuated by otherwise considerate and decent people. Since habits are inherited and acquired, the young pick them up unknowingly. They "create out of the formless void of impulses a world made in their own image."[40]

All of this indicates that solutions to the problems of whiteness cannot be found solely through changes to our legal and political systems, education about the nature of genetics, changes to our environments, or indictments of racial contracts. All of these things are necessary, but even done in concert they are insufficient. Any successful attempt to unweave the fabric of white supremacism must entail an active reconstruction of the habits of whiteness. While the following was written thirty years before the start of the civil rights movement proper, it stands as a fitting description of why white privilege and white supremacist racism persist long after our society's most earnest attempt to rid itself of these taints.

> A social revolution may effect abrupt and deep alterations in external customs, in legal and political institutions. But the habits that are being shaped by these objective conditions, the habits of thought and feeling, are not so easily modified. They persist and insensibly assimilate to themselves the outer innovations—much as American judges nullify the intended changes of statue law by interpreting legislation in light of common law. The force of lag in human life is enormous.[41]

In this equation, the civil rights movement was an extremely significant moment for the United States because it was a step toward realizing the ideals of equality, justice, and freedom upon which it was based. In particular, the social movements of the 1960s radically challenged the concepts regarding race that had been at work in our laws and social institutions. They pointed out that operative concepts (such as those that held that only white people were worthy of respect and the full rights of citizens, and that non-whites were either untrustworthy or morally corrupt) were false, unnecessary, and based upon distorted experiences. They established new laws that singled out these concepts as unwarranted, and initiated an era where all people were to be regarded as equal under the law.

However, Dewey's analysis of habit argues that this change would not be enough to solve the problem of whiteness. This is because the new legislation could not reach down to the level of habits of whiteness: the habit of taking impulses of fear and uncertainty at dealing with unfamiliar people of different races and organizing them into habits of exclusion and control. Further, since habits are stubborn and adaptive to a degree, they change to persist in a changing environment. A change in laws could not alone change the habits, by then 250 years old, that led white folk to believe that they were better than non-whites and deserved better treatment. To fully eradicate whiteness, we need an organized inquiry focused on the habits by which we live race, and then we need to change them. The first stage of this reconstruction needs to focus on understanding the problematic habits and the impulses that drive them as well as imagining new habits that might channel these impulses into habits that are less cruel and dangerous, more compassionate and sane.

The solution to the problem of habits that skew an organism's response to his environment is to develop habits that are more felicitous through *careful and directed inquiry.* Again, the judgment of whether or not a habit works is the degree of fit within an environment. This prevents a lapse into a quietistic and nihilistic response where white supremacist race habits are "just what we do." While the young might know no better, the rest of us are responsible for evaluating our habits and changing them when they are problematic. Perhaps Dewey's most astute observation is that the worst cases of moral travesty are not those committed by people who consciously violate the dignity of their fellow human being. The truly egregious acts of inhumanity are the ones that the perpetrator does not even see as cruel or unjust. Thus, we are judged in this model not so much by our conscious responses to ethical dilemmas, but by the courage and sensitivity with which we inquire into the habits that define the boundaries of ethics. "What is necessary is that habits be formed which are more intelligent, more sensitively percipient, more informed with foresight, more aware of what they are about, more direct and sincere, more flexibly responsive than those now current. Then they will meet their own problems and propose their own improvements."[42] Dewey argues that "habit as a vital art depends upon the animation of habit by impulse; only this inspiriting stands between habit and stagnation."[43] Therefore, our task is to use our impulses to adjust our habits so that they fit as well as possible within our environments.

Whiteness is a network of interrelated habits that gives meaning to what Dewey called "native tendencies," such as pugnacity, fear, pity, and sympathy.[44] It is a pattern that involves biological and cultural components. It is not biological in the way that scientists two hundred years ago believed race was biological: a set of *fixed* behaviors, attitudes, and propensities that emerge, Athena-like, fully dressed from our flesh. Instead, race is, in part, a biological phenomenon in terms of the embodied aspects of human life and our perceptions of the morphology of people around us. Race is at the same time a cultural pattern by virtue of the ways in which we give meaning to native impulses (such as fear or nurturance) and make sense of changes to our embodied experiences. However, we are not concerned here with racialized habits *tout court*. The primary problem is not that human beings respond to each other according to habits that entail certain distinctions that we have come to see as "racial." Indeed, we will see in the following chapter that Du Bois argues that we need to recognize and cherish racial differences as a key to global peace and harmony. In light of the fact that this discussion is focused primarily on the particular invidious habits that are associated with whiteness in America, we are concerned first with habits of racial prejudice that emerged from categories established within white supremacist contexts. For this reason, I will end my discussion of Dewey's notion of habit by looking at his description of how the habits of racial prejudice are formed.

The Formation of Habits of Racial Prejudice

Dewey defines prejudice as "something which comes before reason and cuts it short; it is a desire or emotion which makes us see things in a particular light and gives slant to all our beliefs."[45] He further argues that race prejudice derives from an instinctual "universal antipathy" toward anything or anyone different from our habituation.[46] Dewey believes that after a cursory examination of human anthropology "we are struck by the instinctive aversion of mankind to what is new and unusual, to whatever is different from what we are used to, and which thus shocks our customary habits."[47] It is this apparently universal aversion to the strange that serves as the impetus behind racial prejudice. "The facts suggest that an antipathy to what is strange (originating probably in the self-protective tendencies of animal life) is the original basis of what now takes the form of race prejudice."[48] This habitual aversion to the strange is tightly isomorphic with the relationship between experience and problems: just as strange phenomena or organisms generally lead to an impulsive aversion, experiences that do not fit into the pattern of inquiry disrupt the pattern.

Dewey claims that the root of racial discrimination does not have to do with race per se. In language that we will later see shares much with Du Bois's assessment of the relationship of race and racial friction, Dewey argues that "this friction is not primarily racial. Race is a sign, a symbol, which bears much the same relation to the actual forces which cause friction as a national flag bears to the emotions and activities which it symbolized, condensing them into visible and tangible form."[49] There is nothing inherent about people of African, Asian, indigenous American, and European descent that necessitates violence between the groups. Instead, our political, economic, and social interests, as pressing parts of our social environments, become cashed out along the lines of racial and ethnic categories, much as these factors were cashed out along denominational lines for Europeans during the Reformation. Our original aversion to the different becomes infused with these other factors and over time becomes racial prejudice.

Dewey explains racial prejudice according to his theory of human instincts by saying, "We are carrying old political and old mental habits into a condition for which they are not adapted, and all kinds of friction result."[50] Therefore he suggests that a better understanding of foreign cultures would prevent racism in the future. He claims that most people will achieve a rational control of instinctive biases only through "a change not only in education, and in the means of publicity, but also in political and industrial organization."[51] However, it is useful at this point to see how Dewey's conceptions of habit and racial prejudice might make sense of a current and disturbing phenomenon that clearly involves racial prejudice: the various political and legislative campaigns to stop the "invasion" of would-be construction, hospitality, and agricultural workers who cross the political border that has relatively recently bifurcated the land that has been part of Latin America for four hundred years.

For many white Americans living in places such as Texas or Arizona, increases in the number of non-European people have long elicited unfortunately fearful responses. The self-named "Minutemen" vigilante groups who patrol the U.S. southern border are perhaps the most visible and concerning manifestation of these fears. As the United States become ever more Latino/a, we see these same fears in white communities far from the southern border. In the summer of 2006, city councils for suburban communities such as Hazleton, Pennsylvania, and Riverside, New Jersey, reacted fearfully to increases in the Latino/a population when they voted to "fine landlords $1,000 for renting to illegal immigrants, deny business permits to companies that give them jobs, and make English the city's official language."[52] Dewey would tell us that this unease is in part an organic response (in the very broadest sense of the word "organic"). It has to do with the fact that white Americans are now sharing space with a number of people that they *take to be different*. Of course, it is foolish to think that people of different hair color, skin pigmentation, and sartorial style must necessarily respond to such an encounter by instantiating a legal code that prohibits the other group from using their first language in public contexts or by establishing paramilitary groups who engage in haphazard patrols. In this case, the change in the organic living environment is made meaningful *through the customs that channel the uncertainty arising from a new encounter into fear*. In this context, the customs that make this change in population meaningful are ones that are associated with the idea of whiteness.

The inchoate feelings of unease are channeled into white supremacist habits (such as establishing laws against the use of languages other than English or treating public spaces as if they are the property of all whites) in part because of the white people's habit of believing themselves to be members of a besieged group that causes them to respond to a change in the environment through a political program designed to codify a primary aspect of their culture as normative. It is the concept of whiteness, and its associated aspects (from the simple and pre-reflexive habits of reading certain physical features as indications of moral, intellectual, and psychological propensities to the more complex ones of assuming that people of Latino cultures are dishonest and suspicious) that causes many white people to organize a fairly inchoate and morally inert impulse (the one of feeling a bit out-of-sorts at finding yourself occasionally in the minority, or hearing people in your immediate environment using a language with which you are not familiar) into an anti-democratic and arrogant mode of behavior. We can safely describe these habits as white in that they rely on certain normative assumptions about culture and race that can be traced back to the idea of a culturally superior white race that deserves preferential treatment because of its greater degree of civilization. We see this combative and exclusionary dimension of the habits of whiteness when the mayor of Hazelton responded to news that his municipality was being sued by human rights organizations for passing an unconstitutional ordnance by framing the issue of immigration as a fight from which he will not back down and proclaiming that "a line has been drawn here in Hazelton."[53]

If these people were unencumbered by certain habits of thinking that caused them to see the world in such a Manichean way, they would be free to see the change in their environment in radically different ways. If they had developed better habits vis-à-vis other cultures, they might not take any more than a passing notice of the change in their environment. Southwestern "Minutemen" might look at the families crossing a border as being modern versions of their own ancestors who left poverty and political oppression to make a better life through hard work. In fact, they might want to fight *for* these people since they not only struggle against poverty and the corruption of the countries in which they were born (like the pioneers and pilgrims who are enshrined as civic saints in this country's dominant mythology), but also must struggle against the injustice of a country that begs them come to their kitchens and construction sites, only to call them "illegal" when the work is done. If they were not hardened by the habits of thought that are at the heart of whiteness, they would not think it odd that cities older than the United States with names such as Santa Fe, Amarillo, and San Francisco are populated largely or even predominantly by people whose first language is Spanish. At the very least, they might not take foolish pride in being illiterate in all languages save one.

The Promise and Limits of a Deweyan Critique of Whiteness

Dewey's work offers valuable resources for addressing the problems of racial whiteness. As we will see in chapter 8, whiteness finds its reality in common experiences that are irreducible to biology, and while recent biological findings that refute older ideas of race are significant in that they radically change the way we think about race, they do not prove that race is unreal. This is because our lived experience exceeds the microscope: while a scientist might be able to prove that genetic evidence does not support the biologically rooted racial taxonomy of the last few centuries, we nonetheless still live in a cultural and social world created by these assumptions. Dewey directs us to look to these common, lived experiences for the facticity of whiteness, as well as for clues on how we ought to develop responses to the problems of whiteness.

Dewey's acuity to habit leads us to look for the residues of whiteness from earlier ages that still adhere to our actions and institutions even though the idea of white supremacy has had its overt manifestations purged from American politics. It leads us to attend to the fact that while most white Americans think of themselves as holding to the universal "regardless of race, treat all people equally," we may and do still live by the universal "treat people as people only if they are white or act white." This kind of contradiction is not only possible but even common because of the nature of habit, where inherited kinds and categories become part of our unconscious response to the environment.

Yet despite these important resources, Dewey's work alone is insufficient to develop a pragmatic critique of whiteness. The first and most significant shortfall is that Dewey hardly deals concretely with problems of race in his work. Even when he does mention racial prejudice, it is only as a passing reference to elucidate his central claims about habit formation. Thus, the broad chasm between his subject matter and the particular problems of race leaves us in need of a more particular treatment of race and whiteness in America. However, while I agree with Sullivan that Dewey "underestimates the perversely complex operations of racism and white privilege," the preceding discussion of his sophisticated treatment of the complex interrelation of habit, concepts, and propositions makes me dispute her claim that Dewey assumes "an incredibly simplistic understanding of unconscious habits."[54] The fact that Dewey failed to identify and change the habits of whiteness that he carried in his thoughts and actions does not mean his treatment of habits was simplistic. Far from it, his discussion of habit and its relationship to concepts, impulses, and precepts gives us a nuanced account of how we ought to strive for the obvious pragmatic goal of reconstructing the habits of whiteness, even as his own personal failure to notice these habits offers us a sobering caution as to the difficulty of the endeavor. I therefore agree fully with Michael Eldridge when he claims in his essay "Dewey on Race and Social Change" that we should not look for any particular pearls of wisdom regarding race among Dewey's writings, but that "the Dewey to whom we should be turning is primarily the social theorist" who offers general but applicable models for resolving social strife.[55]

While Dewey's theory of habit offers us a valuable tool to achieve what should be the clear goal for any fully pragmatist treatment of the problem of whiteness, namely the meliorization of the current situation through inquiry and reconstruction, two serious problems with Dewey's work remain. The first is his assumption that we have an instinctual "universal antipathy" toward anything or anyone different from our habituation.[56] As a consequence, Dewey gives us little sense of how or why white Southwestern Minutemen or Mid-Atlantic council members would ever make the move to embrace a change in their environment. If we agree with him, we would have to say that a geopolitical change like the one currently occurring in this part of the world must be met by white folk with greater or lesser degrees of dis-ease. This is because of the deep equation that Dewey makes between *difference* and *discomfort*. The different or unexpected experience spurs an inquiry to make sense of it and corral it within the pen of inquiry. The different person or culture is always in some sense odd and not as desirable as one's own. An encounter with difference is always at root a kind of problem. While certain trends in our politics lend a depressing degree of credence to this idea (such as the alacrity with which white Americans flee neighborhoods that are becoming more culturally and ethnically diverse in favor of exclusive gated communities) we nonetheless need a different account for how we ought to see different people of different races relating to each other.[57] With what Dewey has given us, the best we can hope for is a political reality in which people of different races develop a greater acceptance of their instinctual feeling of discomfort with each other. It is a world perhaps free of violence and oppression, but filled with uneasy smiles and tenuous friendships across racial lines.

The second major problem is the fact that he, like I and any other person living in a white supremacist society, adopted ideas and habits that reinscribe this system and did not fully reflect on or analyze his assumptions regarding race and culture. Even though Dewey was doubtlessly progressive and rare as a white philosopher in the 1930s who believed that "different 'races' are not due to anything in inherent physiological structure," his work is still marked by white supremacist assumptions.[58] I agree, therefore, with Sullivan's claim that not even in his few works on racial prejudice does "Dewey challenge, or even indicate awareness of, the white privileged perspective that operates within it."[59]

The most pervasive example of this is a frequent rhetorical distinction he makes between civilization and savagery, where the first is usually synonymous with European ways of social organization and the later entails only to non-Western peoples.[60] We see that habits of Eurocentric thinking impact his work most readily in his assumptions that peoples who did not pass through the variegated stages through which Europe passed are like children when compared to mature Europe. As he said in *Human Nature and Conduct,* "It is no accident that men became interested in the psychology of savages and babies when they became interested in doing away with old institutions."[61]

We can also see a deeply myopic view of race in his 1932 address to the NAACP. He does not entirely dismiss the role of race prejudice in leading to different lived experiences among people of color, for he does point out that "the group which you represent has suffered more than any other, more keenly, more intensely."[62] However, he quickly claims that people of color do not really suffer primarily because of racism, but because of economic injustice. He thus informs the NAACP that "while members of your group have been discriminated against more than others they are only experiencing in a more intense degree what all the labor groups [. . .] are passing through."[63] When he counsels a "cooperative economic and social order" as a remedy to the discrimination suffered by his audience, he is offering the same medicine he has prescribed to "any white group that is at a disadvantage, since your fundamental difficulties do not come through color."[64] In this work he again argues that racial prejudice is in effect not primarily a matter of race, since "all the laboring groups [. . .] are in the same boat."[65]

Dewey is right to *link* racial prejudice to economics, though he overemphasizes the link to the point that erases the ways that habits of whiteness impact economic prejudice. His rhetorical implication is accurate when he asks his audience, "Why were you kept in slavery except for economic reasons? What was slavery except a manifestation of the motive for private gain?"[66] To this he could and should have added, "Why were Native peoples defined as 'savages' but to justify stealing their land? Why were millennia-old cultures in India and China painted as corrupt but to justify Empire and the opium trade? Why have women throughout history been framed as emotional, docile, or inferior but to deny them control over their own bodies, lives, and labors?" As these and other cases illustrate, human difference is often posited as a hierarchical difference that materially benefits whoever is at the top of the hierarchy. While a pragmatist should be committed to ending these sorts of hierarchies on the grounds that they are undemocratic, contrary to human flourishing, and conducive to great human suffering, a pragmatist mindful of the way that habits direct behavior would *not* treat all these different problems—racism, sexism, ageism, religious intolerance, heterosexism, and economic prejudice—as *the same problem.* While they are wrong for generally the same reasons, they can't be solved at the same time or painted with the same brush. Dewey therefore overstates the economic case when he says that race discrimination is *just* a heightened form of classism, or, as he puts it, "all the laboring groups of the United States [. . .] are in the same boat."[67] This misses the fact that in 1932 a white laborer and a black laborer could not eat in the same restaurant, ride in the same Pullman car, sleep in the same hotel, let alone sail in the same boat. As Du Bois would scathingly point out a year later in his essay "The Right To Work," there are serious differences between the kind of oppression suffered by white laborers and the oppression faced by laborers of color. It is because of this lack of attention to racial difference and the impact of racial prejudice that Du Bois says of "parties of reform, of socialism and communism" that "[n]one of these offers us anything concrete and dependable."[68]

This assumption that Dewey makes—that problems of race are really just problems of economics and class and that the only way to deal with racism is to address issues of class and economics—is still common enough today. In many ways it is a forerunner of the argument that Richard Rorty made in the last decade of his life that progressives would do better to put aside their fight for rights in the arena of "identity politics" and instead stick to the more concrete issue of economic justice by fighting for union and workers' rights. As Rorty put it in *Achieving Our Country,* "Leftists in the academy have permitted cultural politics to supplant real politics, and have permitted cultural politics to supplant real politics, and have collaborated with the Right in making cultural issues central to public debate."[69]

The problem of racism is, like any other form of injustice and cruelty, intertwined with these other problems such as sexism, ableism, ageism, and economic injustice. A full understanding of patriarchy requires looking at issues of class: a full understanding of homophobia requires that we look at how this form of prejudice is manifested differently in different cultures and toward members of different communities. Nonetheless, each of these habits that disguise the wolf of human cruelty in different sheep skins—sometimes "natural law," sometimes "traditional values," sometimes "the free market"—needs to be studied and corrected *both* as an interactive feature of our experiences that interpenetrate each other *and* on its own terms. Further, to collapse one into another risks failing to see and reconstruct a dangerous habit. Thus, Dewey's assumption that class essentially trumps race leads him to tragically elide the extent to which race and white racism impacted his audience in ways he could barely begin to imagine.

I think this is a good indicator of why a good pragmatist never engages is hagiography of any of the canonical pragmatists, because it is a tradition of great promise but also deep flaws. Though Dewey invites nearly worshipful treatment by many of his readers and interpreters, it is clear that he personally would be "weirded out" by his canonization and would pretty quickly cop to his limitations. Eddie Glaude gets right pragmatism's promise and problematic when he writes that pragmatism needs to sing the blues because

American pragmatism emerged in the context of a nation committed to democracy and slavery, to ideas of equality and to the insidious ideology of Anglo-Saxonism. American pragmatism indeed reflects the haunting duality at the heart of this country: a simultaneous commitment to democratic ideals and undemocratic practices. To say then that pragmatism is native to American soil is to acknowledge that it carries with it all the possibilities and limitations that have defined our fragile experiment in democracy.[70]

W. E. B. Du Bois provides resources to solve the problems and deficiencies in John Dewey's work. Du Bois is every bit as concerned with the problem of class prejudice and economic injustice as Dewey. However, Du Bois is able to see race and class as two distinct but interrelated phenomena, and not just two guises for the same face, or worse yet, a merely cultural mask covering a real economic face. Du Bois further offers a model of race that is fully compatible with the basic features of Dewey's theory of inquiry and habit, but is free of his pessimism regarding difference. As someone who has thought and written about race more than any other, Du Bois gives us an unparalleled perspective on the particular nature of the problems at hand. More importantly, Du Bois offers a perspective on cultural and ethnic difference that is both more informed and more optimistic than Dewey's. Where Dewey offers the hope that we can *tolerate* difference, Du Bois argues that we *must* seek it out as a resource, or to use his language, to *embrace it as a gift*. His metaphor that racial difference is a kind of space between the branches of a common human tree that enables or even demands sharing poses questions to white folk that can get us to see why and how we need to grow out of the idea of mere whiteness because, as he showed us, so long as we think and act as if we were merely white, we have no real gifts to share with others.

FIVE

Du Bois and the Gift of Race

This chapter explores the conservationist approach to race that Du Bois developed over the seventy-odd years of his scholarly career. It shows how Du Bois offers his readers a pragmatic view of race that is both constructive (that is, Du Bois recognizes that race came into being over time and is not an absolute or antecedent category system) and interactive (in that it exists at the confluence of morphology and culture). Du Bois should be at the center of our dialogues on race and whiteness since we need the resources found in Du Bois's visionary language of race to make sense of and start resolving the problem of whiteness. Du Bois was not only the first pragmatist to develop a sophisticated and in-depth analysis of race; he was the first major intellectual in the West to draw our attention to the role of whiteness in the prevalent understanding of race and to the fact that whiteness functioned in a way that made it qualitatively different from other race groups. He showed us that whiteness and race should not be treated as insular concepts that only matter in studies of ethnicity; they are ideas that have defined human relations in the West for five centuries. Du Bois also redefined the understanding of race in the West by frequently appealing to the idea that races have at their core a cultural gift.

Du Bois's work demonstrates that the problem of whiteness adheres largely in habits of whiteness that have been uncritically handed down from older generations to younger ones. He leaves us with the recognition that we need to develop a context-rich account of whiteness, one that shows how white folk need to balance two contrary needs: to identify *as white* when it comes to taking responsibility for current and past injustices enabled by the idea of whiteness, and to identify as *not white* when describing an alternative to the current categories of race that equate Europeanness with whiteness.

In order to make use of these Du Boisian resources, I must first defend the coherence of placing Du Bois's work within a pragmatist framework by demonstrating the extent to which his approach toward race and social justice borrows from and advances pragmatist philosophy. The second section will explore his approach to race as developed in his middle and later works (primarily his 1920 work *Darkwater* as well as his 1940 *Dusk of Dawn*). This reading of his concept of race pays particular attention to his deployment of religious metaphor, not merely as a rhetorical strategy, but as a response to the moral framework within which he and his fellow Americans operated. His use of religious metaphor to illuminate his ideal of race is both prophetic (in that it self-consciously places his theory of race within the stream of the African American moral theology) and pragmatic (in that he uses the very same religious language that propped up white supremacist understandings of race in order to develop a notion of race that was more democratic and in line with current experience).

Du Bois's Pragmatism

Philosophers are far from unanimous regarding where Du Bois fits in the history of philosophy, or indeed, whether he was even a philosopher at all. There are ample interpretations in the scholarly literature that place him within Hegelian, Marxist, or existential camps.[1] Without discounting that, as a complex and fecund thinker, Du Bois incorporated analyses drawn from Hegel and existential philosophy and adopted certain Marxist ideals late in life, this section will thematize his pragmatist roots. We also will look to answer the question raised in the title of Paul C. Taylor's excellent study of Du Bois's pragmatism, "What's the Use of Calling Du Bois a Pragmatist?"[2] This follows in the footsteps of Cornel West's classic, *The American Evasion of Philosophy,* in which he claims that "[a]s one grounded in and nourished by American pragmatism, Du Bois . . . allies himself in word and deed with the wretched of the earth."[3] However, in addition to the descriptive value of adding to the evidence that he was indeed a major figure in the advancement of this paradigmatically American school, there is a more immediate value in uncovering Du Bois's pragmatism. Paul C. Taylor explains this value well when he writes that "[r]eading Du Bois pragmatically . . . is doubly illuminating. It reveals aspects both of Du Bois and of pragmatism we might otherwise miss. Whatever its intrinsic worth, this double revelation is extrinsically valuable because it may help restore to us some important resources—or, perhaps better, instruments—for dealing with current social problems."[4]

Reading Du Bois through a pragmatist lens, then, thematizes vital resources that prove invaluable in addressing the problem of whiteness and that might otherwise remain obscured. Such an interpretation unlocks his interactionist view of race, one that is compatible with Dewey's interactionist model of ideas and action. For Du Bois, race is neither a matter of essence or *zeitgeist* (as it might seem from a Hegelian standpoint) nor an artificial tool of false consciousness (as in existentialism or Marxism); instead, race on his analysis inhabits the confluence of certain persistent phenomena over which people have little control (such as morphology, history, and cultural inheritances) and other sorts of things over which people have greater control (such as how a society envisions relations between races and what it holds as a proper goal vis-à-vis race). In his landmark 1897 essay "The Conservation of Races" Du Bois asks us to conserve racial practices and identities as wells of singular and irreplaceable human experience; at the same time he critiques whiteness as a race unlike any other that must be changed in light of its oppressive and undemocratic consequences.

Further, a pragmatist reading of Du Bois helps us interpret the unique role of religious metaphor within his work, a fascinating and underexplored dimension of his work until the publication of Edward Blum's critically acclaimed work *W. E. B. Du Bois, American Prophet: Politics and Culture in Modern America*.[5] Du Bois's consistent reliance upon a very specific sort of religious language shows that he sees race not as a purely or even primarily biological feature of the world that is a kind of given feature we can only observe or suffer through, but as an experiential phenomenon constructed largely through religious discourse that is fully real in its effects on lived human reality. His use of religious discourses also shows his attention to the fact that racial habits cannot be dispelled merely by pointing to the findings of science, but must instead be *reconstructed* into a more life-affirming feature of human existence through this very same language. Further, if we take into account that "the thing which concerns all of us as human beings is precisely the greatest attainable security of values in concrete existence," that is, the use of inquiry to encourage stability and human flourishing, we see that Du Bois was very much a pragmatist in his attempt to use both the scientific and religious elements that contributed to the modern idea of race to achieve an improved racial situation.[6]

Du Bois can rightly be credited as a quintessential meliorist pragmatist for being the first philosopher and public intellectual to fully follow the threads of race that are deeply woven into every pattern of our American cultural cloth. Eddie Glaude highlights the centrality of race to American culture in his essay "Tragedy and Moral Experience: John Dewey and Toni Morrison's *Beloved*" and explains why American pragmatist philosophers need to follow Du Bois: "If American pragmatism is to be understood, in part, as a specific historical and cultural product of American civilization, and as a particular set of social practices . . . that articulate certain American desires, values, and responses, then it must address explicitly the tragedy of race in America."[7]

One of the best places to look in order to see Du Bois's pragmatism is the introduction of his 1940 work *Dusk of Dawn,* because it is in this work that we find one of his clearest pragmatic calls to action:

> The problem of the future world is the charting, by means of intelligent reason, of a path not simply through the resistances of physical force, but through the vaster and far more intricate jungle of ideas conditioned on unconscious and subconscious reflexes of living things; on blind unreason and often irresistible urges of sensitive matter; of which the concept of race is today one of the most unyielding and threatening.[8]

Several facets of this passage reflect Du Bois's pragmatism. First and foremost is the fact that Du Bois, like Dewey, orients his relationship to the future according to a problem. This focus on resolving the problem of race is the most consistent thread in the tapestry of his voluminous life work; the work that won him his first taste of national acclaim, *The Souls of Black Folk,* was organized around a central, haunting question that he posed to himself and other African Americans: "How does it feel to be a problem?"[9] In the same work he penned his famous and frequently quoted prophecy, that "the problem of the twentieth century is the problem of the color-line."[10] This propensity to address race not as a subject for detached reflection, but as a problem that calls out for remedy, indicates just how much his work shares Dewey's claim in *The Quest for Certainty* that "all reflective inquiry starts from a problematic situation."[11]

We also see his pragmatism in that the *sort* of problem he sees has to do with the effect of certain operative ideals of which we are not in full conscious control. Du Bois, especially at the end of his life, comes to the realization that the best way to reform the problem of white supremacism and white-defined racial categories is to approach it as a problem concerning habits. Race is a problem not because it fails to accurately chart a pre-existing, biological reality; in fact, the sorts of scientific discoveries of the thorough genetic intermixture of the human family that current geneticists are still trying to disseminate among the population of nonscientists were already old hat to Du Bois in 1940 when he simply stated that the "scientific definition of race is impossible."[12] The idea of race is problematic because of how we *use it,* either consciously or unconsciously. It is a problem because not only is it one of those "ideas conditioned on unconscious and subconscious reflexes," but it is also "unyielding and threatening."[13] In fact, we will see that Du Bois frames the problem of race in almost exactly the same way that Dewey does in his most detailed treatment of the subject in "Racial Prejudice and Friction": not as an unavoidable clash between inherently different races, but as the correctible effect of habits of prejudice. What Dewey failed to notice, however, is something that Du Bois addressed at length, namely that the problematic habits are inured to a concept of whiteness in particular that organizes society according to a lopsided and destructive logic. Because of this attention to the difference between whiteness and other race groups, Du Bois shifts the focus of his racial analysis over the course of his career. Recognizing that racism in America would not end with the strengthening of African American cultural and intellectual gifts (the sort of thing he urged in "The Conservation of Races" and *The Souls of Black Folk*), Du Bois turned his attention to whiteness, and how its ideas and habits impede democratic community in America. As he wrote in the *Crisis*, "the American Negro does NOT stand in unusual need of moral training. It is the American white man who needs that."[14]

Du Bois advances a pragmatic model of race in that he sees the concept of race as the product of inquiry. Races have a history and reality that involve biology and morphology, but are not reducible to them. Races are furthermore revisable in light of continuing inquiry. But beyond the pragmatic way in which he approaches and defines race is his stated purpose that, more than any other aspect of his work, places him at the vanguard of pragmatism. The following passage refers to the various sociological studies that he supervised at the turn of the last century in Atlanta University, yet it just as accurately describes his life-long efforts to solve the problem of race in the United States: "The object of these studies is primarily scientific—a careful search for truth conducted as thoroughly, broadly, and honestly as the material resources and mental equipment at command will allow; but this is not our sole object; we wish not only to make the Truth clear, but to present it in such shape as will encourage and help social reform."[15] This passage speaks to the fact that Du Bois's work was not merely an instance of pragmatist philosophy, but remains one of its defining manifestations. In these few lines we see myriad threads that run through the works of other pragmatists. We see it in the broad use of "science" that also marked the works of Peirce, James, Locke, and Dewey. His desire to conduct the search for Truth "thoroughly, broadly, and honestly" matches Dewey's imperative to conduct inquiry with the "fullness and range of conditions" in mind; his acceptance that inquiry is constrained by the real limits of available "material resources and mental equipment" shows him to share Addams's concrete meliorism.[16] Aside from all these threads that run through this intricately woven textual tapestry, there remains Du Bois's pragmatist spirit. It is seen in his injunction to make inquiry not merely an enlightening endeavor (in that he wants to "make the Truth clear") but one that lights a path of action to the extent that it "will encourage and help social reform." Just as Dewey says of ideas that "their final value is not determined by their internal elaboration and consistency, but by the consequences they effect in existence as that is perceptibly experienced," Du Bois conducts his inquiries into race, and later democracy and pan-nationalism, in order to make our collective experience more meaningful and peaceful.[17]

No stranger to the tragedy of race, Du Bois was forced to confront white supremacist racism again when the lynching of an African American man, Sam Hose, in Georgia pierced Du Bois's early optimism like "a red ray which could not be ignored."[18] While this incident taught Du Bois that "there was no such definite demand for the scientific work of the sort that I was doing," it did not end his commitment to pragmatic approaches to problems as much as change his tactics.[19] It was not enough to present a racist society with the knowledge of how much misery white supremacism caused: people depraved enough to kill a man because of a rumor are unlikely swayed by the findings of a blue-ribbon panel on race and justice. Habits of racism had been bred into the bone of white folk for so long and granted them such a cheap and easy sense of self-importance that Du Bois learned how to speak to this audience where they stood (or indeed, swaggered). In order to end racism and release the positive value latent in the idea of race, Du Bois had to work with the current state of America: its people, its history, and its dominant ideals.

Du Bois stood at the end of one philosophical tradition, and at the head of another. We see him as a participant in a centuries-old tradition when he says in *Dusk of Dawn:* "Apparently one consideration alone saved me from complete conformity with the thoughts and confusions of then current social trends; and that was the problems of racial and cultural contacts. Otherwise I might easily have been simply the current product of my day."[20] When we read his critique of the fact that most people live their lives and think their thoughts by mimicking the lives and thoughts of people around them, and when we read his relief at being faced with a set of problems that caused him to live and think differently, we see Du Bois as an inheritor of Europe's defining philosophical movement: the Enlightenment. His critique of the ignorant, sheep-like behavior regarding race endemic to most white Americans is isomorphic with Immanuel Kant's critique of tutelage in his epochal 1784 essay "An Answer to the Question: What Is Enlightenment?" His sometimes brutally honest autobiographies are a public answer to Kant's deployment of Horace's ancient challenge to anyone who would be wise: "*Sapere aude,*" or "Know thyself." While there are many differences between Kant and Du Bois, both of their philosophies share roots in the Enlightenment, where "*[e]nlightenment is man's emergence from his self-imposed immaturity.*"[21]

We can also place Du Bois at the fore of an American philosophical movement, traceable to Emerson, Thoreau, Elizabeth Cady Stanton, Charlotte Perkins Gilman, and Native American wisdom traditions that sought to bring human inquiry more fully to bear on the vicissitudes of human existence. He and his contemporaries (such as Alain Locke, John Dewey, and Jane Addams) extended enlightenment beyond its modernist boundaries. They were, as Scott Pratt writes in *Native Pragmatism,* inheritors and promulgators of a distinctly American attitude in philosophy committed to "the indigenous attitude to the principles of interaction, pluralism, community, and growth."[22] Philosophy in their hands did not merely demarcate the limits of epistemological certainty within a basically unknowable, noumenal world; it became intimately wedded to the quest to solve the problems that had vexed humanity longer than history had recorded its struggles: famine, disease, war, sexism, poverty, and racism. It did so not merely by ending each individual's immaturity, but by encouraging society as a whole to let go of outdated ideals in favor of newer ones that promised to expand social justice and succor those in need. Du Bois challenged Americans to rethink our understanding of race, the proper relationship between white folk and people of color, as well as our vision of America's role on the world stage. In each of the cases above, pragmatists joined the rejection of tautology seen in Kant with a progressive and moral mission to increase the meaning within human experience and diminish the sum of human suffering and injustice.

The Context for Du Bois's Idea of Race

Du Bois's view of race was unique for the time, and would become hugely influential among subsequent generations of race theorists. Its originality had largely to do with the fact that he came to intellectual maturity at a time when concepts of race were particularly mercurial. Du Bois says of his early education on race, "The first thing which brought me to my senses in all this racial discussion was the continuous change in the proofs and arguments advanced."[23] That is, just as he was getting used to one explanation for why people of color were treated as non-entities by white-dominated society, "the basis of race distinction was changed without explanation, without apology."[24] Most troublingly peculiar, however, was that though the definition of race fluctuated unpredictably, the conclusion that the white race was superior was as constant as the North Star. This, in turn, led him to see that race was not so much a subject that the great minds of the West had contemplated disinterestedly, but a conceptual crutch used by its European inventors to justify an otherwise unjustifiable system of human exploitation. The selective history of whiteness at the start of this book bears out Du Bois's thesis: we saw how the propositions regarding race evolved through the laws of the early colony in a way that maximized the facility with which white colonists could treat fellow human beings of African and indigenous descent as sub-human. Du Bois cast the dominant understanding of race as a kind of fantasy from which whites were afraid to awaken "because the economic foundation of the modern world was based on the recognition and preservation of so-called racial distinctions."[25]

Recognizing the inconsistency of dominant notions of race, Du Bois hammered out his own view of race that accounted for the things that dominant definitions did not. Du Bois offers his first definition of race in "The Conservation of Races": "What, then, is race? It is a vast family of human beings, generally of common blood and language, always of common history, traditions and impulses, who are both voluntarily and involuntarily striving together for the accomplishment of certain more or less vividly conceived ideals of life."[26] In order to understand this concept of race and his arguments for why it ought to be conserved, we must examine the context within which this concept took form.

Du Bois presented "The Conservation of Races" in 1897 to a nascent group of African American scholars, ministers, and professionals called the American Negro Academy (hereafter ANA). ANA was the brainchild of the Cambridge-educated African American minister and missionary Alexander Crummell, a figure who made a deep impression on the then twenty-nine-year-old Du Bois. Wilson Jeremiah Moses claims in his biography of Crummell that Du Bois "carefully crafted ['The Conservation of Races'] to gratify the emotions of the Academy and its founder."[27] While it may or may not be the case that Du Bois wrote his first acclaimed essay as an attempt to curry Crummell's favor, the impact of the elder scholar on Du Bois is undeniable.

With the death of Frederick Douglass in 1895, Booker T. Washington became the most venerable leader of Black America. Washington, working from his powerful political based at the Tuskegee Institute, urged a conservative course and "hoped to mold the character of the black masses into conformity with the great American industrial machine."[28] In his 1899 work *The Future of the American Negro,* he proclaimed to his fellow African Americans that the only solution to their present suffering was "[f]or the Negro in every part of America to resolve from henceforth that he will throw aside every nonessential and cling only to essentials—that his pillar of fire by night and pillar of cloud by day shall be property, economy, education, and Christian character. To us just now these are all wheat, all else chaff."[29] Crummell was also an African American leader whose star rose higher in Douglass's absence, though he would never achieve the national acclaim and access to halls of power that were open to Washington. His approach to the problems facing African Americans was almost diametrically opposed to Washington's. Indeed, Wilson Moses goes so far as to claim that "Crummell's hidden agenda for the American Negro Academy was to formally oppose the rising power of Tuskegee."[30] Enamored with the ideal of the African noble savage (cultivated during his twenty years as a missionary in Liberia) Crummell resisted attempts to assimilate African Americans into white American society. Instead of the practical trade education and quiet assimilation encouraged at Tuskegee, Crummell argued from his platform at ANA that blacks in America needed to overcome their "cultural deficiencies" in order to receive fair treatment in America, a goal requiring an "intellectual elite who, like Plato's philosopher-kings or France's enlightened despots, would guide the masses for their own good."[31]

This conflict between Crummell and Washington was a powerful influence upon Du Bois's development as a thinker. First, the animosity between Washington and Crummell spilled over into Du Bois's own career. This is seen nowhere more clearly than in the chapter from *The Souls of Black Folk* titled "Of Mr. Booker

T. Washington and Others," where Du Bois took up the anti-Bookerite torch as he critiqued the assimilationist tack advocated by Washington and fostered at Tuskegee.[32] Second, we see that Crummell's idea of a class of black philosopher-kings was the direct forebearer of Du Bois's idea of the "Talented Tenth."[33] Third, Crummell's thoroughly religious and spiritual tone largely defined Du Bois's style for years to come. However, as Du Bois thought of himself more as a freethinker who believed in a Creator than as a practicing Christian, his use of religious language to explicate race and oppose racism differed from Crummell's.

Crummell urged the improvement of black culture in America as part of the process of achieving Christian salvation. Du Bois, on the other hand, illuminated his vision of race through Christian Scripture and language because these ideas, joined with the science of the day, justified the privileges enjoyed by white Americans and the suffering of everyone else. If white folks were convinced God ordained white supremacy, Du Bois would confront their beliefs with the very texts that propped up their power, in order to undermine it. Finally, and most significantly for our study here, is their shared approach toward race. Both Crummell and Du Bois approached race as a *gift of unsurpassable value that must be preserved,* despite the horrific racism that opposed them at every turn, and despite Washington's calls to assimilate and Garvey's calls to leave America. Du Bois's definition of race above borrows heavily from Crummell's own argument, expressed in his 1888 work "The Race Problem in America," that race is "a compact, homogeneous population of one blood, ancestry, and lineage."[34]

Before we address Du Bois's own conception of race in earnest, we need to point out one more significant difference between Crummell and Du Bois concerning their conservationism. Crummell's conservationism was descriptive and rooted in his theology: his work called on his fellow African Americans to recognize that they were a race because God had made them so, and that nothing in the world would ever change the inherent unity of their race. Du Bois's conservationism, on the other hand, was normative and rooted his humanist meliorism: accepting that it was all too possible that the particularities of black culture and identity might get diluted into oblivion within America, Du Bois called on African Americans to *choose* to preserve their racialization. To see why this is the case, we will return to his particular conception of race.

The Idea of Race: A Du Boisian Analysis

Two aspects of Du Bois's treatment of race in "Conservation" and *The Souls of Black Folk* are particularly significant for this project. First, he prioritizes history over biology when defining the boundaries of race. We see this in his claim that races "generally" share blood, but "always" share history and traditions. Thus, for Du Bois race obtains its reality more through human interaction and sociality than through biological taxonomy. Second, this passage points to a normative dimension that Du Bois found in race that adds a unique depth to his analysis. He exceeded commonplace definitions of race by introducing the idea that a race shares a common "striving together" and is organized according to certain "ideals of life." Seen in this way, race is not merely a bunch of people who happen to share a genetic matrix. If this were all that he and later racial conservationists meant by race then all the people with detached earlobes or arch-shape fingerprints would be members of a common race group. Instead, a race is *a people* who are rooted in a common past, which in turn makes them share, to a significant degree, a common disposition toward the future. This normative dimension is crucial for current dialogues about the value of race, as it suggests why we need to preserve racial practices, even if the old eighteenth-century idea of race is false. Du Bois's articulation of race as being real without being a biological essence established a new understanding of race that still continues. For example, the economist and race theorist Glenn Loury argued for a constructivist position on race at the especially apt setting of the W. E. B. Du Bois Lectures at Harvard University. Like Du Bois, Loury defines a contextual and meaning-rich notion of race thus:

> A field of human subjects characterized by morphological variability comes through concrete historical experience to be partitioned into subgroups defined by some cluster of physical markers. Information-hungry agents hang expectations around these markers, beliefs that can . . . become self-confirming. Meaning-hungry agents invest these markers with social, psychological, and even spiritual significance. Race-markers come to form the core of personal and social identities. Narrative accounts of descent are constructed around them. And so, groups of subjects, identifying with one another, sharing feelings of pride, (dis)honor, shame, loyalty, and hope—and defined in some measure by their holding these race-markers in common—come into existence. This vesting of reasonable expectation and ineffable meaning in objectively arbitrary markings on human bodies comes to be reproduced over generations, takes on a social life of its own, seems natural and not merely conventional, and ends up having profound consequences for social relations among individuals in the raced society.[35]

According to Du Bois, race is not a mere biological *genus,* as it involves strivings of life more than strands of DNA. At the same time, it is not a wholly intentional community of self-selecting members like a social club, for it also involves matters of birth, heredity, and family. However, building from the foundational role of heritage and ideals of life in Du Bois's delineation of race (and following Du Bois's penchant for using classical and biblical references), we might liken the concept of race, like concepts in general from a pragmatist perspective, to the Roman God Janus.

This deity of doorways and new beginnings for whom January is named bore two faces: one looked back into the past (or inward toward the hearth) and the other peered into the future (or outward to the uncontrolled wilderness).[36] The aspect of race that is bound to heritage, history, and memory corresponds to the past-looking face of Janus, while the facet that pertains to ideals of life and common strivings is the face of Janus that turns to the future horizon. The past-looking face lends race historical weight and descriptive stability, while the face that looks toward the approaching horizon imbues race with teleological significance. Descriptively, race is a pertinent distinction between peoples that evolved over time. While race and racial differentiation involves certain biological traits and features, race cannot be reduced to biology for Du Bois. Instead, race inhabits a confluence between somatic similarities and ideals of life, where the otherwise accidental and inert body-variations take on meaning as they are variously and gradually wedded to certain ways of life. Races are not different from each other because certain morphological features correlate to certain innate ways of being. Instead, different communities or families that have come to blend their morphological differences into a more or less discernible racial pattern have passed down particular and distinct heritages. Du Bois would later say of the physically inherited racial characteristics of Africans: "The physical bond is least and the badge of color is relatively unimportant save as a badge; the real essence of this kinship is its social heritage of slavery; the discrimination and insult; and this heritage binds together not simply the children of Africa, but extends through yellow Asia and into the South Seas. It is this unity that draws me to Africa."[37] Thus the morphological difference is not an inherent marker of difference, but an indicator that a person bears a relationship to a certain history and a possible future.

The future face of race removes it from being a device of mere taxonomy and description, and locates it as a phenomenon that can offer human beings normative direction in life (what Dewey called "category"). Being born into a certain race means inheriting a course already plotted that need not be unerringly followed, but must be negotiated. Therefore, one's racialization requires one to take a stance on issues that are of particular historical relevance. While any individual person might chose to identify with, oppose, or ignore these ideals of life, Du Bois would say that race still involves normative import in the form of an inherited "striving" or "particular ideal, which shall help guide the world nearer and nearer that perfection of life for which we all long."[38] In addition to a normative value, race has a prophetic element in that each race bears a message for the rest of humanity in the form of its collective, preserved experience. However, he claims that "[s]ome of the great races of today—particularly the Negro Race—have not yet given to civilization the full spiritual message they are capable of giving."[39] This unfinished business—the gift not yet given— is the core of his prophetic vision of race. Yet, Du Bois does not see the Negro Race as one selected by God to preach a divine message to fallen or prodigal races.[40] Instead, Du Bois charges the black race with a *secular and humanist* prophesy, one that emerges from the history of a people, which will guide black Americans, as well as the rest of civilization.

It is important to briefly point out how Du Bois's treatment of race correlates to Dewey's treatment of concepts and habits. One way to place the works of these two thinkers in dialogue as part of a larger project of developing a critique of whiteness is to say that Du Bois's analysis of whiteness reveals that the problem of whiteness largely involves a category mistake, or, better said, a disjunction between our propositions regarding race and our habits regarding race. The aspect of race involving the past correlates to *kinds,* or the propositions that are collected from past experiences, while the aspect of race that relates to strivings and ideals of living relates to categories, or the propositions that shape future inquiries and interactions. In our current system, we almost universally assent (at least publicly) to the idea that the different racial kinds do not correlate to different universals (or more simply that we hold to the belief that all people should be treated the same way regardless of race), while acting according to habituated responses that originated when different kinds did correspond to different universals (or we *habitually* act as if we should treat people differently according to which racial group we think they belong). So while we have largely rejected white supremacist *categories* in the Deweyan sense regarding people of color, we still carry the *habits of action and thought* that were institutionalized centuries ago. If this is so and these habits are ones to be eliminated or transformed, we need to use revised categories of race, especially the least analyzed and most detrimental one—that of whiteness—in order to achieve a situation where our actions match our egalitarian words. To preview a point that will be developed later, Du Bois leads us to attend to the ways in which the white race (not as a biologically discerned genus, but as a stable and powerful form of human identity) is built upon a flawed sense of history. As a consequence, the idea and habits of whiteness not only give rise to the oppression of non-whites, but adversely affect the lives of those within the pale of whiteness. In order to see why it is the case that Du Bois urges us to critique and either revise or reject whiteness, we first need to see how and why race, for him, is a gift.

The Prophetic Dimension of Race

Du Bois communicates his conception of race in a way that appealed to religious and humanist sentiment simultaneously. His unique deployment of religious texts spoke to the absolute moral urgency of the problems of race, while his simultaneous faith in scientific method and the very possibility of eventually healing the wound of racism appealed to the idea that civilization was a dynamic and pan-cultural agglutination. Du Bois made copious use of Christian Scripture throughout his career even though he was not a practicing Christian (indeed he claims to have almost lost his first teaching position because of his brusque refusal to pretend he was one).[41] One might interpret this tendency as mere rhetoric: Du Bois was, after all, a supremely persuasive author and orator, and as such knew that he could make his case all the more persuasive if he tugged at the heartstrings of his audience through familiar spiritual stories. However, Du Bois used religious language as part of a larger strategy to reshape the concepts and habits of race.[42] His purpose was not to understand a thing that was "out there," removed from him and passively awaiting his speculative gaze. Instead, he strove to interact with the phenomenon of race (a part of his experience that powerfully affected him and everyone else) in a way that led to the resolution of pressing human problems. In particular, since he knew that the phenomenon of race as lived in the twentieth century was the offspring of religion and science, he knew that he had to marshal both of these discourses in its reimagination.

Du Bois recognized that white supremacist racism had been legitimized for centuries by white supremacist readings of the Bible.[43] For example, the story of the curse laid by Noah onto his grandson Canaan was one of the most common explanations for why Africans (cast as descendents of Canaan) could be enslaved by white Christians (who saw themselves as descendents of Shem).[44] Similarly, in the Virginia colonies the idea of whiteness emerged from the older idea of a Christian community that was God's elect people. Therefore, like all pertinent aspects of our experience, our understanding of race was formed in the interaction of inherited ideas and habits (in this case ones relating to the tradition of Judeo/Christian morality) and new experiences (the present, dynamic situation of Europeans, Africans, Asians, and indigenous people cohabitating and struggling against each other within industrialist society). As Christians, the scientists and natural philosophers of the seventeenth and eighteenth centuries *could not but* define race through religious language. Europeans had developed the habit of seeing themselves as innately superior to non-Europeans. This habit was so fundamental that it was able to bridge the chasm between religious conceptions of the world and scientific ones. Even in the heady and rebellious days of the European Enlightenment, when ancient ideas and institutions were critiqued and dismantled, the habitual assumption of white or European supremacy was barely dented. Seeing that white supremacism was such a particularly intransigent social force largely because it appeared so natural to whites, Du Bois came to the conclusion that in order to pry white Americans from their false sense of ordained racial superiority he would have to redefine race in part through the very religious language that carries so much weight in American political discourses. He thus used Christian metaphors as a fulcrum to leverage the mass of white prejudice by recasting of the very tradition that, in their minds, justified racism. In particular, he used the idea of a prophetic calling to draw attention to the evils of racism and the urgency with which it must be opposed.

This prophetic mission is one of the reasons that Du Bois urges his fellow Americans to conserve race. A race is a group of people who, through a common history and common plights, have acquired a vision of the world that enables them to speak certain truths about the world that other races have not experienced. On the one hand, each race is equally anointed messenger and errant audience. On the other hand, the Negro race, impeded from presenting its full message, must be more messenger than audience at this moment in history. Du Bois thus radically challenges the dominant relationship between African Americans and oppression. Where Christians at the time, both black and white, succored Africans in America with the image of the *Lamb* (the chosen child of God that humbly bears suffering for the sake of universal salvation), Du Bois calls on his fellow African Americans to read their plight as the trial of a *prophetic people* who must speak the troubles that they have seen, so that the other races might learn the consequences of cruelty and the need for love. The following passage is from his *Credo* (1903), which Ronald White Jr. tells us "was published in scroll form and could be seen hanging in black homes across the country."[45]

> I Believe in God, who made of one blood all nations that on earth do dwell. I believe that all men, black and brown and white, are brothers, varying through time and opportunity, in form and gift and feature, but differing in no essential particular, and alike in soul and the possibility of infinite development.
>
> Especially do I believe in the Negro Race: in the beauty of its genius, the sweetness of its soul, and its strength in that meekness which shall yet inherit this turbulent earth.
>
> I believe in Pride of race and lineage and self: in pride of self so deep as to scorn injustice to other selves; in pride of lineage so great as to despise no man's father; in pride of race so chivalrous as neither to offer bastardy to the weak nor beg wedlock of the strong, knowing that men may be brothers in Christ, even though they be not brothers in law.[46]

The first reference is to Acts 17:26: "From one blood he made all nations to inhabit the whole earth." It emphasizes the inherent equality and unity of all humanity denied by white supremacist conceptions of race. It also sets up the sort of tension and intellectual daring that is the hallmark of Du Bois's work, for this is a treatise in favor of Negro pride, yet opens with a statement that refutes the idea of biologically distinct and ranked races. His second biblical reference is his idea of a "gift" or a "spiritual message" that gives us a deeper sense of how he sees race as having a normatively charged and future-oriented facet. This harks back to Genesis 37:5–10 and the story of the Hebrew prophet Joseph. God gave Joseph the gift of second sight; he is thus able to scry the future through reading dreams. With this gift Joseph warns those around him of impending dangers and helps avoid catastrophe. In one case he interprets a dream that enables the king of Egypt to prepare for a seven-year drought. While the gift is a boon for those *around* Joseph, it is the source of great hardship for Joseph himself. The gift arouses jealousy in those near him (including his own brothers), and incites them to do him harm (by first throwing him down a well, and then selling him into slavery).

If we take Du Bois's biblical orientation to heart, we see that the race-specific ideals of life are prophetic gifts that are of unsurpassable value to those outside the race, yet are also inseparable from incomparable suffering meted upon the gift-bearing race. A race's collective experience can be a gift for another race as it gives the recipient-race a view on life that is outside their experience. A race-gift challenges the recipient to experience the world in startling, often troubling, ways. However, this difference can also potentially incur the wrath of the recipient-race: what seemed a mandated way of life before the exchange might seem contingent, unnecessary, and even inferior after the exchange. Therefore, a race runs the risk of violence any time they offer to make a gift of their ideals of life.

The third significant biblical reference is found in the phrase "strength in that meekness" possessed by "the Negro Race." This is a reference to the Sermon on the Mount from Matthew 5:3–4:

> How blessed are the poor in spirit:
> the Kingdom of Heaven is theirs.
> Blessed are the meek:
> they shall inherit the earth.

This biblical passage encapsulates the novel way of following God that becomes the core of the Christian tradition. In the Hebrew Scriptures being one of God's people meant maintaining the covenant by following the Torah. We see this, for example, in Exodus 19:3–6, where Yahweh promises a covenant to the people of Israel. The Hebrew Scriptures emphasize that one is *born into* God's covenant, and thus into God's community; in this divine-mortal relationship, the Creator chooses his people. Conversely, the Christian passage indicates that being "of God" does not mean being part of a *chosen people,* but *choosing God* by choosing to be meek.[47] This use of Matthew aligns with Du Bois's separation of the concept of race from biology. Just as the Nazarene asked his audience to choose a sacred way of life (thus choosing to walk with God), Du Bois asks his fellow blacks to choose meekness as their source of strength. As Cornel West says in *Prophesy Deliverance!* Du Bois cast the central message of his people to be "that of meekness, joviality, and humility manifest in the Afro-American gift of spirit."[48] Again, this is not a meekness to be equated with weakness or acquiescence; it is a meekness that defines itself through a *rejection of violence and domination.* He imbues race with intentional weight: what do you *choose* to remember about who you are? Do you *choose* to give the gift you inherit to those who need it, or not? Do you *choose* to have "pride of race and lineage and self?" In addition to the questions that Du Bois asks of his reader vis-à-vis their racialization, Du Bois's analysis leaves his reader with at least two pressing questions: How do we keep from forgetting the unity of blood while still finding pride in one's race? Why should we maintain race pride if we ultimately share the same blood?

The racial gift is a bridge across the racial divide made possible by the divide itself. The gift is a possibility that inhabits the rift between the "One Blood" and "Pride of Race." Racial pride relates to the particularity, uniqueness, and originality of the gift. It is the reason the gift is *worth giving.* A gift is most valuable when it is something the recipient does not have, has not thought to obtain herself, but yet needs in some sense. Thus, the racial gift is a gift of *particular human experience,* accumulated, refined, and expressed over generations, that the other does not have. The very *difference* between the giver and the receiver is what makes the gift interesting, new, and valuable. Yet, the gift is *receivable* and *understandable as a gift* precisely because the giver and the recipient are of "one blood." The experience of the other is meaningful to the extent that we can identify, at some level, with the other's tribulations and hopes, even if the actual experiences are different from our own; as common members of a single humanity, we can eventually come to see how and why members of another race-family value what they do. While the racial gift is a path of life alien to the recipient, she can still see that it comes from a human existence that faces the same problems and hopes as her own.

Du Bois maintains a great tension within his critique of whiteness. On the one hand he levels a devastating critique against whiteness as a duplicitous and cruel phenomenon. On the other hand, he does not merely reverse white supremacism by casting white people as beyond the pale of humanity. He always leaves room for the possibility of redemption and for white folk to use their gifts for the benefit of human kind. While he urged that this exchange of gifts was essential for world peace, he also described whiteness as being an inherently false and violent phenomenon. The question at this point is, should white folk participate in the exchange of racial gifts that Du Bois saw as an essential component of a healthy and balanced global community, or does the history of whiteness as self-anointed superlative category exclude the people who inherit whiteness and white privilege forevermore from this cultural exchange? I argue for a resolution of the problem of whiteness first diagnosed by Du Bois through a reconstruction of whiteness according to Dewey's notion of habit. White folk can and indeed must participate in this cultural exchange as a necessary means of building a pluralistic and life-affirming community out of a group of very different communities that sadly still bear the scars of their internecine fights. A pragmatist reconstruction would enable white folk to reclaim the sorts of cultural gifts that Du Bois says we all need, which are in danger of being obliterated by the idea and habits of whiteness. However, before we talk about how to reconstruct whiteness, the case still needs to be made that there is something amiss with the history and habits of whiteness.

SIX

Du Bois's Critique of Whiteness

Dewey and Du Bois in Dialogue

We can now begin to combine Du Bois's view of race with Dewey's notions of concept and habit in order to develop a pragmatic critique of the problem of whiteness. Du Bois's view denied race a simple, biological foundation while granting its very real effect on our collective lived experience and cultural gifts. To use Dewey's language, Du Bois treats race as *a kind,* as *a category,* and as *a set of habits.*

On the one hand, race is a kind (defined by generic propositions). It is an idea that gives shape to our experiences by using sets of traits (a common past and history for example) drawn from past experiences that describe a group of things (in this case, human beings). These conjunctions of traits are not eternal or transcendent, but selected and learned. This correlates to Du Bois's claim that "the scientific definition of race is impossible."[1] Instead, race is a kind in that certain people (and in the case of the particular taxonomy with which we are concerned, these people were Europeans in the seventeenth and eighteenth centuries) were able to achieve stability in their inquiries by appealing to the idea that humanity was divided (either by divine design or by evolutionary co-incidence) into different groups.

Races for Du Bois, like concepts for Dewey, are also forward-looking. Du Bois expresses this through his idea of the racial gift, or the idea that each group's unique experiences give them a perspective on human life that is distinct from the perspectives of other groups, yet at the same time valuable to them. This is similar to Dewey's idea that categorical propositions are "formulations of possible ways of acting or operating."[2] Indeed, the people who first appealed to the idea of race did not do so merely for division's sake; instead the "category" of race (in the Deweyan sense), defined by propositions regarding future disposition, was at the crux of the idea of race. They did not say, "A white child has such and such traits, where a Negro child has such and such traits," and leave the matter there. Instead, the reason the idea was so very appealing to those in power was that it enabled them to develop habitual forms of action in terms of an imagined future, one that benefited their group. As we saw in the first chapter, a child who was "white" had to be treated as potentially autonomous individual, whereas a child who was "Negro" could be treated as property. Here the description of the kind carries forward an expectation of future action that in turn reinforces the concept of racial difference and hierarchy.

Hence, both thinkers show that race is more than just a concept, since concepts are bound up with habits. These habits include the different ways that African Americans acted when they were around other black people, or when they were in the company of white folk. They also included the different ways that white people behaved toward other whites on the one hand, or people of color on the other. Again, both philosophers agree that neither these particular categories nor these particular habits are necessary or beyond our control. They would also agree that some categories and habits are necessary, as people cannot constantly face each new experience or moment of action as a radically unique moment. We need ideas that make sense of the world and scripts that give us starting points as to how to act in the world. Du Bois's diagnosis of our problem—a diagnosis with which Dewey would agree, based on his brief words on racial prejudice—is that we have a set of confused habits.

Du Bois shows us that the problem of racism rests on the shoulders of white Americans, because their habits regarding race are confused at many levels. In the era of colonial Virginia the disjunction was between, on the one hand, the central Christian ideas of free will, love, and charity and, on the other, the ideas and practices that treated certain human beings as unworthy of being treated as free or deserving Christian love. In our current age it is a disjunction largely born of a temporal separation between publicly affirmed ideas regarding race (that we are all equal, and that white people do not deserve better treatment than non-whites because of their race) and habits that are stuck in an earlier era (which includes everything from where the focus of the criminal justice system is to what kind of mannerisms are proper, what features are beautiful, or what counts as intelligence). Du Bois spent his life showing us how racial concepts permeate *all* aspects of our lives and how the injustices they enable challenge the fundamental ideas of what America is and ought to be. Having gained a general sense of his approach to race, we need to see how he relates dominant ideas of race to white supremacism and the deity he sees at the top of white supremacist culture: money.

Race and Money

In *Dusk of Dawn* Du Bois first explicitly draws a connection that was implicit in much of his work, going as far back as *The Souls of Black Folk:*

> I think it was in Africa that I came more clearly to see the close connection between race and wealth. The fact that even in the minds of the most dogmatic supporters of race theories and believers in the inferiority of colored folk to white, there was a conscious or unconscious determination to increase their incomes by taking full advantage of this belief. And then gradually this thought was metamorphosed into a realization that the income-bearing value of race prejudice was the cause and not the result of theories of racial inferiority.[3]

Race is real in the way that money is. In both cases, their definitions are the product of certain agreed-upon conventions, and their value adheres to their ability to determine human action. There is no pertinent difference in the materials that make up a five-dollar bill that makes it five times as valuable as a dollar bill. Indeed, the nature of modern currency *requires* that the different bills be made from exactly the same materials. The difference has to do with the fact that our economic system *treats* a five-dollar bill the same as five one-dollar bills. Similarly, Du Bois would say that there is nothing inherent in a black person and absent in a white person that warrants the discriminatory treatment the former receives. Instead, the social difference between a white person and a black person adheres to a social convention whereby the white person is treated as though he or she were more valuable.

However, the passage above shows that money and race share more than this coincidental similarity: indeed race is real largely *because of* money. That is, it was the economic value of establishing a racial hierarchy where certain human beings (ones from certain European families) were free to profit from the abuse and enslavement of other peoples (ones from anywhere but Europe) that caused racial categories to flourish. Just as James said that the truth of an idea is its "cash value," we can say that Du Bois showed us that the cash value of race really was *literally its cash value:* it allowed Europeans to frame the world and humanity in such a way that they were able to exploit both for their own material wealth. Du Bois expresses the tension between science and economics regarding race in *Dusk of Dawn* when he says that "[e]ver since the African slave trade and before the rise of modern biology and sociology, we have been afraid in America that scientific study is this direction might lead to conclusions with which we were loath to agree; and this fear was in reality because the economic foundation of the modern world was based on the recognition and preservation of so-called racial distinctions."[4] Du Bois here points out that science and economics are at loggerheads because scientific studies of human biology eventually began to erode the older notion of fixed and hierarchically ranked human races. This would in turn threaten the social system of white supremacism, which was immensely profitable for European folk around the world. Thus, racial hierarchies exist not because of scientific findings, but because of monetary holdings.

We see this correlation between white supremacism and money in both of the moments in the history of whiteness examined in the first chapter. We find an example that is truly chilling in the laws of colonial Virginia. Recall the 1667 act called "An act declaring that baptisme of slaves doth not exempt themfrom [sic] bondage."[5] It was a brazen effort to deny people of African descent the ability to claim the status of free-citizenship through the act of baptism. This act made the slave status—a legal status that accrued *only* to people of indigenous or African descent—heritable. While all normative "Christians," that is, all people from the Christian countries of Europe, had the right to expect their children to be born free, with all the rights of citizenship, all non-Europeans had to inherit the status of their parents. Even children born of European Virginian mothers who gave birth as indentured servants were free, since indenture was a temporary suspension of certain citizenship rights. In the case of African Virginians, this law meant that they were almost inevitably born slaves. While this might have been an utterly bankrupt and despicable law from a social or ethical point of view, it was a stroke of financial genius. The colonial elites could have their cake and eat it too. They could sleep with a clear conscience, knowing that their slaves had been lifted out of the doldrums of heathendom because of the slave master's "charity and piety," but could still work them like animals until they left for their eternal reward. Again, this moment is a crystal-clear illustration of the fundamental contradictions and inhumanity involved in the idea of whiteness. To the extent that it was an identity that emerged from Christianity, it had to uphold values of human kindness. To the extent that it was premised upon superiority and the idea that they were God's chosen people, it allowed white folk to oppress all others.

The psychology of these legislators is lost to us for better or worse: we will never know if they actually believed they were being magnanimous, or if this law and dozens like it were part of a conscious and cynical attempt to deny the humanity of fellow human beings for the sake of profit. The question of their intent is a moot one for our purposes nonetheless. What matters for our study is that this law institutionalized a habit of thought that quickly became pervasive. This law, and others like it from this pivotal period, established the legal and conceptual foundation from which the walls of racial habits and behaviors could arise. It made a particular reading of phenotype and morphology into a classificatory exercise that bore significant social, political, and legal weight. It also solidified the conceptual habit of treating certain people with certain perceivable features as ends in themselves, and other people with other features as means. Figuring out whether money created race, or whether a pre-existing idea of race was later used by men for financial gain, is as fruitless as resolving the "chicken or the egg" conundrum. As Du Bois says above, we don't know if race was put to work in the colonies "consciously or unconsciously." The fact remains, however, that racial ideas and habits *were deployed* to great financial gain for a small number of people.

The key to these new financially rewarding habits was the idea of whiteness, the idea that white people were meant to rule over non-whites because of the fact that whites were special. That this sense of entitlement has been tied tightly to the idea of whiteness throughout its history was a point that Dewey missed in his analysis of the problems of racial prejudice. Du Bois, however, as someone who was intimately familiar with whiteness, did not make this mistake. Ironically, he agreed with white supremacists throughout the ages on one point: that white folk were different from non-white folk. His work draws attention to the fact that white folk are corrupted in a way that people of color are not. This is not because white folk are innately evil, but because the sense of superiority inherent in the idea of whiteness leads to particular kinds of cruel behavior.

Du Bois's Critique of Whiteness

Du Bois critiqued whiteness not as a collection of inherently evil people, but as a flawed *idea* and set of *habits* that have ossified around most people of European descent living in America. These ideas and habits have placed these people in disequilibria with their world, their history, and people of other cultures and traditions. Du Bois exerted a great deal of energy on this critique because he saw whiteness as not only a problem that could be solved, but one that had to be addressed in order to realize the democratic potential of the nation.

While Du Bois wrote many works that critiqued the idea of whiteness and the behavior of white Americans, no work does so with more passion than "The Souls of White Folks." The title is a reference to his earlier, more widely read work of literary genius, *The Souls of Black Folk,* that counterposes the mellifluous compassion of the first work with a righteous bitterness toward the idiocy of white America. Its opening passage warrants being quoted at some length.

> Of [White Folk] I am singularly clairvoyant. I see in and through them. I view them from unusual points of vantage. Not as a foreigner do I come, for I am native, not foreign, bone of their thought and flesh of their language. Mine is not the knowledge of the traveler or the colonial composite of dear memories, words and wonder. Nor yet is my knowledge that which servants have of masters, or mass of class, or capitalist of artisan. Rather I see these souls undressed and from the back

and side. I see the working of their entrails. I know their thoughts and they know that I know. This knowledge makes them now embarrassed, now furious! They deny my right to live and call me misbirth! My word is to them mere bitterness and my soul, pessimism. And yet as they preach and strut and shout and threaten, crouching as they clutch at rags of facts and fancies to hide their nakedness, they go twisting, flying by my tired eyes and I see them ever stripped,—ugly, human.[6]

Here Du Bois proclaims that in spite of their conquests, white folk are still fools. To make this charge, Du Bois twists the biblical passage that includes the first phrase passed between humans. When Adam first sees Eve he proclaims in Genesis 2:22,

> This one at last is bone of my bones
> and flesh of my flesh!

Adam makes this announcement out of relief; he is relieved because he had named all the other created beings without finding a suitable companion, but in Eve finds a being with whom he can relate, an equal. It is a passage that speaks the erotic and deeply embodied enjoyment of another that is clearly part of God's blessing of the faithful in the Hebrew tradition, which didn't go over so well in the monastic communities that were the cauldrons of early medieval Christianity. Du Bois also uses this phrase to express an intimate knowledge, but in this case the knowledge does not lead to relief. Instead he uses the phrase to show just how well he understands the extent to which whiteness rests on a lie.

When Du Bois refers to white folks "crouching as they clutch at rags of facts and fancies to hide their nakedness" he is referring not only to Adam and Eve's nakedness, but also to the false idea of a superior white race that is propped up by the slanted science and theology. He sees the white march to civilize the world as merely an attempt to conquer it. Further, Du Bois knows that whites are not above any other member of the human family, but just another branch of the tree's common trunk. As he says in "Credo," the most overtly religious of his works,

> I believe in the Devil and all his Angels, who wantonly work to narrow the opportunity of struggling human beings, especially if they be black; who spit in the faces of the fallen, strike them that cannot strike again, believe the worst and work to prove it, hating the image which their Maker stamped on a brother's soul. . . . I believe that the wicked conquest of the weaker and darker nations by nations whiter and stronger but foreshadows the death of that strength.[7]

In this passage, Du Bois indicates the nature of the challenge ahead and the reason that the human family has not equally shared its gifts. Just as we might imagine a God giving us the opportunity to achieve community across and through differences, we can imagine an opponent that subverts this goal. Du Bois names this opponent the "Devil." It is worth remembering that the Christian idea of a completely evil Devil emerged from the more complex Hebrew idea of "satan." Satan, while cruel, was not the embodiment of evil. Instead, he was God's adversary and one of the primary obstacles facing God's people.[8] Likewise, white folk are not evil per se, but are obstacles to the achievement of human community and peace by virtue of the ideas and habits of whiteness.

While all the branches of the human family have gifts to share in their unique styles of life, certain branches have "fallen" (if we expand his biblical metaphor) in that they have abandoned the collective project of mutual exchange and have taken it upon themselves to oppress others. Certain races thus function as adversaries, or satans, to the other races. Members of these races have used the very gifts they might have used to benefit other members of the family to "spit in the faces of the fallen, strike them that cannot strike again." Finally, since race is defined in part by a collective heritage that becomes the starting point for subsequent generations, these race-families are defined in part by a collective history of oppression.

Du Bois believes that the whiter nations have perverted their gifts to assault the nations that lack their particular gifts: industrial organization and military production. This misuse answers one question but raises others. We now know why humanity has not reached a harmonious equilibrium. The history of European colonization indicates the ways in which whites have used their abilities to rob and suppress darker peoples. But we still do not know what it means to say that whiteness rests on a lie, or exactly what "rags of facts and fancies" whites hide behind. What does he see when he looks at our "souls undressed and from the back and side?" Further, our brief glimpse into Du Bois's critique of whiteness from *Darkwater* indicates a rift, perhaps unbridgeable, between this work and his earlier "Conservation of Races."

Put simply, if the idea of whiteness as a superlative race is a deceptive and coercive one that hides behind "rags of facts and fancies," then how could it be worth conserving? Part of the answer lies in the fact that Du Bois, with his 1920 *Darkwater,* recognizes that the idea of the white race is qualitatively different from the idea of the black race. Both are real in the same way: they are both inherited founts of human meaning that span generations through habits, attitudes, and cultures. They both rely on kinds that use morphology as a badge that marks an individual as the inheritor of a particular history. They are both organized around habits: frameworks of meaning that are passed from old to young that organize inchoate and new experiences. However, they are different in that the history that white Americans inherit is a skewed one that in turn causes them to adopt habits of action that are violent and anti-democratic. Whiteness is a distinct racial identity both because it directs future actions according to past experiences that never happened and because it encourages a violent and exclusionary disposition to non-whites. To fully see how and why Du Bois treats whiteness as both real (as a set of habits that guide the actions of most Americans) and false (in that these habits assume an ideal history and purpose that is fabricated) we need to look to his 1940 *Dusk of Dawn.*

In "The White World," the chapter of *Dusk of Dawn* that most directly addresses the question of whiteness, Du Bois uses the literary device of a fictional white man named Roger Van Dieman to illuminate how white Americans are like the emperor who wears no clothes. By engaging in a hypothetical dialogue with an "average (white) Joe," Du Bois is able to show the effects of the idea of whiteness, particularly the way its concepts and habits make racial prejudice against people of color and the concomitant privileges reserved for whites seem natural and warranted.

The aspect of this critique that is most germane for the current examination of the problem of whiteness is his analysis of the *amnesia and distorted sense of history* that is linked to whiteness. This historical disconnection is what makes whiteness so dangerous and unlike other races. When Du Bois asserts that people of Asia and Africa have made countless contributions to human development, Van Dieman replies, "I have never heard of it."[9] To correct his myopia, Du Bois uses a metaphor of a sled going up and over a hill. The laborious work of getting the sled up the hill is likened to the very first acts of civilization in Africa and India, where humanity first began to develop some measure of predictability and meaning within its environment. The current age is the wild rush down the other side, where the rider feels only the power of his movement, which is the explosion of production and wealth in white nations. The mistake is that the white rider has forgotten the centuries of work that made the current speed possible, not to mention the millions of laborers of color around the world whose sweat drives the engine of American and European commerce.

In addition to suffering from a distorted sense of history, whiteness is also problematic because of its habitual dishonesty. He claims in *Dusk of Dawn* that "[i]ndeed, the greatest and most immediate danger of white culture, perhaps least sensed, is its fear of the Truth, its childish belief in the efficacy of lies as a method of human uplift."[10] This critique is the deepest and most fundamental of all; consequently, it is the one that links Du Bois most firmly to the contemporary critiques of whiteness that we will survey in the following chapter. While Du Bois will come back to this point many times in his long career and emphasizes different aspects of it at different times, his basic claim is that whiteness rests on a heap of colossal lies.

They include some specific lies that he mentions in "The White World," such as the idea that this continent was a *tabula rasa,* unmarked by any civilization, upon which white America could manifest her destiny, or that the indigenous peoples of this land are incapable of rule, or that African Americans are so inferior that they will inevitably die out (thus solving the "Negro Problem" that so vexed white thinkers at the time). We can further add the propaganda (several centuries old by Du Bois's time) that the white race is inherently superior to the other races in every way, and non-whites need white rule to raise them from barbarism. White folk have justified their deferential treatment according to authorities religious, scientific, or both. Yet it is all based on a supposedly natural distinction that is not there. So while white culture doubtlessly *exists* (there really are laws, practices, institutions, and activities that are based on the idea of a distinct, superior white race), it leads a *false* existence (in that the supposed difference is fabricated, and kept in place by legal sanction, social custom, and force of habit) that in turn generates more falsehoods (the ones necessary to maintain the façade of white superiority and civility). The idea of a naturally superior, benevolently civilized, and divinely blessed white race is so deeply appealing to whites that all evidence to the contrary is rejected or explained away. The horrors of the African slave trade are made palatable by the idea that Africans are little more than beasts of burden who barely notice their slavery. Indeed, slave owners praised themselves for passing a law that stated that baptism could free a slave from sin, but not from his master. The genocide of Native Americans and the theft of their homelands are worked into a biblical context; the Lakota or the Wampanoag play the cursed Canaanites to the blessed Israelites from Christian Europe.

As mordant as his critique might be, Du Bois avoids critiquing white *people* as inherently evil or false. This would amount to a double error for Du Bois. Framing whites as devils would contradict Du Bois's arguments that all humans stem from a single blood. Further, such a claim would undermine his meliorism; it would enable white folks rankled by his critique to say, "If we are naturally so evil, why *shouldn't* we keep doing what we're doing?" Instead, when Van Dieman accuses Du Bois of thinking that white folk are "about the meanest and lowest [people] on earth," Du Bois responds that "[t]hey are human, even as you and I."[11] White culture is false not because its members are so, but because it is a cultural group that is premised on a lie (or a myopic view of history) and whose actions are guided by a false sense of superiority. To link this aspect of Du Bois's critique to Dewey, the lie upon which whiteness is premised correlates to a mistaken *kind,* while the concomitant arrogance correlates to a mistaken *category* (or disposition toward the future). Both of these aspects of the concept of whiteness have been active and functional for so long that they cease to draw attention to themselves; they have become habits.

This critique of whiteness returns us to Du Bois's original take on race: that it is a phenomenon as real as anything in the world, but culturally and experientially real rather than biologically. "Human beings are infinite in variety, and when they are agglutinated in groups, great and small, the groups differ as though they, too, had integrating souls. But they have not. The soul is still individual if it is free. Race is a cultural, sometimes an historical fact."[12] Du Bois is pointing to the fact that, as gregarious creatures, our groups define us. Races are then merely ancient groups that have developed over centuries. Their members share certain phenotypical features, to be sure, but the real glue that keeps the agglutination together is experience and history. Thus, while individual humans are located within a spectrum of variety in terms of biological starting points, we are accepted into such-and-such a group. And it is as a member of this race-group that our experience is defined (or at least that is how things have been since we've lived in a racialized world). Lest anyone think that this cultural understanding of race is somehow undefined, however, Du Bois reminds us, in one of his most famous passages, that these cultural groups bear incontrovertible weight in terms of how we live our lives. When, in his last utterance of their dialogue, Van Dieman asks him how it is possible for Du Bois to differentiate himself as a black man when he admits that there are no biological races, Du Bois replies, "I recognize it quite easily and with full legal sanction; the black man is a person who must ride 'Jim Crow' in Georgia."[13]

One further critique of white American civilization merits mentioning: the idea of whiteness and its associated habits cause those considered white to live in a state of almost total contradiction and hypocrisy. This critique further illustrates the way in which whiteness is different from other racial categories. To use Du Bois's most common counterexample, blackness is an identity that is based on a historical inheritance that is more or less accurate (remembrances of African civilizations, the Middle Passage, slavery, struggle for freedom, emancipation, Reconstruction, lynchings, Jim Crow, and the civil rights movement). This historical/cultural identity motivates a particular disposition to the present that correlates to the present situations of African American folk: a response to the continued injustice and marginalization suffered by black Americans marked by a prioritization of social justice and community uplift. Contrarily, whiteness is racial identity based on remembrances of events that did not happen in the way they are remembered. The stories involve harmonious sharing between pilgrims and Native peoples, stalwart and just struggles later on against savages, beatific sharing of Christian salvation among backward pagans, and the development of an industrial system that is the worldly salvation of all peoples. Ideals of equality are set out as goals, but they cannot succeed since the conditions established in the past (exceptionalism, poverty, violence) make the ideals unworkable. The false memory leads to a present condition of almost total contradiction: where ideals of white America are at odds with each other and the actions necessary to maintain the current system. The concept of whiteness leads to defensiveness toward attempts to correct the legalized white supremacism of our past: since our Golden Age, or "good ol' days" are in the past, multicultural initiatives threaten to weaken what was once a great nation. Du Bois shows this attitude in another fictional dialogue (with an unnamed white friend) that presents the different, incompatible value systems that run through white American life: Christianity, Gentility, Americanism, and whiteness.

Du Bois starts by briefly articulating the basic Christian virtues that serve as the moral basis for Anglo-Saxon, Protestant, white American society: the Golden Rule, goodwill toward all human beings, the willingness to bear discomfort to help those less fortunate, and the valorization of worldly poverty over wealth.[14] Unfortunately, this is at almost total loggerheads with the life of a gentleman. In particular, the gentleman's way of life necessitates ample financial resources, for both the material trappings necessary and the leisure time to cultivate the precise air. This reliance on accumulated property and wealth gives rise to a new set of concerns (that further draw the American white man from the Christian values he supposedly holds as the ideal). These are the paradigmatic concerns of the American: the need for a strong police force to protect our wealth from those who are inside our country, and an army to defend our wealth from those on the outside.[15] These three sets of concerns give rise to a "fourth code of action": the code of the white man.[16] While Du Bois's friend had lived much of his life oblivious to questions of race and white supremacy, "[h]e had come to realize that his whiteness was fraught with tremendous responsibilities, age-old and infinite in future possibilities. It would seem that colored folks were a threat to the world. They were going to overthrow white folk by sheer weight of numbers, destroy their homes and marry their daughters."[17]

The white code changed the tenor of the preparedness that defined Americanism. The point was "[n]ot only preparedness nor simply defense, but war against the darker races, carried out now and without too nice discrimination as to who were dark: war against the Riff, the Turk, Chinese, Japanese, Indians, Negroes, Mulattoes, Italians and South Americans."[18] This white code involved three laws. The first was that of self-preservation.[19] This entailed treating the crimes of white people as incidental and those of non-whites as characteristic. While Du Bois did not specifically mention it in this discussion, he could have easily pointed to lynching, the white supremacist act of violent self-preservation in its most depraved and purest form, as proof for this doctrine. The second law was that of exploitation, or making sure that "the poor must be poor so that the Rich may be Rich."[20] The third and final law of the white code is "Empire: the white race as ruler of all the world and the world working for it, and the world's wealth piled up for the white man's use."[21] This pressing problem with whiteness brings us back to Bacon's Rebellion, when the legally articulated idea of whiteness provided a crucial tool of social control to the colonial Regents in Virginia. It is also the aspect of whiteness that Du Bois calls most characteristic of whiteness.

> Yet the fields of Belgium laughed, the cities were gay, art and science flourished; the groans that helped to nourish this civilization fell on deaf ears because the world round about was doing the same sort of thing elsewhere on its own account. As we saw the dead dimly through rifts of battle smoke and heard faintly the cursing and accusations of blood brothers, we darker men said: This is not Europe gone mad; this is not aberration nor insanity; this *is* Europe; this seeming Terrible is the real soul of white culture—back of all culture,—stripped and visible today.[22]

This passage refers to the plight of the Congo at the hands of Belgium's King Leopold.[23] It selects this instance of European conquest of Africa as an illustration of white Europe making use of its gift for its own purposes. Rather than claiming this horror in the Congo (where about twelve million Africans died) as an aberration, Du Bois forces us to recognize that this is but one instance of the blithe violence enabled by the idea of whiteness. That is to say, modern Europe was built upon just this kind of conquest by violent and oppressive means. European civilization might look just and noble from the European point of view (where "the cities were gay, art and science flourished"), but this progress is only a facade that hides the unimaginable pain and destruction experienced by darker races everywhere. The idea of whiteness explains the bounty by appealing to the fact that whites are, and always have been, the wisest, thriftiest, and most advanced of all people. The barbaric violence necessary to bring these riches to the great cities of Europe, and later America, need not be considered.

A word needs to be said, however, about the easy exchange of "white" and "European" in the passage above. It is important to note that Du Bois does not argue that whiteness has always been synonymous with being European. The best source for addressing this equation is his 1944 piece "Jacob and Esau": a commencement address given to the graduates of Talladega College in Alabama.[24] In this speech he returns to the biblical metaphors that marked "The Conservation of Races," *The Souls of Black Folk,* and *Darkwater.* He argues that the legacy of Jacob—the quick-witted, younger son of the elderly patriarch Isaac who tricks his rough-hewn elder brother Esau out of his birthright and his father's blessing—lives on in the civilizations of Europe. In particular, the calculating trickery of Jacob is "typical of modern Europe" and is expressed in the idea that "life must be planned for the Other self, for that personification of the group, the nation, the empire."[25]

Temporality is crucial in Du Bois's analysis here; it is not the case for him that European people have always been this way. Instead, the problem of Jacob-like behavior is traced to the moment that they "begin to lie and steal, in order to make the nation to which they belong great, [because] then comes not only disaster, but rational contradiction which in many respects is worse than disaster, because it ruins . . . the human reason by which we chart and guide our actions."[26] Whiteness became associated with Europe because of the racial taxonomies being developed by European natural philosophers that cast the various fledgling nations of Europe as, though culturally, politically, and religiously distinct, sharing the trait of whiteness. Italy, Spain, Holland, France, and Britain were all Jacobs, in this regard, circling the globe in search for Esaus whose birthright they might steal in the name of Country, King, and Christ. While intra-European violence and competition was all too common, the idea of a superior white race mandated that other Europeans, as fellow Caucasians, be treated with a certain degree of respect (Irish, Romas, Samiis, and Jews excepted).

Demonstrating the increasing impact of Marxism on his work, Du Bois is quick to point out that the imperatives that directed the "white world of Europe and America"[27] were responsible for the fact not only that "peoples of whole islands and countries were murdered in cold blood for their gold and jewels," but also that the "mass of the laboring people of the world were put to work for wages which led them into starvation, ignorance and disease."[28] He goes on to demonstrate that the irrationality of white nation building has climaxed in the wars of the twentieth century, where white Europe and America "commit suicide on so vast a scale that it is almost impossible for us to realize the meaning of the catastrophe."[29]

The four codes amount to an "almost quadri-lemma" for whites (people of European descent who identify and are identified as white and thus able to partake of white privilege) in America. They want to be good Christians (with all its kindness and poverty), but the desire to achieve the social status of a gentleman is as American as apple pie, as are the desires to protect our wealth against the masses of non-white poor people who would take it. The problem is not which to choose: it is that white American culture entails all four sets of habits and uses them at different times for support. Thus, not only is white American culture based on a lie and connected to its history in a selective and distorted fashion, but it is completely incoherent in terms of its own goals and aspirations. It claims to be the greatest Christian nation in the world, but it greedily defends its worldly wealth against the meek who might use it to improve their lot beyond poverty.

Du Bois maintains a great tension within his critique of whiteness. On the one hand, he levels a devastating critique against whiteness as a duplicitous and cruel phenomenon. On the other hand, he does not merely reverse white supremacism by casting white people as beyond the pale of humanity. He always leaves room for the possibility of redemption and for white folk to use their gifts for the benefit of humanity. Du Bois is able to maintain this tension because of an idea that lends his voice to an easy dialogue with Dewey's and demonstrates the extent to which he is a pragmatist. At the end of *Dusk of Dawn*, in the chapter "Revolution," Du Bois hints at this idea when he points out that he "began to realize that in the fight against race prejudice, we were not facing simply the rational, conscious determination of white folk to oppress us; we were facing age-long complexes sunk now largely to unconscious habit and irrational urge, which demanded on our part not only the patience to wait, but the power to entrench ourselves for a long siege against the strongholds of color caste."[30] Du Bois goes on to suggest an apt response to the problem of white supremacist racism must take into account the fact that racism is largely an unconscious affair: "This process must deal not only with conscious rational action, but with irrational and unconscious habit, long buried in folkways and custom. Intelligent propaganda, legal enactment and reasoned action must attack the conditioned reflexes of race hate and change them."[31]

We can now see how Du Bois is able to simultaneously maintain the idea of race conservation and critique white folk so forcefully. Races are generally worth preserving because they involve particular shared cultures and historical perspectives. His analysis reveals the extent to which people of color, as people who have suffered a kind of oppression that white people have not felt, need to speak out against the conscious and unconscious violence that stems from white habits. This is why he says, "[T]he colored world therefore must be seen as . . . a group whose insistent cry may yet become the warning which awakens the world to its truer self and its wider destiny."[32] The white race is different from all others, however, and ought not be preserved. It is based upon distorted ideas, like the idea that white people are naturally superior to all others and carry a "white man's burden" to improve all non-whites by forcing them to adopt white culture. It is also based upon a distorted history, as outlined above. However, what is most troubling about whiteness are the damaging and conflicting habits that attach themselves to it. These include the habitual cruelty with which white folk treat non-whites, as in the myriad laws passed in the Virginia colony that denigrated the lives of non-whites, sometimes even under the guise of saving their souls. It is for this reason that white folk throughout history (and I will argue the same can be said regarding many contemporary white Americans) were able to profess their belief in many high ideals (from the universality of Christian salvation to universal human equality), all the while engaging in habitual behaviors that oppressed their fellow human being. While Du Bois leaves us with the clear sense that the habits of whiteness need to change and that people who now see themselves as white need to develop a new identity, he does not offer much by way of where this alternative would come from. We will address the matter of where white folk can discover or develop gifts worth sharing in the fourth part of this book.

The reading of Du Bois advanced in this chapter also makes us take seriously his consistent use of religious language when describing race and the problem of white supremacism. This language is one of the most consistent features of his work; it is prevalent in his 1898 essay "The Conservation of Race" and is still a central part of his work as late as the 1940s, as seen in his essay "Jacob and Esau." Once we read white racism as a problem of habit, this language is not merely a rhetorical seasoning common to thinkers trained in the nineteenth century. Instead, this language is part of the "intelligent propaganda" that he calls for at the end of *Dusk of Dawn*.[33] This language gives him leverage over the obdurate and age-old habits and ideas at the heart of white racism. In true pragmatist fashion, he uses this religious discourse (one he was not shy about rejecting in terms of his person beliefs) as a resource to redefine the problem of racism. He refutes the quietist biblical reading of race (where people of color are the sons of Canaan who must quietly endure the lot God has chosen for them) with an angry prophetic reading of race. He suggests to white folk and people of color alike that non-whites are more like the meek from the Sermon on the Mount: people who refuse to use violence, but nonetheless will overthrow the contemporary, unjust social order that stands in the way of a just

Kingdom of God on Earth. This consistent use of biblical language is not mere rhetoric, but entails a new logic about how we should understand race generally, and the relationship between white and non-white peoples the world over.

Du Bois, lyrical in his dying as in his living, left this world the night before Rev. Martin Luther King Jr. delivered the most famous and significant speech of twentieth-century American politics. King's oration also invoked the moral force of biblical language to strengthen people of color in their struggle against injustice and to let fall the scales from the eyes of white folk regarding the pain they cause their fellow human beings. The civil rights movement, of which Reverend King was a crucial part, strove to solve the problem of the color line. It succeeded in many ways; white supremacist ideals were exposed as the unjust and artificial norms that they were, and white politicians, judges, and police where no longer able to justify their terrible power over non-white by appealing to these ideals.

Unfortunately, the habits of whiteness did not die, but only changed their trappings. White folks continue to hold disproportionate control over the country, and anti-black, anti-Asian, anti-Latino, anti-indigenous, and anti-Semitic attitudes, behaviors, and policies still abound. Just as the habits of whiteness were able to make themselves seem natural and normal and in line with the spirit of Christianity and America during Du Bois's time, they now work in such a way that they seem in line with the spirit of the civil rights movement. Van Dieman, speaking for the majority of white Americans, told Du Bois to stop agitating about racial justice because "[o]f course . . . you know Negroes are inferior."[34] Nowadays, Van Dieman's grandson, equally inured in the tutelage of his age as his grandfather was in his, tells liberatory theorists that all their work is for naught because "don't you know that racism has been over for thirty years." In order to see how whiteness and white privilege have changed since Du Bois's time, we need to now look to feminists, pragmatists, and other liberatory scholars who try to identify and combat the stain of white racism and privilege.

CONTEMPORARY PROBLEMS AND DEBATES

Whiteness in Post–Civil Rights America

[W]hen, on August 6, 1965, President Johnson signed the Voting Rights Act into law, many thought they had witnessed the culmination of a second Reconstruction. It had started in 1954 with *Brown*, a case which tacitly repudiated the fundamental assumption that the Thirteenth Amendment's abolition of slavery had meant little; it continued through the 1964 Civil Rights legislation that restored black citizenship rights under the Fourteenth Amendment, and was thought to be complete when Congress passed a law restoring black voting rights under the Fifteenth Amendment. What more was there to be done?

This passage is drawn from Anthony Cook's *The Least of These: Race, Law, and Religion in American Culture*.[1] It strings together the different gems of the civil rights movement like a necklace, starting with *Brown v. Board of Education* and ending with the signing of the Voting Rights Act. Cook, able to look back on a justice movement that reached its apogee after Du Bois's death, shares the older scholar's skepticism. He writes the passage above to capture the common belief that this movement completely and utterly satisfied the requirements of justice regarding the legacy of racism in the United States by changing the socioeconomic conditions that perpetuated white privilege and gave white supremacist racism its awful bite. Once the combatants of the movement had won complete citizenship and rights of equal access for people of color, many white Americans answered the question "What more was there to be done?" with a relieved "Nothing."

Such relief was unfounded, however. Cook reminds us that riots broke out in Watts, Los Angeles, five days after Johnson's historic signing. Of the thirty-five people who died, twenty-eight were black.[2] More riots followed. The worst would come almost exactly two years after the culmination of the civil rights movement, when horrific riots erupted in the summer of 1967 across major U.S. cities including Newark, Detroit, and Atlanta. These riots seemed to indicate that the legal changes wrought over the previous decades of struggle were not enough. As a country, we no longer legally recognized white supremacism as the law of the land. However, racial justice was still out of reach.

In the aftermath of these riots President Johnson appointed the National Advisory Committee on Civil Disorders, which came to be known as the Kerner Commission (after its Chairman Otto Kerner, then governor of Illinois). The commission produced an extremely detailed account of the riots and conjectured on potential causes for the riots. With a candor that surprised the people dissatisfied with the moderate-to-conservative composition of the committee, the report stated that

> [r]ace prejudice has shaped our history decisively; it now threatens to affect our future. White racism is essentially responsible for the explosive mixture which has been accumulating in our cities since the end of World War II. Among the ingredients of this mixture are: *pervasive discrimination and segregation . . .* which have resulted in the continuing exclusion of great numbers of Negroes from the benefits of economic progress. . . . *Black in-migration and white exodus . . .* [and] *Black ghettos* where segregation and poverty converge on the young to destroy opportunity and enforce failure.[3]

A later review of the Report (*The Kerner Report Revisited*) criticizes the original attempt to understand the riots. In so doing, the re-visitation not only illuminates how and why the report failed in its attempt to understand the violence of 1967 but also casts significant light on our *current* situation, where white supremacist language is absent from our laws but racism still vexes us.

> The *Report,* however, also had several shortcomings. Its basic finding that "white racism" was the fundamental cause of the racial disorders and the emphasis placed upon that finding by the mass media have given the erroneous impression that the guilt of white society is simply a matter of prejudicial attitudes. The *Kerner Commission Report* failed to specify exactly what was meant by white racism and largely ignored the problem of institutional racism—the less overt, more subtle acts that sustain and perpetuate racism policies in virtually every American institution. Thus, the *Report* placed too much emphasis on changing white attitudes and underplayed the importance of changing white behavior and the basic structure of such institutions as schools, labor unions, and political parties.[4]

On July 27, 2006, President Bush signed the Voting Rights Act Reauthorization and Amendments Act of 2006. While this signing is obviously more commendable than refusing to sign it, as several conservative politicians from southern states urged the president, his statements at the signing ceremony present a picture that the original voting rights act was necessary only to address the aberrant violence of a few sheriffs and miscreants. While the *Kerner Report* at least acknowledged the existence of white racism, even though it failed to talk about its systematic and institutional nature, President Bush made no such statement. He spoke instead of President Johnson's intention to "bring African Americans into the civic life of our nation."[5] The violence that met the marchers is acknowledged, but is stripped of its context as an act of white supremacy. President Bush acknowledged how "[w]hen the marchers reached the far side of the bridge, they were met by state troopers and civilian posse bearing billy clubs and whips— weapons they did not hesitate to use."[6] The fact that the "civilian posse" was made up entirely of white men acting out a ritual of violence that was older than the nation itself was of course not mentioned. Indeed, the word "white" appears nowhere in his address at all. It remains unspoken by the president, invisible to many of the white politicians on the dais, but surely felt and seen by the representatives of the African American community who experienced the rare phenomenon of being invited to a ceremony at the Bush White House.

This chapter tries to bridge the gap between Du Bois's time and our own. It assumes that the last thirty-five years have changed whiteness: its ways of manifesting, its public profile, and its problematic. Further, it argues that though the civil rights movement was a singular event in our history that effected a drastic change in the way that race functions, it was nevertheless a therapy that was not allowed to fully run its course. It made us, as a nation, admit to the evils and injustices that had grown up around our ideas of race and whiteness. Its moral imperatives changed America in myriad positive ways, especially in terms of legal rights and access to economic opportunities. Nonetheless, white resistance and force of habit prevented it from going deep enough to affect a full recovery. The signing of the Voting Rights Act is rightly considered a monumental achievement in the quest for real democracy because it was the boldest and most widespread effort to change the legal and economic structures that variously inflamed racial tension and legalized white supremacy. However, we are in the state we are in now, where these efforts are being systematically undermined before they've fully balanced the lopsided economic and legal privileges of whiteness, because it did not fully address the habitual dimensions of whiteness. For all the hope it gave and still gives fair-minded people and for all the real change it effected, it did not eliminate the habits of white supremacy or "the problem of institutional racism" discussed by the political scientists reviewing the *Kerner Report*.

In the first section of this book we saw how white privilege was created and maintained by legislators, scientists, and intellectuals through fiat and explicit appeals to white racial superiority. The civil rights movement brought an end to such above-board appeals. Brave people such as the women of the Birmingham bus boycott, Rosa Parks, Rev. Martin Luther King Jr., Malcolm X, and Bill Moore (a white man killed by other whites during his solitary civil rights march through Alabama) put their lives and bodies in harm's path in order to speak truth to power.[7] The power was white hegemony that had existed in this continent since before the foundation of the nation; the truth was that this hegemony was unjust, undemocratic, unfounded, and unnecessary.

However, as the *Kerner Report* plainly points out, white Americans still received benefits over and against non-whites soon after the civil rights movement, and the same can be said of our current situation. Law enforcement targets minorities disproportionately to whites as the very ideas of criminality and innocence are still racialized by white supremacists' assumptions. Culturally determined notions that equated professionalism, beauty, intelligence and responsibility with European American norms prevented non-whites from achieving the employment opportunities necessary for advancement within a capitalist society. White folks still held the wealth and land that they had accumulated during the times that non-whites were either marginalized or treated as legal nonentities. Finally, while the civil rights movement shone the light of conscience on the horrors of white violence, it did not eradicate the public and psychological wage (as W. E. B. Du Bois called it) that white folks had received since the aftermath of Bacon's Rebellion.

It is for this reason the problem of whiteness reemerged, but in a manner distinct from other historical attempts by white folk to improve their situations vis-à-vis people of color. Of course, some groups did try the old methods; the Klan marched on the Capitol to urge the protection of white rights and neo-Nazis publicly lamented the fall of Aryanism through similar means. However, these tactless calls for white privilege met widespread public denunciations from whites and non-whites alike. The civil rights movement salted the earth where these overt forms of hatred grew. It was simply impossible to look upon these overt white supremacists as responsible human beings after the civil rights movement had forced white America to glimpse the horrors they had wreaked upon their fellow human beings. Instead, whiteness adapted to the new, post–civil rights climate.

The old habits of thought regarding whiteness persist in the post–civil rights era. While many, if not most, white people came to change their concepts of race (and whiteness in particular), they generally did so in ways that did not challenge some of the well-established habits that perpetuated racism. These habits powerfully determined the ways that white folk understood and responded to myriad political issues: fair labor practices, the "war on drugs," the preservation of the authoritative university canon, family values, the "war on terror," and the "defense of the border." These programs were dressed in the values of equality and fairness, but marginalized non-whites and reinforced white privilege. While many people striving to reassert and maintain white privilege were doubtlessly doing so in a conscious manner, many more were invested in the idea that we now live a racially free and fair society, disconnecting the habits formed with the long-established concept of race from a conceptual frame. This in turn broke the circuit linking kind to category to habit back to kind, thus blocking reconstruction of the habits of race and whiteness.

In this chapter, continuing the point that whiteness persists as a problematic cultural and political phenomenon, I will use the work of prominent race theorists as well as research conducted by social scientists to support the claim that white supremacist habits persist in the post–civil rights United States. These contemporary theorists echo the basic critique of whiteness pioneered by Du Bois in the early and mid twentieth century, most notably regarding the ignorance that whites cultivate regarding racial injustice as well as the relationship between whiteness and economic profit. Further, I will argue that the *primary* (though not only) problem of whiteness inheres in the habits of white supremacism that survive in the actions and thoughts of whites who are by and large not consciously invested in the older, blatant kind of white supremacism. I will also show how whiteness is also problematic for people who identify as white, because of the culturally alienating affect of whiteness.

We will then look at how white supremacism can persist in an environment where almost nobody ascribes to white supremacist views and where all intentionally white supremacist laws have been removed. Much of the current literature on whiteness suggests that we face this confusing situation regarding whiteness because it is transparent or invisible to white folk. I agree with the theorists who use language of transparency or invisibility to describe the persistence of white supremacist habits, I argue that when they are referencing the invisibility of whiteness they are speaking about the *habitual dimension of whiteness* as seen through a Deweyan and Du Boisian lens. It is precisely this invisibility or unconscious habitual aspect of whiteness that calls for a pragmatist methodology to conceive of and resolve the problem. In particular, a pragmatist assessment of the current situation suggests that we need to reconnect the habits of race to racial concepts in order to regain the possibility of reconstruction.

Whiteness as Problematic

Historical pragmatists such as Dewey and Du Bois initiate their inquiries in order to respond to pressing problems. Following their lead, I am developing a pragmatist critique of whiteness in order to respond to the political and social problems that still vex us as a consequence of the lingering effects of whiteness. The most pressing problem from a pragmatist standpoint has to do with the fact that *whiteness still adversely affects the lived experiences of individuals and communities.*

One of the most prominent and jarring studies of the intractability of white privilege in the post–civil rights era is Andrew Hacker's *Two Nations: Black and White, Separate, Hostile, Unequal,* which was originally published in 1997 and was most recently revised in 2003.[8] Not only was this book instrumental in re-invigorating a national discussion on race and white privilege, but it is still one of the starkest indicators of the disparity between the conditions of whites and African Americans in America.[9] Here are just a few of the statistics from Hacker's work that indicate the prevalence of white privilege:

> Black households earned $606 for every $1000 earned by white families in 2000.[10]
>
> Black Americans in 2001 suffered unemployment rates nearly double those of whites.[11]
>
> Black Americans are more than three times as likely as whites to live under the poverty line.[12]
>
> Black people in 2000 comprised 46.3% of the prison population while comprising only 12.3% of the US population. Conversely, whites made up only 36.1% of the prison population though they comprised 75.1% of the national population.[13]

A report by the Public Safety Performance Project also showed that white people are far less likely to be incarcerated than blacks or Hispanics. The study found that only one out of 106 white men over the age of eighteen was behind bars, compared with one in 15 for black men the same age and one in 36 for Hispanic men.[14]

This disparity is largely due to the much touted "war on drugs" that directs billions of federal, state, and municipal dollars toward paramilitary operations conducted exclusively within neighborhoods that are predominantly black, Latino, or Asian. This warehousing of people of color offers white folks economic advantages in various ways: it artificially lowers unemployment figures that in turn stabilize or strengthen wages; it also provides employment for the largely white rural communities where the prisons are built. It is important to remember that this war focuses on people of color even though white Americans consume most of the illicit drugs in this country. A finding by Human Rights Watch points out that "twice as many black men and women are being imprisoned for drug offenses than are whites, even though studies show that there are five times more white drug users than black ones."[15]

Perhaps the most blatant instance of white prejudice in the post–civil rights era concerning law enforcement was the "crack epidemic" of the 1980s. Clarence Lusane demonstrates the impressionistic and knee-jerk nature of the Congress's response to the perceived "crack epidemic" and notes that the new crack legislation made it onto the House of Representatives' docket only after Speaker of the House Tip O'Neill was outraged at the death of Lenny Bias, the star basketball player who overdosed on crack cocaine in the summer of 1986, after he had been drafted by O'Neill's beloved Boston Celtics.[16] Randall Kennedy, in his article "Racial Trends in the Administration of Criminal Justice," outlines how a 1986 federal statute radically increased the minimum mandatory sentences for crack cocaine (which is powder cocaine that is mixed with baking soda and amphetamines to make a solid "cookie"): "Under the law, a person convicted of possession with intent to distribute 50 grams of more of crack must be sentenced to no fewer than 10 years in prison; by striking contrast a person has to be convicted of possession with intent to distribute at least 5,000 grams of powered cocaine before being subject to a mandatory minimum of 10 years—a 100:1 ratio in terms of intensity of punishment."[17]

This, on its face, might seem to have little to do with race. However, these sentencing guidelines disproportionately targeted minority drug users, because although whites comprised the majority of cocaine users in the United States, they generally used powder cocaine, while crack was marketed within mostly minority communities. Kennedy related the sentencing guidelines above to the issue of racial discrimination when he points out that "[i]n 1992, 92.6 percent of the defendants convicted for crack cocaine offenses were Black, and only 4.7 percent were White. In comparison, 45.2 percent of defendants sentenced for powered cocaine offenses were White and only 20.7 percent were Black."[18]

At no point did any legislator say (on record, at least) something like "Let's criminalize crack cocaine in a way that is more severe than powder cocaine *because* we'll throw more black people into jail that way." This is the sort of blatantly white supremacist attitude that a Jim Crow politician might have been proud to profess. However, in the post–civil rights era political world, such a profession would likely terminate a career. None of this changes the fact that we still have laws on the books in 2008 that disproportionately target black and Latino people. This is because the habits of thought that direct disproportionate negative attention to the behaviors and lives of non-whites still persist.

Scandals from the late 1990s involving white cops killing, torturing, or harassing people of color also indicate the extent to which law enforcement in this country still works according to a bias in which whites are presumed innocent and non-whites are presumed guilty. To list only a few of the most recent and egregious examples: the "racial profiling" by the New Jersey state troopers that led them to pull over (and in at least one case fatally shoot) minority drivers four times as frequently as white motorists, the sexual assault and torture of Haitian immigrant Abner Louima by four white New York City police officers in the restroom of a Brooklyn precinct, the fatal shooting of African immigrant Amadou Diallo by four white New York City police officers as he stood in the vestibule of his apartment, and the fatal beating of Earl Faison while in the custody of the Orange, N.J. Police Department under mistaken suspicion for the murder of a police officer. In all of the cases above, white officers violated the human rights of the people they were charged to protect and serve because the race of the victim marked them as "suspicious" or worse.[19]

The habits of whiteness have always been most extreme in moments of scarcity, such as colonial Virginia in the seventeenth century, or in inter-group violence, such as the American Civil War. It is no surprise, therefore, that whiteness plays an important, if largely unacknowledged, role in the global "war on terror" declared in the aftermath of the horrors of September 11. George Yancy aptly uses this issue in the introductory chapter of his edited volume *White on White/ Black on Black*. Commenting on the fact that President Bush and others were at a loss for words when they saw pictures of the grotesqueries performed in the American run prison in Abu Ghraib, Yancy writes,

> Indeed, President Bush announced, "This is not the America I know." But "Whose America?" and "Whose knowledge?" Perhaps it is here that Bush's "knowledge" about America might be framed within the context of the epistemology of ignorance, whereby he is blinded by a certain historically structured and structuring (white) opacity. . . . Bush's comment only further confirmed my conviction that critics and pundits had failed to explore and interrogate the subtext of race that I theorized had been performed at Abu Ghraib. Such themes as sadistic brutality, sexual violence, xenophobic paranoia, the reduction of fellow human beings to brute beasts, played themselves out against a silent, thought familiar, backdrop of a long history of America's racist drama: the racializing, stigmatizing, and brutalizing of the marked "Other."[20]

As egregious as these examples are, far more national attention has been directed at the problem of racial profiling by police.[21] The issue of racial profiling (which is the use of race along with other indicators by police in determining which individuals are most likely engaged in criminal activity and therefore worthy of special attention) has largely replaced the issue of police brutality as the central issue regarding race and criminal justice because, as Kennedy points out, "[a]lthough no persons in positions of governmental authority publicly defend racial discrimination in the infliction of force, some officials and commentators do defend some forms of racial profiling."[22]

This has led many commentators, most notably Henry Louis Gates Jr., to claim that racial profiling has ratified a de facto law that penalizes "a moving violation that many African-Americans know as D.W.B.: Driving While Black."[23] This sort of official suspicion directed disproportionately at non-whites is a problem not only because it entails bad policing (as it encourages a lazy and inaccurate correlation between color and criminality) but also because it is becoming mainstreamed. Racial profiling is but a new name for an old habit, one first encouraged legally in 1680, whereby law enforcement officials direct their suspicion at non-whites in a way that makes the possession of the sort of morphology common to Europe an advantage while making the features common to Africa, Mexico, the Middle East, Asia, and South America a detriment.

It is important to assess these disturbing facts regarding racial inequity in criminal justice in concert with one of the claims from the first chapter of this book, namely, that whiteness became more and more valuable to the extent that non-whites bore the brunt of more and more violence and negative attention. Whiteness became valuable in the late seventeenth century not because of new benefits enjoyed by European Virginians, but because African Virginians and Native peoples living with the colonies *lost* important rights (the right to vote, to walk free on roads, to choose to marry or not, etc.). In colonial Virginia after Bacon's Rebellion, laws that called for the capture of *all* escaped slaves and servants were replaced by similar laws that focused *only* on escapees who were of African descent. Similarly, our current situation is not one where white people are privileged because white skin amounts to a "get out of jail free" card; white people still get arrested, fined, and jailed in large numbers. Instead, white people are privileged in that they, by and large, do not have to suffer the *disproportionate* law enforcement attention that people of color do face. Further, whites are also privileged vis-à-vis criminal justice in that the face of law enforcement is still predominantly white.

While the disparities between whites and people of color in the criminal justice system show how the habits of white supremacism survive and privilege white folk by *disadvantaging* people of color, it is important to indicate that, over the centuries of white supremacism, white folk have also garnered considerable *positive* privileges. To see the how our society still grants white people unjust advantages over and against non-whites, we can look to George Lipsitz's *The Possessive Investment in Whiteness: How White People Profit from Identity Politics*.[24] Here Lipsitz lists some of the more salient ways in which white folk still benefit positively from their whiteness: "[I]t accounts for advantages that come to individuals through profits made from housing secured in discriminatory markets, through unequal educations allocated to children of different races, through insider networks that channel employment opportunities to the relatives and friends of those who have profited most from present and past discrimination, and especially through intergenerational transfers of inherited wealth that pass on spoils of discrimination to succeeding generations."[25]

In looking at the investment that white people still have in their whiteness, Lipsitz fleshes out the argument developed by Cheryl Harris in her groundbreaking "Whiteness as Property" that whiteness should be seen as a form of property constructed during the era of slavery that continues to hold sway today.[26] It is a valuable commodity to the extent that it is a powerful guarantor of justice and fairness. It does not mean that you get to have rights that exceed those of basic citizenship, but that you can assume that your rights will not be violated, and that you will be treated fairly under the law, assumptions people of color generally cannot make.

When we look at the different treatment that white people and people of color experience under the law, we see how the idea of whiteness still plays a powerful role in our society, even though almost all people in authority happily condemn the idea of white supremacism. To use the framework we saw in Dewey and Du Bois, the habits formed during centuries of legalized and enforced white supremacism outlasted overt language that codified white supremacism in our laws. These habits perpetuated all of the aspects of white racism against which Du Bois fought. They encourage systematic violence against people of color (as seen in cases of police brutality, the war on drugs, and racial profiling). These habits benefit white people economically and socially, as Lipsitz outlines above. This obduracy of habitual whiteness that is still sadly similar to the kind of white racism against which Du Bois railed is in and of itself a sufficiently serious problem to warrant a concerted social response.

However, other theorists of color have looked at whiteness from another angle and reveal a subtler problem, one that Du Bois pointed out as well. To their eyes, the most serious problem goes even deeper than the way in which it skews the enforcement of our laws and the distribution of justice. To their eyes, the most serious problem with whiteness is that it is totally detached from the ebb and flow of life. Whiteness is, for them, a culture that has grown critically ill. To reference Du Bois's idea that races are valuable and worth preserving because of their gifts, whiteness is a race group grown disconnected from its past whose gifts have become toxic.

Culture comes from the Latin word *cultus,* which means "to care for." At its heart, it has to do with growth: of crops (as in the word "cultivate") or of peoples. Culture can be understood as a set of ideas, practices, and rituals that help human beings develop morally, intellectually, and spiritually. It gives us a sense of purpose, community, and context. It nourishes all parts of our being: body, mind, heart, and soul. Whiteness, however, is a culture that does not do these things; indeed, it works in the opposite fashion. It is a culture in the apparent sense: it is made up of a set of rituals, ways, and traditions that define who we are: consumerism, militarism, and patriarchy. It has its seminal figures and myths: Christopher Columbus, George Washington, Theodore Roosevelt, and John Wayne. However, to recall the Du Boisian interpretation of whiteness, the culture of whiteness is one whose primary artifacts and gifts—technology, trade, and military might—have overgrown their role within life and have taken it over. People who are now identified by others and identify themselves as white doubtlessly inherit rich cultural traditions. However, these valuable cultural traditions are not originally white, but stem from the heterogeneous milieu of European peoples.

Gloria Anzaldúa's work, particularly her book of essays and poetry titled *Borderlands*/La Frontera, names almost exactly the same problem at the heart of whiteness that Du Bois described in *Dusk of Dawn*. The primary purpose of her collection is to describe her idea of *mestiza* consciousness: a new, amalgamated sense of self that seeks to bridge the different dichotomies that she is forced to live between (man/woman, straight/queer, Catholic/pagan, American/Mexican). One of the primary reasons that she offers this new model of consciousness is that the dominant culture, white culture, is a necrophilic force that threatens the life and growth of all beings. The following passage from the chapter "*Tlilli, Tlapalli/* The Path of the Red and Black Ink" is important to cite at length, as it powerfully describes how whiteness is a culture that has grown disjointed and toxic.

> Whites . . . have cut themselves off from their spiritual roots, and they take our spiritual art objects in an unconscious attempt to get them back. . . . White America has only attended to the body of the earth in order to exploit it, never to succor it or be nurtured in it. Instead of surreptitiously ripping off the vital energy of people of color and putting it to commercial use, whites could allow themselves to share and exchange and learn from us in a respectful way. By taking up *curanderismo,* Santeria, shamanism, Taoism, Zen and otherwise delving into the spiritual life and ceremonies of multi-colored people, Anglos would perhaps lose the white sterility they have in their kitchens, bathrooms, hospitals, mortuaries, and missile bases.[27]

At this moment I want to set aside her recommended therapy: her suggestion that white folks adopt the cultural ways of non-whites. It is a suggested solution to the problem of whiteness that will play an important role in the final chapter of this work, where it will serve as both guide and foil for the proposal that this work will advance. Instead, we need to focus on her diagnosis: that "whites . . . have cut themselves off from their spiritual roots." This passage crystallizes the idea that whiteness is a culture that has become so disconnected with certain fundamental human needs that it has become toxic. Her work highlights the various constituents of this problem (that whiteness is spiritually unrooted, that it rapaciously acquires aspects and pieces of indigenous and chthonic culture to balm the wound in its heart, that it values commercialism, sterility, and militarism) and the likely result if it is left unchecked: that we will ruin the earth for all life if we don't eradicate it first in a nuclear holocaust.

It is worthwhile to point out the isomorphism between Anzaldúa's critique and Du Bois's. Both mention whiteness as being out of touch with itself as well as its dangerous lack of memory. This is, on the one hand, troubling, for it shows that Anzaldúa in 1987 still sees the same problem that Du Bois critiqued at the turn of the last century. However, this similarity is also encouraging in a way, for it reinforces the fact that the answer to how to solve this problem lies in somehow *building up connections:* between different groups of people now living, between the present and the past, between the human and the natural. In the next part we will focus on how we can use Du Bois, Dewey, and contemporary theorists such as Anzaldúa, Rich, and Outlaw to envision how we can shape new habits designed to counteract the disconnection that Du Bois and Anzaldúa see in whiteness.

The white feminist poet Adrienne Rich also casts light on the dangers of white American culture. However, where Anzaldúa focuses on its desires and directions (its future possibilities, as it were), Rich explores its relationship to the past. She offers us the insight that white Americans are starving our cultural selves by substituting the junk food of nostalgia and amnesia for the robust, if often difficult-to-swallow, histories and herstories that force us to account for our current conditions.[28] Rich's critique of whiteness, like Anzaldúa's, is an integral part of a pragmatic critique of whiteness because she highlights the ways in which whiteness encourages a form of amnesia that clouds our vision of crucial historical moments and collective experience that, if remembered, would lead us to act differently. Furthermore, her critique of whiteness as an identity that encourages a kind of collective forgetfulness strongly echoes Du Bois's critique of whiteness, especially when he talked about the role of forgetfulness in enabling the arrogance that impeded the sort of inquiry in which white people needed to engage. Further, the amnesia and nostalgia of whiteness prevent us from making decisions based on all the facts, or the widest "range of conditions" as Dewey would put it.[29] As a consequence many white people respond to present situations according to historical memories or experiences that never actually happened. Amnesia and nostalgia function in tandem to dampen any memory of injustice and suffering within our history and herstory that might encourage a critical reappraisal of the status quo.[30] Amnesia is the desire to forget the racism, classism, homophobia, genocide, slavery, and misogyny that created the current social order, while nostalgia is the attempt to sugar-coat these chapters in our history so they seem to be a golden age.

Rich claims that the complacent forgetfulness of whiteness in the United States is supported by two interrelated impulses: "[o]ne is the imperative to assimilate; the other, the idea that one can be socially 'twice-born.'"[31]

> The pressure to assimilate says different things to different people: change your name, your accent, your nose; straighten or dye your hair; stay in the closet; pretend the Pilgrims were your fathers; become baptized as a christian, wear dangerously high heels, and starve yourself to look young, thin, and feminine; don't gesture with your hands; value elite European culture above all others; laugh at jokes about your own people; don't make trouble; defer to white men; smile when they take your picture; be ashamed of who you are.[32]

This helps us see why whiteness is deracinated in the way that Anzaldúa describes. It is a culture that offers real social and economic advantages, but at a price. The price that white folks have paid is to give up their inherited, ancient ways of relating to the world, other people, and themselves and cut and stretch themselves till they fit the Procrustean bed of Anglo-American culture. We pay for economic and social privileges with our gifts in the Du Boisian sense. All this leaves us "unanchored when the storms arise," which in turn leads us to disrespectfully help ourselves to some cultural system, practice, or tradition that looks like it might help.[33] While, as Anzaldúa suggests, any and all of these things might succor the dull pain caused by the amputation necessary to join whiteness, Rich shows us that until white people come to terms with our nostalgia and amnesia, it will simply be an act of cultural theft that grants temporary relief to the pain.

The impulse to be twice born that is emblematic of American Christianity in particular and Americanism as a whole also reveals the instability and danger inherent in whiteness. Rich rightly points out that the desire to be twice born is "a very old American pattern, the pattern of the frontier, the escape from the old identity, the old debts, the old wife to the new name, the 'new life.'"[34] Aside from the inherent irresponsibility of the idea that we can just walk away from our messes and sins left at points east, there is the problem of self-hatred: "In the desire to be twice-born there is a good deal of self-hatred. Too much of ourselves must be deleted when we erase our personal histories and abruptly dissociate ourselves from who we have been. We become less dimensional than we really are."[35] We saw this desire to be twice born clearly at work in the motivations of the rioters in 1863. Their violence was their way of rejecting their old identity as oppressed and downtrodden by participating in ritual whiteness. They tried to claim the whiteness that Anglo-Americans denied them.

Whiteness has become toxic and imbalanced. Instead of offering a well of ancient, accumulated wisdom that helps us know who we are and how to face the future, it perpetuates the myth that we can always change ourselves and the world to fit our fancy. As Du Bois pointed out, it is a race-consciousness that cultivates not exchange and participation, but taking and owning. With consumerism, we can just buy a new identity (though we have to keep up with the Joneses). Through military superiority, we can either move to new lands or control distant ones so that we can get the commodities we want at the prices we want (though at the price of the very democratic ideals that are our collective spiritual core). All of this is to the obvious detriment of non-whites and non-Americans. Less obvious is the fact that this is of unparalleled detriment to white folks. White people have been encouraged to forget all the other ways that our ancestors thought of themselves: according to clan, family, nation, language, music, vocation, and place. While whiteness (now understood as a complex of habits and practices disconnected from geography, history, group commitments, etc.) has been the ticket to economic privilege and social power here in America, it has bleached us of our ties to the things that offer human beings the sustenance we need to live.

So, despite the advances of the civil rights era, habits of whiteness still skew our nation away from racial equity and toward unjust privilege for white folk. Whiteness as a lived script or habit for whites has also caused the people within the pale of whiteness great harm. It is important to acknowledge that the civil rights movement did make significant, positive gains: white supremacist firebrands such as George Wallace experienced true moral conversions and publicly begged forgiveness of African Americans for their crimes, the Voting Rights Act helped close the gap between white and black voting statistics, increased voting by people of color led to an increase in representatives of color in state and national congresses, and repressive law enforcement officials who colluded in the murder of people of color were largely swept out of office.[36] We need to remember these improvements to steel ourselves against the hopelessness and nihilism that comes with thinking that white racism is unchanged in our country and that it will always be with us.

However, the movement had at least one significant negative impact on the state of race in America: it fostered an atmosphere where white folks assumed racism to be dead and buried, and were even less aware of the privileges that they still carried by virtue of the accident of their skin color. Whenever topics of race and racism come up in the classroom, on the street, or in the media, whites are now able to disarm any concern about present racial imbalances by pointing to a few set images that have come to represent the end of racism in America: the desegregation of schools in Alabama and Mississippi under the supervision of white National Guard troops sent by a white president, the proud defiance of the Black Panthers marching down the streets of Chicago and New York, and above all the poignant image of Rev. Martin Luther King Jr. presenting his "I Have a Dream" speech at the Mall in Washington, D.C. These important moments in our history, and their constant repetition in our present age, have ended the days of extreme and overt white supremacism, but initiated the age of white privilege through invisibility. The circuit between habits, on the one hand, and concepts, on the other, was broken; we have relinquished the propositions defining the old concepts, but still have the concepts in the habits. Indeed, since the habits of whiteness (habits of thought and behavior formed after the advent of concepts of whiteness) have been disconnected from the concepts of whiteness, they are less noticeable than before as they impact our perceptions and behaviors.

Whiteness as Invisible to Whites

A number of race theorists have argued that whiteness, in one way or another, functions according to invisibility.[37] White people remain ignorant of white privilege because of the fact that all aspects of our lives—our institutions, practices, ideals, and laws—were defined and tailored to fit the needs, wants, and concerns of white folk. As we saw in the first chapter, the very idea of citizenship assumed whiteness (as well as maleness). Going further back, the religious ideas that predated the founding of the current political system assumed that whiteness was a privileged, even divinely chosen, group. White norms and values have so defined American society, in its laws, rhythms, and expectations, that they are not even visible to white folks *as racialized, as white.* When we study the invisibility of whiteness we realize that the theorists are describing the fact that the intellectual and behavioral habits of whiteness have survived the changes in the 1960s that wiped away the terms and symbols of white racism.

Charles Mills, in *The Racial Contract,* describes the way that white people relate to issues of race through "*an inverted epistemology, an epistemology of ignorance, a particular pattern of localized and global cognitive dysfunctions (which are psychologically and socially functional), producing the ironic outcome that whites will in general be unable to understand the world they themselves have made* [italics in original]."[38] In the introduction to their anthology *White Trash: Race and Class in America,* Matt Wray and Annalee Newitz offer a succinct summary of the relationship between the invisibility of whiteness in America and white privilege: "It has been the invisibility (for whites) of whiteness that has enabled white Americans to stand as unmarked, normative bodies and social selves, the standard against which all others are judged (and found wanting). As such, the invisibility of whiteness is an enabling condition for both white supremacy/privilege and race-based prejudice."[39]

Perhaps the most consistent and insightful critic of white supremacy in our current era is bell hooks. Two of her earliest works, *Ain't I a Woman* and *Talking Back,* were at the vanguard of critiques fashioned by women of color against the persistence of white supremacism and its ability to poison the thoughts and actions of liberatory and well-intentioned thinkers (such as white feminists).[40] In *Killing Rage,* she illustrates how whiteness is now dangerous because of its invisibility to white folk. The current problem with whiteness in the present era is that we have made a

> very small but highly visible liberal movement away from the perpetuation of overtly racist discrimination, exploitation, and oppression of black people which often masks how all-pervasive white supremacy is in this society, both as an ideology and as a behavior. When liberal whites fail to understand how they can and/or do embody white supremacist values and beliefs even though they may not embrace racism as prejudice or domination (especially domination that involves coercive control), they cannot recognize the ways their actions support and affirm the very structure of racist domination and oppressions that they profess to wish to see eradicated.[41]

Where white privilege had historically perpetuated itself through conscious and premeditated actions, whiteness now maintains itself by convincing white folk that it isn't there, and that they, like all decent human beings in the aftermath of the civil rights movement, are not racist. The invisibility of white supremacism is such an intractable problem because it enables white folk to perpetuate white supremacist values while simultaneously decrying them. We are able to pay lip service to the ideal of anti-racism in a way that leads us to believe that racism is over. However, authors like hooks show us that white supremacism lives on in terms of practical impact on the lives of human beings.

Motivated by critiques from hooks and other feminists of color such as Gloria Anzaldúa and María Lugones, white feminist scholars began to offer analyses of the invisibility of whiteness from "the inside," as it were. Marilyn Frye's chapter titled simply "White Woman Feminist" from *Willful Virgin* contains a useful analysis of the relationship between the accidental morphological feature of being light-skinned and the constructed nature of "whiteliness," which is a "deeply ingrained way of being in the world."[42] This is a way that, among other things, encourages the "whitely" person to think that she or he "knew right from wrong and had the responsibility to see to it that right was done,"[43] "is not prejudiced, not a bigot, not spiteful,"[44] and generally thought of him/herself as an authority "in matters practical, moral and intellectual."[45] These "whitely" attitudes and behaviors collude to prevent the critical and widespread challenging of white privilege that would be necessary to abolish it. As Allison Bailey says of Frye's notion of "whiteliness" in her article "Locating Traitorous Identities: Toward a View of Privilege-Cognizant White Character," it comprises a set of racial scripts that "are internalized at an early age to the point where they are embedded almost to the point of invisibility in our language, bodily reactions, feelings, behaviors, and judgments."[46] Thus, white people still apply standards to our lives that are based upon the assumption of white privilege and supremacy, but they have been so long a part of our conceptual parlance that they no longer seem racialized.

This privileged projection, whereby white people assume their ways are normative, affects all whites, even those who spend their lives combating racism and drawing out its effects. In his work on African American autobiography and white identity, *Act Like You Know,* the white philosopher Crispin Sartwell discusses this propensity to assume the objective, authorial invisibility of whiteness: "Left to my own devices, I *disappear* as an author. That is the 'whiteness' of my authorship. This whiteness of authorship is, for us, a form of authority; to speak (apparently from nowhere), for everyone, is empowering, though one wields power here only by becoming lost to oneself."[47] In part this invisibility has to do with the historical identification of whiteness with Americanness, just as "American citizen" for much of our history was shorthand for "free, white, male citizen." Despite the powerful moral awakening of the civil rights movement, it could not in a few years' time expiate the biases that had accumulated over three hundred years. Whiteness has been the norm for the entirety of our republic's existence, or as Sartwell says, "What is 'normal' in our culture is always, invisibly, raced white."[48]

This equation of normalcy and whiteness amounts to a powerful social privilege for white people. In her study of the isomorphism between male denial of male privilege and white denial of white privilege, Peggy McIntosh claims that "white privilege is like an invisible weightless knapsack of special provisions, assurances, tools, maps, guides, codebooks, passports, visas, clothes, compass, emergency gear, and blank checks."[49] While many of the privileges that she goes on to list in her article are *positive* in that they entail things that her whiteness affords her (for example, "[w]hen I am told about our national heritage . . . , I am shown that people of my color made it what it is"), a great number of the privileges are negative, or involve things that her whiteness protects her from.[50] Some of these include that "I can go shopping alone most of the time, pretty well assured that I will not be followed or harassed. . . . I can talk with my mouth full and not have people put this down to my color. . . . I can speak in public to a powerful male group without putting my race on trial. . . . I can do well in a challenging situation without being called a credit to my race."[51] Another way in which whiteness entails a kind of invisibility for white folk is that white folk by and large are oblivious to many of the ways that people of color are disadvantaged and oppressed by habitual and institutional white supremacist racism. For example, Randall Kennedy mentioned how racial profiling is a serious concern largely because it is a practice that is becoming "insulated from scrutiny."[52] This point indicates how the problematic invisibility of whiteness becomes even more dangerous when combined with the well-intentioned but ill-conceived movement for "colorblindness." Though the movement for colorblindness started as a liberatory attempt to fight the explicit white supremacism of our laws and policies, it has since become what Ruth Frankenberg calls "color evasiveness," or the attempt by whites to sidestep all issues of racism by branding *any* use or mention of race as racist.[53]

So how are we to relate the contemporary analysis of the invisibility of whiteness to the pragmatist approach developed in part 2? A pragmatist analysis agrees entirely with what Frye, Frankenberg, Sartwell, and others say regarding whiteness, but uses a different framework to approach the problem. When these theorists say that "white privilege is invisible to white people," they are pointing to the fact that white people are not aware of the extent to which habits of thought and behavior that stem from the era of legalized white supremacism still control their behavior and perceptions. White people still function according to habits of thought that make all of the things that white privilege comprises (treating people of color with suspicion; assuming respectful treatment by authorities; assuming that one's culture, behavior, and appearance will be accepted as normal; etc.) seem normal and not like a privilege at all. The civil rights movement ended conscious and legalized support for white supremacist racism, and further changed many white folk's conscious disposition regarding race, but it did not eliminate the deeper habits that determined how white people thought of themselves and others. Therefore, when these contemporary theorists indicate how white people reject white supremacism but still behave and think in ways that betray unconscious white supremacist attitudes, they are pointing to habits regarding whiteness that are conservative and pre-reflexive. These habits of thought and behavior have affected how white Americans relate to each other and to people of other races so that they will continue to function "below the radar," as it were, until we engage in a careful inquiry into how these habits work and how to reconstruct them.

EIGHT

Contemporary Debates on Whiteness

Three Approaches to Whiteness in Scholarly Literature

Now we can locate the pragmatist response developed heretofore within the literature on whiteness. With the exception of *reactionary theorists,* a pragmatist approach borrows from these approaches in terms of how to understand the problem of whiteness and how to respond to it. At the same time, when seen through a pragmatist lens, these approaches have certain shortcomings; we will see why the discourse on whiteness would benefit from the sort of analysis through habit that the fourth part of this book develops.

We can divide the different theorists who respond to the issue of whiteness and white privilege into three rough categories. The first, *reactionary theorists,* do not see a problem with white folk or white privilege, but instead react against the injustices they perceive in the multicultural programs and movements. The second large group is the *eliminativists:* theorists who start from the fact that the discursive categories of race lack the biological ground that Enlightenment era theorists thought they had, and therefore call for the removal of the idea of race. *Eliminativists* can be subdivided into two groups: *total eliminativists,* or people who want to remove the *entire* taxonomy of race, and *white eliminativists* (who refer to themselves as "race traitors" or "new abolitionists"), who hold that the category of the white race is the nexus of the real problem of racism, and only it should be abolished. The third and most heterogeneous category is that of the *critical conservationists.* These are the theorists who agree with the general spirit of the *eliminativists* (namely that the idea of race lacks a biological referent) but for various reasons do not think that race should be eliminated, either because it might make the problem worse or because the idea of race has taken on such significance that eliminating it would be either impossible or undesirable.

Reactionary theorists, whose study of whiteness is motivated by defensive concerns, treat whiteness as an ahistorical and biologically superior race whose survival is threatened by multiculturalism and affirmative action programs.[1] The primary spokesperson for this confederation is Jared Taylor, whose book *Paved with Good Intentions* assaults affirmative action as an attack on white America and claims that "unless [white men] defend our racial interests and put them first, we will disappear."[2] Also of note is Samuel Francis, a columnist and editorialist for the *Washington Times,* whom Chip Berlet and Margaret Quigley identify as one of the most mainstreamed proponents of white nationalism; they cite his claims that multiculturalism is but an attempt to "wipe out traditional White, American, Christian, and Western culture" and his suggestion that in order for the white race to survive, white Americans "need to kick out the vagrant savages who have wandered across the border, now claim our country as their own, and impose their cultures upon us."[3] In 1995 (when he was one of Patrick Buchanan's earliest advisors for his presidential campaign) he proclaimed that "whites must reassert our identity and our solidarity, and we must do so in explicitly racial terms through the articulation of racial consciousness as whites."[4] Finally, we can add Paul C. Roberts and Lawrence M. Stratton, the authors of *The New Color Line,* who can find a historical parallel to the madness of our current, perilously multicultural society only in the Nazi Reich, claiming that "attacks on white heterosexual males . . . parallel those used by Nazis against Jews."[5]

I will omit any deep engagement with the white preservationists who react to discussions of race and racism in order to defend the white race against liberal attack, and will instead focus on the more worthwhile issue of how to reconcile different liberatory approaches to whiteness studies. In so doing we should not write off these agents only because they are relatively few in number: they remain a daunting and well-organized force in American politics whose long-term approach, access to mainstream media, and deep pockets combine to make them an obdurate impediment in the road to social justice.[6] Instead, even a cursory glance at the statistics of education, housing, unemployment, and, above all, criminal justice shows that white folks still benefit from the accident of our skin and that indigenous, Asian, Latino, and African American people are subjected to continuing discrimination.

On the opposite end of the spectrum we find commentators who start from the insight that the reactionary commentators studiously ignore: that white-defined ideas of race fostered deeply inhuman and oppressive practices. These theorists, *eliminativists,* respond to the issue of racism generally and white privilege specifically by expunging racial terms from our lexicons, laws, and policies.

Eliminativists' approach often starts to undermine the feasibility of using race talk by appealing to scientific research on race and genetics. They point to the almost universal scientific consensus that discursive categories of race do not have biological correlates. For example, recent evidence produced by evolutionary biologists Masatoshi Nei and Arun K. Roychoudhury in their article "Genetic Relationship and Evolution of Human Races," shows that "the genetic variation within and between the three major races of man . . . is small compared with the intraracial variation."[7] More recently still, the epoch-making Human Genome Project (or HGP), which is an effort by government and corporate researchers to decode human DNA, refutes the Enlightenment-era belief in biologically discrete races. Speaking of just one of the many possible positive outcomes of the HGP, Dr. J. Craig Venter, head of Celera Genomics, said that one of the purposes of this project was to "help illustrate that the concept of race has no genetic or scientific evidence."[8]

It is important to contextualize a discussion of the eliminativist response within the scientific dismissal of discursive categories of race because these scientific findings are essential conceptual underpinnings for eliminativists. The most consistent feature uniting the work of the two most prominent total eliminativists—Kwame Anthony Appiah and Naomi Zack—is their frequent use of biology and genetics to develop a rhetorical assault on the idea of race. Their deployment of scientific findings undeniably casts significant light on the topic of race. However, from a pragmatist point of view, they make rather too much of the findings, and do not adequately account for how their rhetorical assault on the idea of race relates to the problematic invisibility of, or habitual dimension of, whiteness.

In his critique of Du Bois's "The Conservation of Races," titled "The Uncompleted Argument: Du Bois and the Illusion of Race," Appiah cites the findings of geneticists who seem to eliminate any biological foundation for discursive conceptions of race. He points out that "[e]very reputable biologist will agree that human genetic variability between the populations of Africa or Europe or Asia is not much greater than that within those populations."[9] Resting upon their authoritative assessment of the biological facts, he is able to make the claim (radical in 1986, but almost commonplace now in academe) that "[t]he truth is that there are no races: there is nothing in the world that can do all we ask 'race' to do for us."[10]

Naomi Zack's advocacy of eliminativism rests on a wider base, though she makes a similar appeal to the authority of biologists to settle the question of race. Over the course of her many articles and books on the subject of race and mixed race she offers several arguments for why we should eliminate the idea of race. In her first book-length treatment of race, *Race and Mixed Race*, Zack problematizes our collective use of race on grounds both biological and ethical: "The concept of black American race has no uniform factual or moral foundation, and when people are identified as racially black, they do not get the same treatment as people who are identified as racially white. So perhaps the time has come to reject the concept of a black American race, because the concept is coercive."[11] Earlier in the same work she argued that since "racial designations are racist, then people ought not to be identified in the third person as members of races. And if people ought not to be identified as members of races, then individuals in the first person ought not to have racial identities."[12] Her argument here is that since science finds no correlation between discursive categories of race and genetics, "in effect, . . . races do not exist."[13]

Zack levels a multi-pronged attack on the idea of race in her article "Race and Philosophical Meaning," where she applies different theories of meaning to the common concept of race and finds that race fails all tests of meaning available, and is thus a vestigial conceptual organ.[14] As if this were not enough, she later develops an existentialist critique of the concept of race that maintains that using racial categories as part of one's personal identity is an act of bad faith, and that to endorse the lie of race is to "impede one's freedom as an agent."[15] Finally, in her anthology, *Women of Color and Philosophy,* she maintains her close use of biology and genetics in her statement that "I do not think that racial categories have the physical reality they are assumed to have in common sense. There are no general genes for race, there is greater variation within, than between, any of the three or four major racial groups, and racial categories change historically and geographically."[16] While this work continues her argument that since there is not biological proof for racial categories we must accept that "racial categories are made up," she concedes that race might play a useful cultural role because the socially constructed categories of race play powerful roles in identity formation.[17]

Before offering a critique of total eliminativism that would outline the relationship between this approach and the pragmatist approach developed in the final chapter, we need to note that both Appiah and Zack have modified their stance on the issue of race in recent years. Where Appiah once proclaimed in 1986 that "the truth is that there are no races," he offers the markedly more reserved assessment of the significance of race in 1992 in his work *In My Father's House: Africa in the Philosophy of Culture*.[18] Where he once rejected the idea of race in toto, he later distinguishes between its biological irrelevance and its potential cultural relevance: "To establish that this notion of race is relatively unimportant in explaining biological difference between people, where biological difference is measured in the proportion of differences between people, where biological difference is measured in the proportional of differences in loci on the chromosome, is not yet to show that race is unimportant in explaining cultural difference."[19] Appiah moved even further from his 1986 stance in "Race, Culture, Identity: Misunderstood Connections," where he maintains the idea that race lacks a biological referent, but later accepted the social value of race and even argued for "an account of racial identity . . . which places racial essences at its heart."[20] Further, Zack has not repeated her claim from 1993 that "racial designations are themselves racist" in her subsequent work.[21] Instead, she ends the 2006 edition of her book *Thinking about Race* with the suggestion that we might develop new paradigms of race and ethnicity: "A new paradigm of race might begin with knowledge that there is no biological foundation for the different racial groups. As a result, what was previously thought of as race might now be thought of as ethnicity."[22] She goes on to describe a paradigm that maintains her strong and consistent commitment to an individual's freedom of self-definition while making room for the possibility of non-invidious race talk that is very much in line with the approaches to race advanced by pragmatist thinkers such as Taylor:

> When people attach strong differences to what they think of as racial difference, these attachments could be viewed as beliefs that individuals are entitled to, much as they are entitled to varied religious beliefs. When the practice of these beliefs is a source of fulfillment and self-expression, they would merit the same respect as the practice of other beliefs that derive from cultural traditions. When the beliefs about racial difference result in harm to other human beings, they would be viewed as moral defects, or sadistic and criminal delusions and treated accordingly; when such beliefs are self-destructive, they would require both psychological and social treatment.[23]

This mutual shift in the works of Zack and Appiah highlights the first negative critique of the total eliminativist approach, namely, that in its early, most extreme forms it treated the findings of "hard" scientists (mostly biologists and geneticists) as the final word on races. While their more recent, reserved claims about the impact of biological findings on the question of race are certainly valid (basically that biology *now* disproves the biology of the eighteenth and nineteenth centuries), total eliminativists still rely too heavily on these scientific findings to remedy a situation that includes many variables that exceed the issue of chromosomes and alleles.

Total eliminativist theories of race also run afoul of Dewey's critique of the spectator theory of knowledge. Their mistake is rather like the spectator theory of knowledge in reverse: they argue that since our best specialists in discerning the world *out there* (in this case geneticists and biologists) tell us that our racial categories do not rest on biological evidence, then whiteness and race aren't *really* real. Thus, where early Greek thinkers of the Ionian Revolution who first engaged in this ocular approach to knowledge said, "I know X is true because I (or someone reliable) saw it," the eliminativist says something like "Since we (or rather our best scientists) do not see racial genes, then race is not really real." In both cases, the idea of the real or the true rests upon the reportage of spectators, who claim to be looking at the relevant thing(s) without affecting them. It assumes that if we want the cold, hard truth about race, we need to go to the scientists who try to ignore history and culture in their analysis of matter.

In so doing, they fail to see (or more recently, unduly minimize) that many powerful and meaningful categories are based more on cultural symbolic meanings than on a pre-existing material reality, or better said, *all* meaning is found at the confluence of material and cultural streams. Just as a five-dollar bill really counts more than a one-dollar bill (even though they are materially nearly identical under a microscope) we must still say that, despite advances, white skin counts more than non-white skin in many contexts (even though white people are less similar to some other white people than to some non-white people when their genes are examined). Finally a pragmatist is motivated to pursue anti-racist programs not to keep from falling afoul of biological findings, but because of the ill effects of racism upon the lives of all people. The goal is not scientific orthodoxy, but the process of human flourishing. This is why I agree with Paul Taylor in his essay "Pragmatism and Race" when he argues for the legitimacy of making use of racial concepts:

> I am claiming that the vocabulary of race is a useful way of keeping track of a number of features of our conjoint social lives all at once—specifically the features involved in the histories of systematically inequitable distributions, and in the continued patterning of social experiences and opportunity structures. It is a useful device because the concept has over the years come to connote registers of human experience—bodies, bloodlines, sex, and individual embedment—that might otherwise get obscured in social analyses, and because it can be used to abstract away from dimensions of experience—ethnicity, culture, and national origin—that receive adequate explanations in accounts that nevertheless fail to shed much light on specifically racial phenomena (involving the connections between bodies, bloodlines, and social location).[24]

We see that when assessed through the lens of a Deweyan theory of inquiry, the eliminativists make too strong a correlation between the findings of highly specialized scientists who study human biology and the world of common experience in which we all (even the scientists themselves) live. Thus, while they are right to say something like "these findings force us to relinquish the idea of a biologically grounded racial taxonomy," that does not at all mean that race doesn't exist, or that "there is nothing it can do for us," or that the best way to respond to the complex historical, sociological, cultural, spiritual, economic, and legal dimensions of race is to get rid of racial terms and categories. They miss the point that most of the ways in which the conceptions and habits of race impact our lives have precious little to do with anything that a biologist could even talk about as a biologist. At the very least, they largely miss the point that the crux of racial issues has always been more cultural than biological.

The second problem with total eliminativism has to do with the invisibility of whiteness and the extent to which liberatory "colorblindness" has become problematic "color evasiveness." In a context where white people have a vested interest in eliminating race talk in order to minimize the extent to which we notice and discuss the lingering effects of white racism, eliminativism might potentially undermine the liberatory intent of its advocates. In our current situation, where white supremacist racism exists not as a legally sanctioned political system but as a series of unthematized and largely unnoticed set of habits and behaviors, claims that "there is nothing race can do for us" or "racial designations are themselves racist" are just as likely to be used by white preservationists fighting multicultural programs and initiatives designed to correct white supremacist habits as they are to be used by people who share the eliminativists' desire to end racism. The current problem involves what Mills calls the "inverted epistemology." It involves the habitual sense of entitlement fostered by whiteness that led white politicians, starting with Ronald Reagan, to appropriate Martin Luther King Jr.'s "I Have a Dream" speech for ammunition in targeted attacks on Mexican-American laborers and immigrants or general assaults on government affirmative action campaigns.[25] Ian Haney López also points out how even well-intentioned attempts to fight racism through colorblindness can in practice solidify a racist status quo:

> Invoking the early civil rights movement's formal antiracism, colorblindness calls for a principled refusal to recognize race in public life. This ideology espouses a deep commitment to ending racial hierarchy, but in fact wages war not so much against white dominance as against the idea that white dominance persists. By rejecting all race-conscious government action, even that designed to end subordination, color-blindness prevents the state from addressing structural racial inequality. Moreover, by eschewing all talk of race, color blindness forecloses debate regarding racism's continuing vitality. Color blindness protects racial supremacy from both political intervention and social critique.[26]

The pragmatist concern is that the results of all the micro-inquiries that contribute to the macro-inquiry of race and racism need to be coordinated and integrated in a way that will most likely address the problem. The chief problem with eliminativism is that if something as totally and completely anti-white supremacist as the work of King can be misused and perverted into a bulwark supporting white privilege, then the findings of scientists can also be misused if they are not carefully integrated into the larger inquiry directed at solving the problem of white racism.

To some eliminativists, this concern might seem like a cynical effort at social engineering. However, if we accept an interactivist model, then concerns about how a claim will likely affect a discussion are every bit as valid as scientific findings that go to great lengths to ignore such social impacts. This is because the ultimate goal of the critique at the heart of this book is to respond to the ways in which whiteness (and to a certain extent, race) adversely affect human flourishing. Following Dewey and Du Bois, we are focused on addressing the *problem,* not on describing a static state of nature. If, following Dewey and Du Bois, all knowing is *knowing for the sake of doing,* then concerns about how a particular way of describing and approaching a situation (in this case the eliminative response) are likely to affect the situation are more pressing than attempts to describe the situation as it is in isolation from the social needs and problems that motivated the inquiry in the first place. If knowing is intimately tied to doing, then any approach to the problem that strives to have a positive effect *must* pay close attention to the likely social ramifications, for, as Glenn Loury writes in *The Anatomy of Racial Inequality,* "one cannot think sensibly about social justice issues in a racially divided society if one does not attend to the race-mediated patterns of social intercourse that characterize interpersonal relations in that society."[27] D. Micah Hester, in conclusion to his essay "Situating the Self," explains well why a pragmatist model urges us to preserve race talk despite the arguments of eliminativists: "A thoroughgoing ethic of race demands that *neither* (1) we ignore race *nor* (2) we jettison the concept; instead, a deeper ethic of race demands a sociology of what function race plays in our ethical deliberations and in what ways it hinders or helps a particular moral inquiry and its outcome(s)."[28]

Having pointed out these two weaknesses in the total eliminativist position, I must point out that this critique is not absolute, but determinate. Most people do ascribe to a folk concept of race that assumes races are simple biologically determined essences that are ahistorical. Many people ascribe to the even older racist assumption that these biologically fixed categories entail pertinent moral and intellectual differences that enable us to hierarchically rank different races. In this context, the eliminativist use of contemporary science to debunk outdated science opens a door that many people assume doesn't even exist, the door to the possibility that we could reject or reconstruct the racial categories we have inherited from earlier ages. Also, the untrammeled liberatory spirit of both theorists—their desire to free people from constraining and largely divisive ideas—must also be part of any effective response to the problem of whiteness. A pragmatist response differs primarily in how to integrate the findings of science. For a pragmatist, the findings of geneticists are the consequences of a particular kind of inquiry that is very valuable, but has no more or less inherent merit than the inquiries of historians, sociologists, and journalists. The point is to engage in a discourse that strives to synthesize these different findings in order to develop the plan of action that will most likely improve the situation. In the current context—where part of the problem is the propensity on the part of white people to downplay or minimize the significance that race still plays in our lives—any claim about the lack of biological evidence for race must also acknowledge that we still need talk about and inquire into how racialized habits of thought and action affect our behavior. A pragmatist analysis strives to add to the conversation this second voice that is often lacking in eliminativist analyses.

In addition to total eliminativists such as Appiah and Zack, we can point to a small group of theorists who remain largely agnostic on the issue of non-white races, but strenuously argue for the elimination of whiteness. The two main proponents of this approach are Noel Ignatiev and John Garvey, and they refer to themselves as "race traitors" or the "new abolitionists." In their co-edited book *Race Traitor,* they lay out their central thesis: "The key to solving the social problems of our age is to abolish the white race. Until that task is accomplished, even partial reform will prove elusive, because white influence permeates every issue in U.S. society, whether domestic or foreign."[29]

Virtually all of the work by Ignatiev and Garvey is marked by a defiant, even militant, tone that informs both their understanding of and their solution to the problem of white privilege. For example, their guiding principle is *"treason to whiteness is loyalty to humanity."*[30] They explain the persistence of whiteness as a divisive identity in a manner that assumes white people are consciously and intentionally using whiteness to their own advantage: "The existence of the white race depends on the willingness of those assigned to it to place their racial interests above class, gender, or any other interest they hold. The defection of enough of its members to make it unreliable as a determinant of behavior will set off tremors that will lead to its collapse."[31] What is most telling for my analysis is their consistent use of militaristic language to characterize the problem of whiteness. Their struggle against white supremacist racism is war, and they plan to win the war by getting enough soldiers who are fighting for the white army to "defect" or commit "treason" and fight for the anti-racist side. Their zeal is admirable and a tonic for the studied ignorance of most white people. However, their characterization over-determines the extent to which white folk are intentionally and consciously fighting to protect their white privilege.

Ignatiev, in "Immigrants and Whites," asks, "[C]an [whiteness] be made to unhappen? Can the white race be dissolved? Can 'white' people cease to be?"[32] Abolitionists, like total eliminativists, hope the answer is "yes." This is the same answer that a Du Boisian critique of whiteness leads us to as well. Du Bois's later work pointed out the especially recent construction of whiteness, as well as the dangerous behaviors attached to whiteness. The critique developed here agrees with the race traitors that the goal should be a situation where white folks no longer think of themselves as white when it comes to developing their own identity. It is crucial to point out, however, that a Du Boisian/Deweyan critique suggests that white folk need to keep their whiteness for instrumental reasons that will be outlined in the following chapter. Specifically, in a climate where more and more white people are dodging the issue of how we have benefited from our whiteness, people who are now considered white need to affirm their whiteness *as part of their democratic responsibility.* This is not white pride (against which all eliminativists rightly rail) but recognition of white responsibility.

The pragmatist critique of whiteness and the abolitionist one part company in terms of how to get to the point where people who are now considered white no longer think of themselves as white. The problem with the abolitionist approach from a pragmatist perspective has to do with their focus on intent and their failure to consider the ramifications of either habit or the transparency of whiteness. If our primary problem now was that white folk, by and large, *intentionally and consciously* perpetuated and participated in whiteness as part of a carefully planned effort to maintain economic dominance, then the abolitionist approach would be fruitful. However, whiteness is not a problem because white people know about and intentionally claim white privilege; it is a problem precisely because most white folk *do not* recognize how they benefit from whiteness. Indeed, if Frye and the other theorists mentioned above are right, most whites, invested in the idea that they are morally decent human beings, would happily answer "Yes" to the question "Do you oppose white supremacism?"

We can better understand why it is not useful to respond to white supremacist racism as a primarily *intentional* stance when we look to social science research on white attitudes toward race. For example, David Sears, in his article "Symbolic Racism," shows that most whites do not espouse the older, intentional, "Jim Crow" racism prevalent before the civil rights movement.[33] Lawrence Bobo argues that Sears's "research on symbolic racism establishes that narrow, objective self-interest has little bearing on why Black candidates for political office become controversial . . . or why Whites mobilize against school busing, . . . or may oppose affirmative action."[34] Bobo himself uses the term "laissez-faire racism" to characterize the post–civil rights climate:

> We have witnessed the virtual disappearance of overt bigotry, demands for strict segregation, advocacy of governmentally enforced discrimination, and adherence to the belief that Blacks are categorically and intellectually inferior to Whites. . . . Instead, the tenacious institutionalized advantages and inequalities created by the long slavery and Jim Crow eras are now popularly accepted and condoned under a modern free-market or laissez-faire racist ideology.[35]

If we therefore combine the sorts of observations made by scholars like Frye with even more carefully conducted research of Sears and Bobo, it becomes untenable to think that the primary reason for the continuation of white supremacist racism is the intentional ill-will of white folks and a concerted effort on their part to oppress people of color.

While the abolitionists' uncompromising stance against racism is clearly admirable and much needed in our society, they do not fully take into account the role of habit in perpetuating whiteness. Whiteness, as a centuries-old system of thought and behavior that is intimately related to myriad aspects of identity, law, and culture in the United States, cannot simply be abolished by getting people to renounce the idea, or their conscious use of the propositions. As Dewey said in *Habit and Human Nature*, "Habits once formed perpetuate themselves, by acting unremittingly upon the native stock of activities. They stimulate, inhibit, intensify, weaken, select, concentrate and organize the latter into their own likeness. They create out of the formless void of impulses a world made in its own image."[36] In such a context as our own, the emphasis on abolition dovetails too neatly with the impulse to avoid the question of white racism by evading the question of race all together. We could well have a group of people who heartily reject the categories of whiteness or even race, but have not taken the careful effort to see all the linkages between whiteness and other aspect of their lives, and so continue to carry around the problem of whiteness. While a pragmatist critique borrows from abolitionism, it cannot share the idea that we can solve the problem by emphasizing intention in lieu of habit.

Having rejected the reactionary preservationists as woefully misguided, and having distinguished between the great part of eliminativism that is useful and the small but significant ways in which eliminativism is off the mark, we can now consider the field in which to locate the pragmatist critique. We can call this extremely large and heterogeneous group *critical conservationists.* They are *conservationists* to the extent that all of them want to conserve race (as either an idea or an identity). They are *critical* to the extent that they both recognize the scientific findings that motivate the *eliminativists* (and thus know that the discursive racial taxonomy outlined in the Enlightenment era does not have a biological referent) and also want to purge race (or in some cases just whiteness) of hierarchical and exclusionary racism. As the number of theorists in this field is ever expanding, we must limit our discussion to the theorists who look specifically at the issue of whiteness and to those who offer resources valuable to a pragmatist critique.

Some *critical conservationists* who deal specifically with the issue of whiteness are the editors of *White Trash,* Matt Wray and Annalee Newitz, whose anthology offers "a critical understanding of how differences within whiteness . . . [help] to produce multiple, indeterminate, and anti-racist forms of white identity."[37] Similarly, the orneriest of their contributors, Jennifer Reeder, created a performance art persona ("White Trash Girl") as a strategic deployment of stereotypes about poor, white, rural women that, nonetheless, accepts whiteness as an irremovable racial identity.[38] Reeder, Wray, and Newitz all accept whiteness as either an acceptable racial identity (in the cases of Wray and Newitz) or an identity white folk are stuck with. However, all three motivate their scholarship with the desire to reform whiteness of its exclusionary and elitist elements through a reassertion of "white trash" identity.

Despite the undeniably liberatory intent of people such as Wray and Newitz, Du Bois's analysis casts grave doubt on the possibility of envisioning a non-racist version of a category whose primary effect was the creation of racism as we know it. Indeed, when he surveys the carnage of the Belgian colonies in the Congo, Du Bois says, "[T]his is not aberration nor insanity; this . . . seeming Terrible is the real soul of white culture."[39] If it is true, as Audre Lorde says, that the *"master's tools will never dismantle the master's house"* then Du Bois's critique of whiteness makes us ask, "What are the chances that we will be able to dismantle the master's house *while standing inside it?*"[40] Anti-racist preservationists hit the nail on the head when they say that we need to unlearn the white supremacist racism we have all inherited in a way that maintains the possibility of a healthy sense of self-worth. In light of Du Bois's work, we must say that they miss the mark by cleaving to *whiteness* as a cultural identity. Du Bois described the asymmetry between whiteness and all other racial identities, where whiteness fosters a kind of arrogance that exceeds the simple pride that is a healthy part of group identities.

Further, our historical analysis demonstrated the especially strong relationship between whiteness and exclusionary violence. Indeed, certain features of the history of whiteness—the way that "white" was a category that emerged only after decades of systematic oppression directed at "negroes, mollatoes, and indians," the way that the Irish tried to assert their whiteness through a horrible frenzy of violence against African Americans—indicate that whiteness evolved as an identity that offered its members carte blanche to commit violence against those outside of the club. To this extent, Du Bois would argue against addressing the problems of white supremacism by finding a kinder version of *whiteness*. Instead, white people, like all people, are entitled to an identity that they can have pride in (which is the point of Wray and Newitz). However, if whiteness itself is not a valid candidate for such an identity, then we need to look for ways of developing or recovering an alternative.

Lucius Outlaw and Shannon Sullivan are two prominent contemporary philosophers of race who follow in the footsteps of W. E. B. Du Bois as they search for a critical conservationist understanding of race and a political solution to the problem of racism. They both agree with the general thesis that the solution to the problem of race is not found in the elimination of the idea or mention of race from our discourses, as suggested by Naomi Zack and Kwame Appiah, but in a critical conservation of race that is non-hierarchical and committed to addressing the pain and suffering of non-white racial groups. It is this moral and critical conservation of race that makes these two thinkers contemporary standard bearers for Du Bois's idea of the racial gift, which, as John Shuford writes, entails the insights that "'race' and race-consciousness are not the causes of racism and racial injustice, [and] that 'race' may be employed toward collective and mutual liberation."[41] However, despite this intellectual kinship regarding their broad approach to race, Outlaw and Sullivan come to a significant and illuminating disagreement over the issue of whiteness. To use Du Boisian terms, they disagree about whether white people, qua white, have a gift worth conserving.

Outlaw is one of a small but growing number of theorists who recognize the illegitimacy of the hierarchical racial taxonomies established during the Enlightenment era but accept race as socially constructed and yet fully real. Revealing a strong affinity for Du Bois's approach to race, Outlaw imagines his work as an inquiry into raciality and ethnicity via a treacherous "third path" between racism and invidious ethnocentrism, on the one side, and anti-racism and anti-invidious ethnocentrism, on the other. What I propose can help us to recognize and nurture races and ethnies as we reconsider raciation and ethnicization as processes by which we humans produce and reproduce ourselves as crucial aspects of our "social construction of realities."[42]

He goes on to say that "the challenge is to find ways to conserve a sense of raciality that is both socially useful and consistent with democratic justice."[43] The key to this process for him is to look at race and ethnicity through the lens of what he calls "philosophical anthropology" instead of merely through biology and genetics.[44] Outlaw argues that when we look at races and ethnicities in the way he suggests we glean "an understanding and appreciation of senses of *belonging* and of shared *destiny* by which individuals are intimately connected to other individuals in ways that make for the constitution of particular kinds of social collectivities, what I term *social-natural kinds*. Races and ethnies are such 'kinds.'"[45] Outlaw thus uses an idea of race that is fully transactional, to use a term coined by Dewey and rewardingly reclaimed by Sullivan. Race is created in the confluence of culture and biology, to the extent that certain biologically determined traits, primarily morphological features, are the tags or badges that play an important role in terms of how specific inherited and socially meaningful groups are formed. The goal is not to get rid of race, because people long have and likely always will use appearance as one of the many determinants in terms of how they form groups. The question in terms of race as a whole is how to form groups in ways that encourage human flourishing "consistent with democratic justice," as Outlaw says.

While Outlaw does not much concern himself with the question of how whiteness fits into this "philosophical anthropology," he does make the contentious suggestion that white and non-white ethnies are more or less symmetrical in terms of their need to be conserved. In an oft-quoted passage from *On Race and Philosophy,* he suggests a general parity across all racial groups with his question, "[H]ow might we work to conserve 'colored' populations and subgroupings (and white is a color as well), races and ethnies, without making it easier for racialism and ethnocentrism to 'go imperial'?"[46] Outlaw, like all racial conservationists, walks a fine line: his concern about "go[ing] imperial" shows that he is aware of the fact that the history of racism is a bloody one and that whiteness is freighted with moral concerns, but nonetheless he is willing to be ecumenical when it comes to whiteness. He seems to hold open the possibility that white folk do have a gift and that we could conserve a collective white identity that is not hierarchical or invidious.

Sullivan's transactional theory of race is largely compatible with Outlaw's desire to conserve race. The idea of transactional bodies that is the heart of her work *Living Across and Through Skins* emphasizes the same Du Boisian insight that different groups are distinct from each other (and thus have a unique gift that they can share) but are distinct in large part because of their interactions with other distinct groups. As Sullivan says, "Using transaction to understand race means conceiving of races as dynamically co-constituting each other in such a way that their distinctiveness is preserved."[47] While her broad approach to race is compatible with Du Bois's and Outlaw's, she diverges sharply from Outlaw on the question of whiteness.

After a careful and sympathetic reading of Outlaw in her work *Living Across and Through Skins,* she voices her suspicions about the possibility of a white gift when she states that "the symmetry between white and nonwhite people suggested by Outlaw does not hold in the matter of valorizing one's race because, in a society built on privilege, valorizing one's racial group has very different meanings for white and nonwhite people."[48] She points out that whiteness is different from other racial groups in large part due to the historical and abiding reality of systemic white privilege. In other words, Sullivan worries that a white racial group cannot be conserved without its "going imperial."

This fruitful disagreement between these two thinkers draws our attention to a Gordian knot that still resists a resolving cut by a critical conservationist. Should white folk participate in the exchange of racial gifts that Du Bois saw as an essential component of a healthy and balanced global community, or does the history of whiteness as self-anointed superlative category exclude the people who inherit whiteness and white privilege forevermore from this cultural exchange? Many other scholars, most notably feminist thinkers like Linda Martín Alcoff and Alison Bailey, have inquired after the ethical responsibilities of white folk in light of the history of white supremacist violence.[49] However, the question raised by Sullivan and Outlaw is slightly different. Both thinkers would agree with the fact that white folk have a special responsibility to disinvest themselves of white privilege and confront, in John Shuford's words, "whiteness as an ontological condition of indebtedness that presents a need, opportunity and responsibility to engage in liberatory culture making."[50] Yet, their disagreement raises the issue of the racial gift: whether white folk have something *positive and culturally valuable* to exchange *after* they engage in the sort of critical introspection and behavior modification called for by feminists.

This divergence on whiteness echoes ambivalence in Du Bois's work regarding the possibility of a white gift. While he urged that this exchange of gifts was essential for world peace, he also described whiteness as being an inherently false and violent phenomenon. Outlaw and Sullivan respectively voice these two sides of Du Bois's thinking on whiteness. Outlaw matches the early Du Bois of "The Conservation of Races," who hopes for an exchange of racial gifts in his famous characterization that "[r]ace groups are striving, each in its own way, to develop for civilization its particular message, its particular ideal, which shall help to guide the world nearer and nearer that perfection of human life for which we all long."[51]

Sullivan on the other hand matches the later Du Bois of *Dusk of Dawn,* who has largely lost hope for a universal racial exchange because of his recognition that whiteness is an inherently false and destructive identity.

What makes this disagreement fruitful for critical race theory generally and whiteness studies specifically is that each thinker has a finger on part of the solution. Outlaw is right in his ecumenism: the goal of a peaceful and pluralistic world obliges us to cleave to the hope that everyone on the planet, no matter who they are, has some cultural gift that is worth sharing and preserving. Sullivan is right when she points out that "whiteness" is not where white folk—that is, people who benefit from white privilege because they are seen by others as white—should go searching for their gift. This is because whiteness, as a category, is not like the other groups: it is built on exclusion and negation. Whiteness does not fit well into the racial transaction described by Sullivan because, since whiteness is defined through exclusion, it cannot preserve the distinctions of other racial groups.

Adrienne Rich urges white folk (men in particular) to let go of the stories of whiteness, and to look further back: "White men need a history that does not simply 'include' peoples of color and white women, but that shows the process by which the arrogance of hierarchy and the celebration of violence have reached a point of destructiveness almost out of control. In other words, white men need to start questioning the text handed down from father to son, the dominator's version."[52] Perhaps what we are missing is the untold histories of how we became white. Perhaps this sort of attention to how people from Europe became white would not only highlight how whiteness has become habitually associated with exclusivity and cruelty but also reveal where white folk might find the gift that they could share with other human families. When we read Adrienne Rich's poetry or Noel Ignatiev's *How the Irish Became White,* we learn how the habits of whiteness came into being as well as what was lost (or at least let go off) in order for certain people to partake of whiteness.

Toward a Pragmatist Response to Whiteness

Before moving on, we need to stop and account for what this critique of race and whiteness has shown. Whiteness is not an ahistorical category that has existed for all time, but a constructed one. It is not an unimportant and insignificant holdover from another era, but a web of beliefs and practices that still hold powerful currency in terms of how people are treated, relate, and think of each other. Whiteness is no one thing: it affects every person differently depending on race, gender, class, and sexuality. Even within the pale of whiteness there is no one pattern of behavior, no one script. For people of color, it is a pervasive and tangible set of practices, biases, and attitudes that hinder their ability to live their lives and receive just treatment. For white folks it is a currency that still pays for deferential and preferential treatment. At the same time, given the nature of these practices and habits, whiteness is also a kind of cultural illness that holds out the promise of social and economic power in exchange for relinquishing the traditions, connections, and histories that affirm and nurture life. Whiteness is one particularly thorny bramble in a thicket of overlapping oppressions; however, it is just one piece, and it must ultimately be understood alongside all the other ways in which we have divided ourselves out of selfishness and fear.

So how should we approach whiteness with an eye on resolving its problem? It is not a biologically fixed race. It is not a consciously constructed club. It is not a creed whereby all whites swear to help each other and thereby hinder the progress of all non-whites. It is something that is so close to white folk that we don't even see it, until someone tips us off to its presence. It is a set of habits, ideas, and practices that have accumulated over the years, but this is still too diffuse a definition or understanding. To fully make sense of whiteness, we need to focus our attention on its effects and the proper way in which it ought to be handled. We need to find a way to talk about it that takes into account its complexity and why the civil rights movement was insufficient to remove it from our midst.

Contemporary philosophy of race and whiteness offers invaluable resources for a pragmatist critique of whiteness, and also indicates the usefulness of a pragmatist approach. The next two chapters describe how a pragmatist critique would use the resources found in Du Bois and Dewey to develop an approach to the problem of whiteness that hopefully includes the best and eliminates the worst of the theories above. Before doing this, we can assess the theories above through a Du Boisian/Deweyan lens and point out the most valuable contribution that a pragmatist analysis would make for the current situation.

There is little to salvage from the reactionary theorists. If anything, they give us a sense of just how much the ideas and habits of whiteness can pervert our relationship to the past and to racial justice in the present. If there is one insight that we can glean, it is that they demonstrate just how important it is for people to be proud of their group, however they define it. While the way that the reactionary theorists express and define this pride is bankrupt, their need to be proud shows us that people currently defined as white will not likely be active in anti-racist struggles unless they can think of themselves as members of accepted groups.

We can take much more from the two kinds of eliminativists. Both sorts of eliminativists share a focus on dispelling myths about race that still perpetuate racism. The total eliminativists thematize the wide gap between academe (where the social construction of race is old news) and the public (who by and large still use a folk notion of race that assumes a biological referent underneath discursive categories). The new abolitionists recognize that whiteness is unlike other racial categories and that the problems of racism involve the idea of whiteness more than any other category. However, the total eliminativists, even in their later, softer manifestations, place too great an emphasis on pointing to science to settle the issue of race and not enough emphasis on how their theories are likely to actually improve the situation of race. Finally, both kinds of eliminativists fail to fully account for the habits of whiteness. As a consequence, they do not look enough at how to address the problem of white racism in light of the fact that most white folk don't know they are perpetrating it.

A pragmatist critique of whiteness would borrow most from critical conservationists. These theorists, by and large, accept race as socially constructed but do not see it as therefore unreal. This is compatible with Dewey's interactionism as well as Du Bois's notion of race. What a Du Boisian/Deweyan critique would add to the debate is an inquiry into the role of habit in the creation, maintenance, and deconstruction of whiteness. Taking Du Bois and Dewey to heart, this response will attend closely to the *habits of whiteness* as well as to the impulses and instincts that drive the habitual ways that white folk respond to issues, people, or things that they see as racialized.

Next we will take a first step in what needs to be an organized *inquiry* into the problem of whiteness that is directed at envisioning a solution to the various problems Du Bois and contemporary theorists associate with whiteness (its exclusionary violence, its prioritization of money over humanity, and the historical, cultural, and social disjunction that it breeds in white folk). Part of the reason that we are now facing largely the *same problem* that Du Bois identified at the dawn of the twentieth century is that we did not engage in a careful or consistent enough *inquiry into the problem.* The responses of the civil rights movement were courageous and fruitful, but not yet complete. The very ugliness and difficulty of the problem made it such that we hoped that the terminological, legal, and procedural changes would be enough. While the problem of *legalized* white supremacism has (for the most part) been solved, the problem of *habitual* white supremacism remains. The following chapter will use Du Bois's diagnosis of whiteness and Dewey's theory of habit and impulse to conceive of a way to address this deeper, subtler, but in many ways more dangerous facet of the problem of whiteness.

RECONSTRUCTING
WHITENESS

Habits of Whiteness

The Moral Equivalent of Whiteness

Many of our current problems surrounding issues of race and whiteness can be better understood and solved by applying the Deweyan model of race. To briefly recap: habits within a Deweyan framework are organic functions of an organism that facilitate its survival and growth within an environment. A habit is "an acquired predisposition to *ways* or modes of response."[1] They are the means through which we make our experiences meaningful because "the *meaning* of native activities is not native, but acquired."[2] Habits work by organizing more basic or "native" feelings that Dewey variously calls instinct or impulse. The native activities occur before habits and emerge within each individual organism, but ultimately depend on acquired habit for any meaning. The key to this relationship for us is to reorganize the impulses into new habits. Dewey says in *Human Nature and Conduct:* "Impulse brings with itself the possibility but not the assurance of a steady reorganization of habits to meet new elements in new situations. The moral problem in child and adult alike as regards impulse and instinct is to utilize them for formation of new habits, or what is the same thing, the modification of an old habit so that it may be adequately serviceable under novel conditions."[3] From what we have seen already of whiteness (in the discussion of Bacon's Rebellion and the New York Draft Riots of 1863, as well as in Du Bois's critique and contemporary accounts) it makes sense to describe it as a set of habits, on the one hand, and a concept, on the other. Most basically, the concept of whiteness is the idea that there exists a certain group of people who are, by virtue of their heredity, entitled to greater rights and privileges than other groups. We see the conceptual aspect of whiteness in the assumptions that linked political freedom and suffrage to whiteness, as well as in the broader taxonomy of race articulated during the Enlightenment. We see the habitual dimension of whiteness in the ease with which these concepts modified preexisting habits into new forms framed by the concept of whiteness. In our current situation, we have deleted the propositions that defined whiteness as a superlative racial category, but the concept and habits of whiteness persist.

In addition to giving us the conceptual framework that will support this critique of whiteness, Dewey also gives us the method with which to address this problem. While I agree with Sullivan's desire to "change the space(s) one inhabits" as part of a response to white racist habits, I also believe she does not make full use of Dewey's model of habit when she writes off the possibility of "gaining direct access to unconscious habits of white privilege" for its "difficulty, if not impossibility."[4] While it is certainly difficult to reconstruct the habits that have undergirded systemic white racism for over three hundred years, Dewey and Du Bois offer us vital tools that would enable us to thematize the specific habits that are problematic, that we might better reconstruct them. If we take full advantage of Dewey's work on the interrelation of ideas, impulses, and habits as well as Du Bois's historically and sociologically informed critiques of whiteness, we can move from seeing whiteness as a vague and murky problem to a determinate problem that can be engaged through inquiry.

The Deweyan/Du Boisian method that I propose for reconstructing the habits of whiteness has two stages. The first is to get white people involved in an inquiry into whiteness. Inquiry in the pragmatist sense is a response to a problematic situation that starts when an organism's experience becomes imbalanced and unsure. Generating an inquiry into whiteness, however, will be difficult. Du Bois and various contemporary theorists have argued that whiteness is difficult to engage because it does not seem problematic to white people. For example, the all-white Minutemen and city councils of places such as Hazelton, Pennsylvania, Riverside, New Jersey, and Carpentersville, Illinois, never frame their actions to monitor, incarcerate, or expel people of Hispanic descent as having anything to do with race or whiteness.

A pragmatist analysis of these situations diagnoses this perceptual slipperiness of whiteness by describing it as a concept and habit that functions very smoothly in the short-term for many white people. As a consequence, it does not draw attention to itself. The first task, therefore, is to make white folk *diseased* with whiteness, and to see that racism does persist in practice. The people who participate in the anti-immigrant and anti-Latino/a vigilantism at the border need to see the connection between these activities and the slave posses that poor whites were duped into during the period of slavery. They need to see the problem with conducting prejudicial and discriminatory actions even as they profess to hold principles of universal fairness.

Second, since we are dealing with a form of racism that is primarily subtle and habitual (as opposed to a form that is codified and overt) we need to inquire into how to reconstruct our current habits regarding race. The reconstruction of the habits of whiteness by re-focusing the impulses behind it finds a ready historical analogue in the history of American philosophy. When William James wrote "The Moral Equivalent of War" he hoped that people could find a way to keep the aspects of warfare that he found uplifting (the sense of camaraderie that can come only when a group faces the threat of death together and the selfless patriotism that can cohere an entire society during times of threat) without having to engage in the haphazard and wasteful act of war itself.[5] He suggested that we find an equivalent conduit for the impulses that have traditionally found their outlet in warfare because warfare itself has changed so much that the inherited habits regarding these impulses have lost their usefulness. When discussing the possibility that we can use these impulses in liberatory manners, Dewey says of James's work that "the suggestion of an *equivalent* for war calls attention to the medley of impulses which are casually bunched together under the caption of belligerent impulse; and it calls attention to the fact that the elements of this medley may be woven together into many differing types of activity, some of which may function the native impulses in much better ways than war has ever done."[6] Therefore, just as James outlined a moral equivalent to war—that is, a practice that harnesses the impulses behind war, but in a fashion that is less wasteful and more moral—we need to find the *moral equivalent of whiteness*. When looking for the moral equivalent to whiteness we need to find an alternative to the current habits and concept of whiteness that is free of the problems outlined in the previous chapters (exclusionary violence and cultural vacuity being the most prominent) and more conducive to human growth and flourishing. We need to find a way to weave the impulses behind whiteness into a different pattern that will avoid exclusion and violence while fostering the sort of trans-racial human connectedness that it has thwarted. The impulses that drive the behaviors are the fulcrums: they are the points at which we can apply intelligently directed pressure to move the mass of habits.

In addition to the method of using impulse to change habit, Dewey gives us the broad outline of our goal. In *Human Nature and Conduct* he states that "[w]hat is necessary is that habits be formed which are more intelligent, more sensitively percipient, more informed with foresight, more aware of what they are about, more direct and sincere, more flexibly responsive than those now current. Then they will meet their own problems and propose their own improvements."[7] However, it is not enough to simply say "we need habits of whiteness that are more intelligent and more sensitively percipient." We need a much more nuanced account of where such a revision should be headed. For such direction, we need to look to the critique of whiteness Du Bois developed, as well as contemporary critiques of whiteness.

Du Bois gives us a sense of the ultimate goal of such a reconstruction in "The Conservation of Races" when he claims that "race groups are striving, each in its own way, to develop for civilization its particular message, its particular ideal, which shall help to guide the world nearer and nearer that perfection of human life for which we all long, that 'one far off Divine event.'"[8] When we relate this hope to his later critiques of whiteness in *Darkwater* and *Dusk of Dawn,* we see that the reconstruction of whiteness needs to address the ways in which the habits of whiteness (with their emphasis on purity and exclusion, and the legitimization of violence as a means of maintaining its own borders) impede the sort of cultural sharing that Du Bois associates with race. If race is worth conserving, for Du Bois, because it serves as a cultural fountain that not only is crucial to individual identity but also is a vehicle for human sharing and community, then we need to find a way for all people to have a race in this regard. Therefore, a reconstruction of whiteness needs to work in two directions at once: it needs to remove the aspects that cause white folk to impede the gift-giving of other races as it also fosters white folk to manifest, develop, or reclaim gifts that are life affirming for the human family. In order for the method developed by Dewey to meet the goal set by Du Bois, we need to assess the present situation of whiteness in terms of habit. We have to find the impulses behind whiteness that are equivalent to the pugnacious impulses that James saw behind warfare.

The Habits and Impulses of Whiteness

Many contemporary theorists of race use terms such as "transparency" or "invisibility" to describe the phenomenon whereby white folk manifest racist behavior but in a way that escapes notice. This aspect of whiteness can be explained through the pragmatist notion of habit as a set of behaviors that are pre-conscious responses to an environment and that rely upon certain inherited categories. While further study will likely produce a more complex understanding of the habits of whiteness, we can start to make sense of the contemporary and historical nature of whiteness by describing three habits: *habitual antipathy to what is strange, habits of entitlement,* and *habits of guilt.*

The *habitual antipathy to what is strange* is a wide-ranging and complex habit that impacts white responses to issues white folk perceive as racialized. We see this habituated response now in the temerity that many white people have toward issues of race. I feel it in virtually every conversation I have ever had with white students about the issue of race. Even after years of speaking about race in public and private environments, I still have to fight the habits that make me want to change the subject. The phrase itself is borrowed from one of the rare passages where Dewey addresses the question of race. It is worth being quoted at some length here as it is not only identifies one of the crucial impulses that need to be reorganized into new habits, but even highlights how fears regarding race and economics underpin nativist movements, both in Dewey's America of the 1920s and in ours of the twenty-first century.

> The facts suggest that an antipathy to what is strange (originating probably in the self-protective tendencies of animal life) is the original basis of what now takes the form of race prejudice. The phenomenon is seen in the anti-foreign waves which have swept over China at different times. It is equally seen in the attitude of the earlier immigrants to the United States toward later comers. The Irish were among the first to feel the effects; then as they became fairly established and the older stock became used to them and no longer regarded them as intruders, the animosity was transferred to southern Europeans, especially to the Italians; later the immigrants from eastern and southeastern Europe became the suspected and feared party. And strikingly enough it has usually been the group which had previously been the object of hostile feelings which has been most active in opposing the new-comers, conferring upon them contemptuous nicknames if not actually abusing them. Witness, for example, the fact that it was largely the Irish who took the most aggressive part in persecuting the Chinese upon the Pacific coast.[9]

Historically we see this habit in the response that the European colonists had toward the indigenous people of this continent. The idea of a "savage" bespeaks someone, or *something,* that is so utterly foreign that it is effectively beyond the pale of humanity. We also see it in the myriad laws and insults directed at people of African descent by Europeans. When we look toward issues of aesthetics and beauty we see how the difference in complexion between people from Africa and people of Europe has caused many members of each group to recoil. Even a thinker who was quite Promethean in many ways, Thomas Jefferson, was deeply impacted by this habit. As he says in his *Notes on the State of Virginia,*

> The first difference [between people of European and African descent] which strikes us is that of color. . . . And is this a difference of no importance? Is it not the foundation of a greater or less share of beauty in the two races? Are not the fine mixtures of red and white, the expressions of every passion by greater or less suffusions of color in the one, preferable to that eternal monotony, which reigns in the countenances, that immovable veil of black which covers the emotions of the other race? Add to these, flowing hair, a more elegant symmetry of form, their own judgment in favor of the white, declared by their preference of them, as uniformly as is the preference of the Oranootan for the black woman over those of his own species.[10]

Here we can clearly see the sad effects of this habitual antipathy to the new or different. The very idea of beauty for Jefferson is completely based on the European features and skin-tones that are familiar to him. The ones that are less familiar to him, those common to people of African descent, are ugly.

We also saw this aversion at play in the moments leading up to the Draft Riots of 1863. The U.S.-born Yankees excluded the Irish because of their rural and pagan customs. The habit of exclusion was so strong that it made a fissure within the previously smooth category of whiteness. Even though the Irish were European and therefore white according to the Immigration Act of 1790, they were so odd in the eyes of Anglo-Americans that the latter developed a discourse of ranked white races, with the Celts at or near the bottom.

Despite our contemporary pretensions to colorblindness and worldliness, we still see this habit of antipathy to what is strange in various places. We see it among the white Americans who engage in hagiographies of poor immigrants to this land who came from corruption and starvation in Europe, but revile so severely against poor immigrants to this land from Latin America and Asia that they will organize armed mobs and call for their incarceration. We see it in the crutch of lazy policing that we call racial profiling. Of course, the "war on terror" lives of a logic that calls only violence committed by Muslims, whether Arab, Persian, or Southeast Asian "terror," whereas the violence of America, Europe, and Israel is framed as a "responsible response."[11] The pain of the despicable attacks of September 11, 2001, also fanned the flames of xenophobia. Many major metropolitan cities in the United States experienced violence against mosques and Muslim households. Some people, like Congressman Tom Tancredo, a Republican from Colorado, actually called for the United States to respond to these attacks by "bombing Islam's holy sites, including Mecca."[12]

If the habit is the habit of antipathy to what is strange, we need to inquire after the impulse that lies beneath it in order to then conceive of a more fruitful way to organize it. We should look for the force behind this habit in the impulse of simple *antipathy*. All people have feelings of antipathy regarding certain things. For example, it is fair to say that all people share an aversion to feeling biting cold or coming into contact with open flames. While so called "Polar Bear Swimmers" (people who swim in near-freezing water) and fire-eaters have clearly controlled or suppressed this impulse, they are odd and attention grabbing because their actions elicit a strong response from their viewers. We find fire-eaters so entrancing precisely because something deep inside us says, "I would never put fire inside my mouth!" We can see why impulses are important features of our psychologies when we consider the usefulness of an aversive impulse to organic survival. A strong organic impulse to avoid biting cold or open flames has obvious survival value. From this perspective, the feeling of antipathy is in and of itself neither good nor bad; it is just a strong inclination away from certain things taken to be risky or dangerous.

It is important to note that while I am using Dewey's framework regarding habits and impulse, I disagree with him regarding where to place the antipathy to what is strange or novel. He argues that we all share an "instinctive aversion . . . to what is new and unusual."[13] He thinks that aversion from the new is itself an impulse; we all are more or less stuck with the feeling that new things are strange. It is true that we all can have the impulse of antipathy, or the feeling of wanting to get away from something, or wanting something to be changed or gotten rid of. However, we can just as easily respond to new experiences, situations, and people with *feelings of enjoyment or curiosity.* Therefore, we should situate the *antipathy to the strange* at the level of habit, and describe the impulse behind this habit as mere *antipathy.*

This distinction is necessary for two reasons. First, it is simply false to think that we all find new experiences or people odd or disquieting. Just think of those early, rosy days of any intimate or erotic relationship. There is an electricity and even magic to the first caress, or embrace, or kiss in a relationship. People are so preoccupied in these early stages precisely because it is *new.* We can think also of the times that entire new horizons of meaning open to us when we encounter a new style of music, or literature, or way of life. While Dewey is right to say we *can* have an aversion to the new, he was wrong to say that we all share a deep-seated, impulsive aversion to all things new.

Second, a generalized antipathy to what is strange or different would undermine survival. Impulses are part of an organic response to environment that facilitates an organism's survival. A feeling of antipathy is essential to survival, so long as it is habituated in the right way. However, in light of the fact that every being, human or otherwise, will almost certainly contend with new organisms and situations, it would be counterproductive in the extreme if we always wanted to avert ourselves from difference or new experiences.

If there is just a general impulse to be averse to something, the objects of aversion are learned and conditioned by one's environment. If the only instinct we are stuck with is a *general* feeling of antipathy, the task becomes a way to better channel it. When discussing our relationship to the instincts or impulses behind the habits, Dewey claims that "in the career of any impulse activity there are speaking generally three possibilities."[14]

> It may find a surging, explosive discharge—blind, unintelligent. It may be sublimated—that is, become a factor coordinated intelligently with others in a continuing course of action. . . . Such an outcome represents the normal or desirable functioning of impulse; in which to use our previous language, the impulse operates as a pivot, or reorganization of habit. Or again a released impulsive activity may be neither immediately expressed in isolated spasmodic action, nor indirectly employed in an enduring interest. It may be "suppressed."[15]

Since we obviously need to avoid the first and last possibilities, we need to find a way to reconstruct the habitual aversion to the strange into a new, more desirable habit.

This phenomenon, whereby an older habitual framing of a certain impulse is changed into a different habit, is already familiar to the history of whiteness. Indeed, when we look at it through a Deweyan lens, we see that this is precisely what happened when whiteness emerged in the seventeenth century after Bacon's Rebellion. One way of reading the solidarity between the laborers of African and European descent in the Virginia colonies is that they did *not* have an aversion to each other, even though many had never seen someone from a continent other than their own until they arrived in Virginia. Instead, they seemed to identify with each other as laborers, even though most came from radically different lands and did not share a common history or language. Of course, they did, by and large, respond to the Doegs and the Pamunkeys with a sense of aversion and hostility. Equally significant is that they also responded this way to the colonial elites—Governor Berkeley and his petty-noble clique—who controlled their lives and profited from their labor. Furthermore, while Bacon's forces saw the Native peoples as enemies, European servants and African slaves had long infuriated their masters by turning to the Native peoples for succor from the pain and suffering of their forced labors. The polyglot community in Roanoke in the Albermarle Sound, made of "European and African American slaves (with and without indentures), felons, landless paupers, vagabonds, beggars, pirates, and rebel of all kinds who beginning in the 1640s lived . . . under the protection of the Tuscarora Indians," is a clear example that laborers were every bit as able to see Native peoples as friends as they were to see them as foes.[16] Therefore, we see no sign that their instinctual antipathy was channeled into habits that were primarily racial. They felt antipathy both toward people of their same racial group and toward people outside it. They held solidarity with people of their same groups and with people outside their group. While Bacon's soldiers were definitely hostile to the Native peoples, they were equally hostile to the elites who were from exactly the same culture and nation as many of Bacon's rebels. In other words, we are certainly not "stuck" with feelings of antipathy across ethnic lines. Indeed, one of the great values of integrated public education is that children become familiarized with children and adults whose ancestors come from all parts of the globe. In their case, the idea of ethnically based antipathy hopefully won't even enter their minds.

We can also make sense of what happened after Bacon's Rebellion through Dewey's conception of impulse and habit. After the rebellion, the elites used sticks to repress non-European laborers, and small carrots to encourage European laborers to break their solidarity with workers of African descent. Instead of being antipathetic to the injustice of the monoculture of the tobacco plantation, they started to be antipathetic toward people who were reified in the laws as different. Before, almost all laborers could enjoy the little but essential things in life: going into a pub, walking the road, choosing whom to marry or befriend. Once these things were taken from non-European laborers, those laborers came to be seen as inferior and dangerous by laborers of European descent. They were inferior in that they were not eligible for the same privileges as whites, and they were dangerous in that they might want those privileges at the expense of white laborers.

Once the European colonists were living in a different social world than they were before Bacon's Rebellion, their instinctual antipathy took on a different target. They changed from having an *antipathy to those people and practices that were associated with oppressive systems of labor to having an antipathy to people they saw as dangerous and strange.* Without the laws and discourses that focused on race, this sort of habit could not have taken form in the way it did. The impulse needed the vessel of racial taxonomy and racial categories for the habit of racial aversion to even be possible. What we need to do now is work another alchemical transformation: one that takes the base impulse of antipathy and remakes it into another form that better meets the needs of a culturally heterogeneous, democratic polity. We can't help having raw feelings of antipathy; we can and must take control of the form that these feelings take.

The second relevant habit of whiteness we need to examine and reconstruct is the habit of entitlement. We see this habit most clearly at work in the reactionary theorists. We see a less extreme but more widespread manifestation of this habit in the behavior and attitude of white folk who think that multiculturalism has gone too far. Tony Horowitz in his essay "Immigration—and the Curse of the Black Legend" describes how politicians such as Representative J. D. Hayworth of Arizona and Representative Tom Tancredo of Colorado, chairman of the House Immigration Reform Caucus, frame Latino/as as invaders who are trying to steal privileges that are reserved for whites. We see this habit of entitlement at work when we read that "Hayworth proposes calls for deporting illegal immigrants and changing the Constitution so that children born to them in the United States can't claim citizenship" as when he tars those who "oppose making English the official language saying they, 'reject the very notion that there is a uniquely American identity, or that, if there is one, that it is superior to any other.'"[17] Tancredo is even more disturbing, saying, "The barbarians at the gate will only need to give us a slight push, and the emaciated body of Western civilization will collapse in a heap."[18] Sadly, these extremely fearful statements made publicly by elected officials are only timid versions of the "*reconquista*" conspiracy theory proposed by many of the people involved in the Minutemen vigilante projects which holds that "Mexico is quietly infiltrating a fifth-column of revolutionaries into the United States with the purpose of territorial conquest. Moreover the infiltration is being accomplished with the treasonous collusion of various 'liberal elite' institutions, e.g. the Catholic Church and the Ford Foundation, and the applause of muddle-headed multiculturalists."[19] The connection between politicians like Tancredo and the Minutemen is more than coincidental: reporter Nicole Colson has long followed anti-immigration groups and writes that Tancredo "was the keynote speaker at the Minuteman Project's opening day rally in Arizona . . . April [2006]," where Tancredo's appearance brought the crowd to its feet and was followed by two men in Nazi uniforms who gave the crowd the Nazi salute.[20]

In these cases we see a response to the insufficient advances of the last three decades that assumes that multiculturalism amounts to an attack on either white people or white culture. We see this habit at work in Jared Taylor's claim that "unless [white men] defend our racial interests and put them first, we will disappear."[21] When Samuel Francis intones that white men "need to kick out the vagrant savages who have wandered across the border, now claim our country as their own, and impose their cultures upon us," he reveals a pattern of thought that assumes white privilege does not cut against the demands of fairness, but is itself just.[22] This habitual response is perhaps the most detrimental of the habits of whiteness, because it treats the therapy for white racism as an attack and the imbalance of white privilege as the mark of a healthy polity.

The habit of entitlement often twines with the habit of antipathy to the strange, to disturbing and violent ends. We see this combination in the actions of the rioters in 1863. On the one side they felt assaulted by an uncaring federal government and Anglo-American society that denied them the opportunity to earn a decent living, but drafted them to be cannon fodder in Grant's bloody war of attrition with Lee. We see their habit of entitlement when they burned down the draft office and drove off the federal officers in charge of the draft. In their minds their whiteness entitled them to be free of such coercion. Sadly, we also saw their antipathy in their bloodlust toward African Americans, whom they saw as different from and beneath themselves. The riot itself, which Jacobson described as a kind of ritual enactment of whiteness, was, from a pragmatist point of view, a complex manifestation of both of these habits.

If we look back on many of the moments in the history of whiteness that motivate past and present liberatory theorists to speak out against whiteness, we see these same two habits working together. The act that for centuries served as the paradigmatic expression of white violence and domination, lynching, combines both of these habits. It is whites' habitual antipathy toward them that makes African Americans the target of disproportionate attention. It is a habitual response triggered by the gross stereotypes that reinforced the idea that they were *different* or the *Other* and that they were sexually different.[23] The habitual of entitlement leads white folk to think they are entitled to control how, when, and if their group mingles with other groups perceived as different or strange. In a manner that is of course powerfully informed by centuries-old patriarchal habits that conditioned women and men alike to assume that women were passive and incapable of making their own decisions or protecting themselves, lynching was the most violent and flagrant example of how the ideas of blood purity reinforced by laws regarding hypodescent and the one-drop rule shaped certain basic instincts into habits of entitlement.

As with the habit of the antipathy to the strange, there is an instinctual response beneath the habit of entitlement that is, in and of itself, neither good nor bad, but that requires intelligent harnessing in order to correct the habits of whiteness. Though we could imagine several phrases aptly describing this impulse, I will settle on the *impulse of pride.* With this I do not mean the complex and quite culturally specific idea of *hubris,* because this Greek idea entails a sense of human defiance of Fate or divinity that exceeds the simple feeling with which we need to contend. Instead, I mean simply the feeling that *who you are, or the group of which you are a part, is valuable.* This impulse in and of itself seems, on its face, to be not just acceptable, but absolutely essential requirement for a healthy, human psyche. It seems impossible to live a contented and worthwhile life without thinking that at some fundamental level, you—as an individual and as a member of a group—are all right.

A pragmatist reading of the habit of entitlement that is manifested in a particular way according to the habits of whiteness is that this habit simply hooks this impulse to the wrong content. We can't help wanting to be proud of ourselves. We *can* choose of *what* we are proud. The problem with whiteness is that it encourages the people who fit the category of whiteness to be proud of the wrong things, namely being *proud of not being oppressed.* We see this infelicitous channeling of pride in one of the most oft-cited problems with whiteness, namely the way it distorts history and memory. Since whiteness has been defined from its earliest days through exclusion, pride in whiteness entails being proud of *not being the excluded other.* We see this in the cultural amnesia that Rich described so powerfully. Going further back, we can recall Du Bois's claim in *Dusk of Dawn* that "[i]ndeed, the greatest and most immediate danger of white culture, perhaps least sensed, is its fear of the Truth, its childish belief in the efficacy of lies as a method of human uplift."[24]

The history of whiteness in America is bloody. When we assess the moments in U.S. history where European Americans appealed to ideas of whiteness to justify their actions—genocide of Native Americans as part of the white race's manifest destiny, lynching of black men to protect the flower of white womanhood, colonization of Caribbean and Pacific island nations as part of the Monroe Doctrine, exclusion of people of color from enfranchisement to protect white civilization, terrorism by the Klan in order to save the White Republic—we see that a wider and more careful history of whiteness presents it as uniformly brutal and inhuman. It is hard for anyone whose heart is not as hard as a millstone to not be ashamed of this history. Therefore, as Du Bois and Rich and many others point out, the impulse of pride impacted by the idea of whiteness results in a habit of entitlement that protects white privilege by inventing a false history. In the past, before the civil rights movement, this habit resulted in the picture against which Du Bois was forced to rail. It resulted in a nostalgic picture of the past that presented the legacy of whiteness in this continent as munificent and kind. D.W. Griffith's *The Birth of A Nation* was the runaway cinematic phenomenon of 1915 and the first summer blockbuster because it so perfectly painted the version of American history that white people wanted to see. In the present situation, where historians and scholars write more nuanced accounts of whiteness that challenge the older stories, many whites feel under attack. In this new social environment the habit of entitlement results in the white backlash prevalent in universities, conservative political movements, and the media. It is what causes some students to feel that programs designed to increase the cultural diversity of an overwhelmingly white campus are in fact attacks on them as white students.

Regarding this habitual aspect of whiteness to want to defend the legacy of whiteness in this country, the task is to channel the impulse of pride into another direction. Put simply, *we need to find something else of which white folk can be proud.* Following Du Bois, it needs to be something that fosters a kind of connection to the past through the past-looking face of race. It also needs to produce the sense of striving which we see in the future-looking face of Du Bois's notion of race: the aspect that suggests certain ways of being that are dynamic and indicate some goal or path toward which we need to strive. So far, the idea of whiteness has proved a flimsy resource in both regards. As Rich so aptly described in the previous chapter, its past-face was looking at a fabricated history, which offered no real cultural sustenance, but only the sugar rush of a false history. Noel Ignatiev gives us a good sense of where to look for this source of non-hierarchal, not-imperialist pride when he answers the question "Is there such a thing as 'white culture'?" this way:

> No. There is Italian culture, and Polish, Irish, Yiddish, German, and Appalachian culture: There is youth culture and drug culture and queer culture; but there is no "white" culture—unless you mean Wonder Bread and television game shows. Whiteness is nothing but an expression of race privilege. It has been said that the typical "white" American male spends his childhood as an Indian, his adolescence as an African-American and only becomes white when he reaches the age of responsibility.[25]

A pragmatist inquiry would follow Ignatiev's distinction to look for an alternate source of pride in the very cultural traditions that European immigrants let go of when they became white. In addition to this we can add the cultural traditions that grew up organically in healthy communities of all sorts that are threatened with extinction within a society that has grown over-commercialized and over-sanitized. Perhaps by looking at the rich and varied histories of actual people's lives and struggles that were papered over with nostalgic and jingoistic stories of white America we might find the sorts of cultural gifts of which people who now identify as white might be justly proud.

Finally, we need to look at the *habit of guilt.* While there have been white people throughout our history who felt guilt regarding aspects of white violence, this habit became most prominent only in the last few decades. This habit entails the opposite response to the history of white violence that we saw at play in the habit of entitlement. Where Taylor, Smith, Gilchrist, Hayworth, and Tancredo respond to current attempts at multiculturalism by digging in and defending the privileges to which they believe their whiteness entitles them, people who act according to the habits of guilt do the opposite. They look at the history and present reality of whiteness, and feel nausea. They feel sick at what happened and what happens because of whiteness. Furthermore, they feel sick because they, as white folk, are linked to this shameful history.

This habit is problematic primarily because of how it directs white folk to remedy the problem of being linked to the violent history of whiteness. As many Native American authors point out, it leads to a kind of cultural plundering, whereby white folk try to fill the cultural void of false white history, as well as distance themselves from whiteness as an identity by appropriating other people's cultures. Margo Thunderbird of the Shinnecock Nation says of this troubling propensity, "They came for our land, for what grew or could be grown on it, for the resources in it, and for our clean air and pure water. They stole these things from us, and in the taking they also stole our free ways and the best of our leaders, killed in battle or assassinated. And now, after all that, they've come for the very last of our possessions; now they want our pride, our history, our spiritual traditions."[26] Thunderbird, and other indigenous theorists such as Ward Churchill, Vine Deloria Jr., and Russell Means all point to the fact that some whites in America have a disturbing habit of turning to indigenous spirituality and traditions as a means of reconnecting with the "primitive" without addressing the privation generating this cultural thirst. These scholars identify groups such as Robert Bly's men's movement and uncritical Indian hobbyists as contemporary "culture vultures": white imperialists who steal cultural practices and traditions from Native peoples in order to fill the spiritual gaps within white hegemony.[27] To add insult to injury, not only are Native traditions stripped of their cultural contexts and meaning, but they become trinkets of commodity fetishism. It is not enough to offer Native traditions as cures for white racism or violence. As our relationship toward nonwhite peoples has been overwhelmingly one of imperialism and domination, any large-scale cultural exchange risks re-inscribing historical patterns of theft.

Of course, white people who feel guilt for being white don't invite themselves just to Native cultural traditions. The cultural traditions of African Americans have long been attractive tropes for whites, since at least the heyday of minstrelsy. The constant demand for youth culture to be edgy and disturbing to its consumers' parents has driven white entertainers to repeatedly pillage black culture for its musical and sartorial styles. From blackface minstrelsy, to Elvis, to the Rolling Stones, to Eminem, white youths have long sought to scare their parents by following the white guy who acted black on stage. We see more complex reactions to the habit of guilt among groups like "white Rastas" and "wiggers" who appropriate Rastafarianism (a religious movement that was established to specifically establish a pure black "Zion" in opposition to the corrupted world of white, capitalist

Babylon) and "gangsta rap" as alternatives to whiteness.[28] In an excellent sociological study of young male white fans of hip-hop music in New England, Jason Rodriquez analyses "how white youths practice color-blind ideology in a local hip-hop scene, justifying their participation and unwittingly wielding their racial power to culturally appropriate hip-hop."[29] One of the most interesting interviews focuses on a subject named Ryan, who eschews the colorblind ideology of the majority of the other subjects in favor of a sensitivity to the racial context of hip-hop that makes him deeply ambivalent about the hip-hop culture he clearly loves. Rodriquez writes that "what separates Ryan from other hip-hop enthusiasts is that establishing this part of his identity comes at the cost of taking on guilt."[30] Rodriquez then quotes Ryan saying, "'I guess I'm concerned about, Blues and Rock 'n' Roll and everything sort of started, was started by African Americans, and look at where that is now? Those roots were in Black culture, but that has been totally taken away, and it's white music now. Rock 'n' Roll is white music."[31] As each new culture form develops organically it is appropriated and deracinated through commodification.

The act of cultural exchange itself is not necessarily problematic. In fact, it is part and parcel of the sort of democratic community building that Du Bois hopes we can achieve if we use the resource of race and race history appropriately. It is of course possible for any individual from one culture to learn from and become a respectful participant in cultural traditions that originate from other groups. For one example of many, we could point to the proliferation across the Western Hemisphere of academies teaching martial art systems from China, Korea, and Japan. In well-run schools, we see deeply cherished cultural traditions that are hundreds of years old being shared with anyone, regardless of background, who is willing to come to them with the spirit of humility and respect that they demand. Far from being acts of theft, these exchanges keep alive and even sometimes improve these traditions; for example, the Gracie family in Brazil has for three generations dominated international competitions in the Japanese style of grappling called *jujitsu*. The problem with the habit of guilt is that is motivates cultural exchanges for the wrong reasons and in the wrong way. The sort of cultural exchange that Du Bois envisions is a mutually respectful giving and taking of learned arts and experiences. The habit of guilt causes people to take cultural gifts without either consent or exchange. Indeed, since it assumes that whiteness is nothing but cruelty and violence, it assumes that white folk have no real culture and nothing to give. It therefore leads white folk who have a sense of the atrocities involved in whiteness to get as far away from being white as possible without trying to either resolve the problems with whiteness or reclaim value beyond whiteness.

Sadly, this habit is every bit as damaging as the habit of entitlement. It encourages a subtle but powerful cultural theft in the attempt to fill the void where a rich cultural connection should be. The cultures of people of African, Asian, Latino, and indigenous descent become mere platters in a cultural smorgasbord. Irresponsible martial arts academies disgrace Asian cultures by casting about symbols of mastery, like black belts, as if they were trinkets to be bought. Native American dream-catchers are treated like fancy versions of fuzzy dice to be hung on the rearview mirror. Following long-standing descriptions of evil not as a thing, but as a lack, we can characterize the impulse beneath this habit as an *impulse of emptiness.* When some people study the history of whiteness they develop a feeling that they, as white people, lack any real culture. Native American sweat lodges and African American blues or hip-hop then beckon as traditions that promise a kind of cultural sustenance that many cannot find elsewhere.

As before, we need to direct this feeling to fill emptiness in a different way. As with all other impulses, the feeling of lack or emptiness can and does play a vital part of life. We see it in everything from the simple physical hunger that leads us to make or find the food we need to survive, or in the more complex situation where an artist is jolted to innovate their style because of the feeling that their current mode of expression is somehow flat or repetitive. Just as we need to address the problematic habit of entitlement by finding something else to be proud of, we need to address the habit of guilt by redefining our sense of how or why we are empty.

In this Deweyan approach to habit, the impulses are largely "given." If we ignore them, they will manifest in a discharge beyond our control, and we can suppress them for only so long. The better alternative is to study them and engage in a directed inquiry about how to best control them. Some people cannot help getting hungry after dinner. We can control whether we direct this impulse into unhealthy and uncritical habits (like grazing in the fridge until stuffed) or critical and healthy habits (like drinking water and eating a set amount of low-calorie snacks). While the habits of whiteness are extremely complex and have wrought countless agonies, from the point of view of impulses and human behavior, they are just habits that we can either try to direct with intelligence or leave alone to their own uncontrolled manifestation. I have outlined what I take to be the basic impulses behind the most destructive of the habits of whiteness. In the next chapter I will suggest how we might direct these impulses into habits that not only are more conducive to the basic ethical requirements of fairness and equality, but also foster the far-off human flourishing toward which Du Bois directs us.

TEN

Whiteness Reconstructed

New Habits of Whiteness

We gain a more functional understanding of our problems with racism once we examine their connection to habits of whiteness. These habits remain problematic because of both their negative effects and their transparency or invisibility to white folk. A pragmatist critique of whiteness seeks a middle ground between eliminativism and essentialism; it would follow thinkers such as Outlaw and Taylor between these two poles because either these positions are out of sorts with the needs of democratic community or they try to achieve a democratic response to whiteness in a problematic manner. This chapter will use the medicines that we find in Dewey to treat the sociocultural illness diagnosed by Du Bois and contemporary race theorists. Du Bois explained why the habits of whiteness are so toxic: they encourage violence, undermine the formation and sustenance of community, put money before humanity, and leave white folk culturally undernourished and rootless. Contemporary theorists show us that racism is now less overt though no less oppressive than before. We have seen how concrete, structural changes to our economic and political systems initiated in the 1960s are now being eroded due in part to a failure to notice or address the habitual dimensions to this problem.

In Dewey's work on the relationship between concepts, habits, and social relations we find a valuable but underused tool with which to reconstruct our social relations into patterns more in line with the requirements and promise of democratic community. However, in order to fully leverage this tool we need to put into action his idea that bad habits cannot be ignored or willed away: they must be reconstructed through careful inquiry. A Deweyan approach to the problems of racism that stem from the habits of whiteness involves first understanding how these habits lead to undesirable consequences and then reconstructing these habits into new ones. As stated before, our goal here is the flourishing community of face-to-face democratic interaction of which Dewey wrote, which I think is the same ideal that Du Bois held in his hope of a global and mutually humanizing exchange of the gifts of race. An apt reconstruction of the habits of whiteness is a necessary step for achieving community because, as we've seen in this analysis, these habits—like habits associated with patriarchy, heterosexism, and ableism—impeded the realization of a truly pluralistic and democratic community. All people interested in the health of our democratic community, regardless of their personal identity, therefore have an interest in the successful reconstruction of these detrimental habits. In fact, the reconstruction of whiteness I think white folk should do is analogous to efforts by thinkers such as Eddie Glaude to envision a new racial and political framework for a "post-soul generation" in part by "encourage[ing] a more imaginative and intelligent politics for the twenty-first century."[1]

Before discussing what the reconstructed habits of whiteness might look like, I will briefly recapitulate some of the virtues that I see in a pragmatist approach to the problems of white racism that makes full use of Dewey's theory of habits. First, assessing whiteness as a bad habit ("bad" meaning out of sorts with our commitment to democracy and human equality) moves our discussions on race away from the defensiveness and recrimination that perennially impede our ability to reach some kind of meaningful agreement on race. It would move away from the issue of intent (such as the pointless "You're a racist!" "No, I'm not!" back-and-forth), and toward the more productive question of "how do we, white people especially, *actually* treat each other, apart from our conscious beliefs about race?" This would enable us to see with Rich that white folk are both innocent and accountable: we are innocent in that very, very few white folks want or consciously perpetuate white supremacist racism per se, yet as beneficiaries of the myriad economic, political, social, and psychological privileges perpetuated by the habits of whiteness, we are accountable for whether we perpetuate, ignore, or change these habits. Such an understanding of racism as a set of habits would enable us to see how racism in the post–civil rights era survives primarily by not being noticed; we would see that someone might have the best intentions in the world and even consciously reject the explicit idea of white supremacism (or for that matter, sexism, heterosexism, ageism, ableism, or environmental irresponsibility), but if the individual has not inquired into how their habits affect their *actual practices in the world,* then they might well be a vessel for age-old and withering venom.

Second, it would suggest a reconstruction of the concept of whiteness as opposed to its elimination. This would be a better response to what other theorists call the invisibility of whiteness, and what a pragmatist analysis terms the habitual aspect of whiteness, because it would require white folk (indeed all folk, but white folk especially) to look at whiteness as a kind (by studying its history as a concept powerfully shaped our social habits and laws) and as a category (as a concept that directs further action). It would dispel the comforting but erroneous belief that white supremacism ended with the elimination of explicitly white supremacist codes from our laws and economic policies or the biologistic argument that we don't have to talk about race because geneticists tell us that the racial categories that shaped our sociocultural landscape do not really match our genes. The civil rights movement doubtlessly moved us closer to the realization of a truly democratic community, but it is also clear that we still have a ways to go before we get there. It is doubtlessly encouraging to learn from geneticists that we are far more biologically similar than different. However, the findings of geneticists in the last ten years have not really cast new light on the sociocultural problem of racism: Du Bois already knew in the 1950s that the biologists in the middle of the twentieth century had shown that the racial categories invented by empire-building Enlightenment-era Europeans were total bunk. The recent findings of geneticists that there is no "race gene" does not mean that the way to *solve the problem of racism* is to simply stop talking about it now that we know race is not in the flesh the way the Enlightenment taxonomists thought it was. Saying that race is not "real" because the categories don't match the genes is a bit like saying the five-dollar bill in your pocket has no "real" value because Fort Knox doesn't hold five dollars' worth of gold to materially back up your symbolic note.

We saw that pragmatism's meliorist power rests largely in its refusal of the "spectator theory of knowledge," which assumes truth is "out there" in our genes or under a rock, waiting for us to sneak up on it unawares. Du Bois outlined a pragmatist model of race that understands the value of race as being a complex interaction of physical signs and sociocultural valuations of those signs, especially in the law. A full solution to the problems related to the complex interaction of laws, behaviors, ideas, and biological features that we call race requires an inquiry into the habits that direct our practices and a careful reconstruction of these problematic habits. This reconstruction would require not only the sorts of concrete political and economic changes initiated in the 1960s, but also a reconstruction of the relationship between ideas, impulses, and experience as described in previous chapters. Such a reconstruction would reestablish the connection between concept and habit in order to better promote reform, instead of disconnecting the concept from action by eliminating the concept from discussion.

Third, a reconstruction of the problematic habits of whiteness would complement the economic and legal changes made in the 1960s that are being dismantled before they've had an opportunity to fully run their course. The civil rights movement produced laws that forced governments to take "affirmative action," to correct our legacy of legally enforced white supremacism by ensuring as much as possible that people of color gained fair access and support in areas such as hiring, university admissions, and government contracts. This movement engendered sweeping and desperately needed reforms of the external legal, economic, and political structures that had perpetuated white privilege for centuries. This sort of concrete, environmental change is necessary for a fully pragmatist reconstruction of habits, since habits are interactive phenomena formed at the confluence of an individual's impulses and her environment. John Dewey addressed exactly this issue in "Racial Prejudice and Friction," one of the few works where he explicitly spoke to the problem of racism.

> In the case of racial prejudice we are still largely under the influence of moral superstition. We fancy we can get rid of moral evils by vigorous condemnation and by preaching to people about how evil they are. Of course sometimes the method succeeds just as mental healing does, but only in special cases, and where conditions are already favorable. It is a good thing to cure even a few cases, but the remedy does not go far. What is needed is the destruction of the thing itself. This will not occur until we can remove the causes which produce it. And as in the case of physical disease we cannot deal with causes until we have made a study of the thing itself free from moral emotion. We need to change men's minds but the best way to change their minds is to change the conditions which shape them rather than to go at it by direct appeal and exhortation.[2]

In the case of the problems of race and racism, Dewey believed that economic conditions were some of the greatest factors behind problems of race and racism. He well described how economic pressures could inflame feelings of antipathy into full-blown racial hatred and violence, especially when dealing with large-scale immigration. The following passage is worth quoting at length since it was written during America's last worst spasm of nativist violence in the 1920s and it aptly describes the situation then as well as the problems now.

> We now come to the most rational factor in the confirming of racial animosities, the economic. In calling it rational I do not mean that it always operates in a reasonable way, but that it has the largest element of thought and calculation in it as compared with instinctive factors. Modern immigration is mostly due to economic causes. This means of course that immigrants believe they can better their condition by removal to another country. This fact means, in turn, that as a rule the economic standard of living is higher in the country of new residence. The immigrants thus bring with them the lower standard of living developed in the country of origin. Only slowly does their standard rise. Industrial competition on the part

of factory employees, small shop keepers, and land owners in agricultural products tends to arouse the antagonism of those previously upon the ground who were already hard put to it to make their livings. When the competition comes from those who persistently maintain a lower standard of living, who save rather than spend and who are willing to work longer hours, the feeling against the immigrant is much increased. Thus there is at the present time in America a strong movement for the restriction of all foreign immigration.[3]

The fact that he so succinctly describes the link between race tension and a globalized labor market is impressive; the fact that what he wrote in the early 1920s is still true and relevant in the twenty-first century should be troubling because it shows that we've learned very little about these problems and have not directed enough energy in the right direction.

Fears over economic competition certainly drive much of resurgent nativism among white Americans. We can discern these economic fears behind the Minutemen posses in the Southwest, anti-immigrant laws passed by city councils across the country, the formation of hundreds of anti-immigrant organizations, and even the Republican mutiny President Bush faced in the summer of 2007 when he tried and failed to strike what he thought was a reasonable compromise between national security and compassion for immigrants with his immigration bill. Of course, the interaction between race and economics goes back much further than the 1920s. We saw this dynamic between economics and racism when whiteness was quite literally invented as a powerful legal category to undercut class solidarity among the African and European workers in the tobacco fields of colonial Virginia. We saw it again when fearful Irish Americans and Irish immigrants in the nineteenth century rioted to violently prove their difference from and superiority to black people because they worried that the lines of racial taxonomy would be redrawn by the proper white Americans in a way that would lump the Irish in with the economically and politically disenfranchised African Americans. We saw how Du Bois linked white racism to the accumulation of wealth when he wrote in *Dusk of Dawn* that

> even in the minds of the most dogmatic supporters of race theories and believers in the inferiority of colored folk to white, there was a conscious or unconscious determination to increase their incomes by taking full advantage of this belief. And then gradually this thought was metamorphosed into a realization that the income-bearing value of race prejudice was the cause and not the result of theories of racial inferiority.[4]

We see how much of the problem of racism stems from vague but powerfully felt feelings of economic dread when we study the illogic of the anti-immigration movement that simultaneously rails against Latinos (excuse me, "illegal immigrants") for somehow being both *lazy* (with the "they come here and mooch off our tax dollars when they go to the hospital or get food stamps" discourse) and *diabolically hard-working* (with the "they work so hard, so long, and for so little money that they take our jobs" routine). While this doesn't make a whit of sense, it does clearly illustrate the fact that economic concerns fuel much of today's racial antagonism.

This is why Dewey called anti-immigrant prejudice "a striking manifestation of the importance of the economic factor in present international jealousies and rivalries. It is a recognition . . . that only by profound economic readjustments can racial friction be done away with."[5] It shows that in addition to what we might call the *internal dimension* to the problematic habits of whiteness (by which I mean the ideas that structure the habits and the feelings that fuel them), there is also an *external dimension,* including but not limited to things like wages, commodity and service pricing, access to health care and education, property values, and job availability, which can either alleviate the problem when they combine to create a feeling of abundance or exacerbate the problem if they combine in a way that creates a real or even perceived environment of scarcity.

As important as this external and economic dimension is, it would be a mistake to say either that racial tension is really just a by-product of economic competition in a capitalist system or that the only real solution to the problem of race rests solely with economic or structural issues. Remember the discussion of the civil rights movement; in the 1960s Americans took great strides toward solving the problem of white racism through significant changes to our economic and political structures, such as laws that ended over three hundred years of legalized white privilege and segregation and initiatives that took affirmative action to redress the inequities of the present, produced by centuries of white racism, by legally mandating the private and public sectors to diversify their workforce. All of these modes of action focused on the external factors such as economics and laws, and they accomplished a great deal. However, while this movement changed for the better the material practices surrounding race in America, it did not sufficiently address the ideas, impulses, and habits that *also* perpetuated and sustained white privilege. The law can punish a wrong-doer, enforce non-discrimination in the workplace, and even largely ensure equal access to collective resources; however, it can't change a person's mind, turn his heart, or change his habits. The law changed the external structures of race in many positive ways, but it was incapable of helping enough white folks to see the reality of their habits regarding race, or the need to reconstruct them to better fit a racially pluralistic and fair democracy. As a result, many white Americans felt aggrieved and put-upon by these economic and political reforms and saw this movement not as justice long overdue, but as a travesty to be reversed in time. The Southern Strategy was such a successful political gambit for the GOP because it tapped the feeling, widespread among white voters in the South, that the civil rights movement had offered minority voters a set of federally supported citizenship rights that many whites felt were their entitlement alone. In the decades since the civil right movement, law schools and think tanks have been carefully and consciously seeded with true believers in the idea that non-violent instruments designed to correct generations of violent white supremacy are themselves racist. It seems that with the Bush-appointed Roberts Court their seed has come to fruit.

We are just forty years into a treatment designed to gradually correct the massive political and economic disparities produced by three hundred years of legalized white supremacism, and many white folk seem to have forgotten why we as a society needed to take affirmative action. What's more, white folk have not suffered any vengeful "payback" for the indignities suffered by people of color, nor should they. White Americans do not live under all-black police departments that turn a lazy eye away from black posses that lynch white teenagers for looking at black teenagers. Nor do we suffer forced expulsion from our properties and jobs as did Asian Americans, peonage and cultural denigration like Latinos, or the biological warfare, broken promises, and land theft endured by our Native hosts. Nonetheless, many white Americans are committed to the delusion that we are now the victims of "reverse discrimination" to such an extent that we need to run to the courts for protection. Bodies even as august as the U.S. Supreme Court indulge this fantasy with rulings that manifest a lack of awareness of white privilege and ignorance of the history of whiteness.

We see this habitual whiteness at play in the majority decision from June of 2007 that programs such as affirmative action and public school integration that were designed to *correct* the economic and legal underpinnings of racism are now *themselves racist* for requiring an adjustment on the part of all citizens to achieve social parity. Chief Justice Roberts ended his opinion on the court's 5–4 decision that a school district in Seattle may not take a student's race into account as they try to maintain integrated public schools with the zinger, "[t]he way to stop discrimination on the basis of race is to stop discriminating on the basis of race."[6] Sadly this bumper-sticker-ready quip rests on a definitional fallacy; it appears reasonable to call integration racial discrimination only if you forget or ignore the very problem that led the court to mandate integration in the first place, namely, the economic, political, and social advantages enjoyed by white folks to the detriment of people of color. It avoids the very issue at hand by simply *defining as discriminatory* careful and intentional steps taken to preserve racially integrated and pluralistic institutions within a society that was for hundreds of years carefully and intentionally segregated in a way to grant people defined as white an unfair privilege in every arena of public and private life.

If America had had a very different racial history in which different groups had spent centuries hurting each other more or less equally, then the court's remedy of colorblindness might be warranted. If the different groups were like a car-load of unruly children, each of whom was as much aggressor as aggrieved, then the Court's majority ruling would be just since it would be like the parent laying down the blanket edict "Everybody quit it!" However, that is not at all our history of race: our actual history—the one I think Du Bois urges us to recover that is notably *absent* from Roberts's opinion and *present* in the dissenting opinions—is a history of *one* legally defined group of people abusing *all the other* legally defined groups for its own economic advantage for generations. In light of our own actual historical and present inequities, it seems that we need to keep race in the analysis at least in order to redress clear and persistent harm, not to mention the arguments made by the likes of Du Bois and Taylor that race is valuable in and of itself.

All this is a sign that *either* a change of habits *or* a change of economic and legal structures will be insufficient to engender the sort of lasting change that is needed to achieve a truly pluralistic and fair community. This is why I will agree with Dewey when he says that fear produced by economic uncertainty largely fuels racial conflict. However, when I read him say that "only by profound economic readjustments can racial friction be done away with" I have to read "only" in the inclusive sense that the only way we will do away with racial friction is if we have a profound economic readjustment *along with some other stuff*, which, in my mind, must include a reconstruction of our habits.[7] Profound economic readjustment is certainly necessary, but I think the last forty years show us that it would be insufficient alone. Economically minded reformers often point to America's postwar period as a shining example of economic justice since that was when a worker with a high-school degree could work a forty-hour week and afford a mortgage, send his kids to well-funded schools, and greet a boss who only made ten times his salary. While it is the case that in the middle of the last century our industry was generally run more fairly since it balanced shareholder profit with community health, we have to remember that the worker got a good deal in the 1950s if and only if he was seen as white and male. A worker who was black, Latino or female was out of luck.

I agree therefore with Justice Breyer when he reminds us that in order to achieve the ideal of a just community, we need to take corrective measures that work back through the categories used in the past to unfairly privilege some over others. In order to correct for how race was used in the past to prevent community, we need to see, think, and talk race in order to solve our legacy of racism.

> Today, almost 50 years later, attitudes toward race in this nation have changed dramatically. Many parents, white and black alike, want their children to attend schools with children of different races. Indeed, the very school districts that once spurned integration now strive for it. The long history of their efforts reveals the complexities and difficulties they have faced. And in light of those challenges, they have asked us not to take from their hands the instruments they have used to rid their schools of racial segregation, instruments that they believe are needed to overcome the problems of cities divided by race and poverty.[8]

Breyer is making a very Deweyan point here. While we all want human flourishing, and we want all people to be free, it is ridiculous to think that in order to be free all we need is to remove people's chains and then let them have at it.

Freedom requires the presence of conditions that enable us to act freely in the world. Education is not only one of the most essential conditions, but is one of the conditions over which we have the greatest degrees of control and can thus best provide for our citizens. This is why Breyer's race-conscious argument echoes Dewey's point from "Philosophies of Freedom":

> The notion that men are equally free to act if only the same legal arrangements apply equally to all—irrespective of differences in education, in command of capital, and the control of the social environment which is furnished by the institution of property—is a pure absurdity, as facts have demonstrated. Since actual, that is, effective, rights and demands are products of interactions, and are not found in the original and isolated constitution of human nature, whether moral or psychological, mere elimination of obstructions is not enough. The latter merely liberates force and ability as that happens to be distributed by past accidents of history. This "free" action operates disastrously as far as the many are concerned. The only possible conclusion, both intellectually and practically, is that the attainment of freedom conceived as power to act in accord with choice depends upon positive and constructive changes in social arrangements.[9]

Since we start in very different places in terms of wealth and access to capital, we need to consciously and constructively change the social arrangement to ensure as much as possible that each individual has the necessary conditions to be a fully free member of her community. An inquiry into and reconstruction of the habits of whiteness is crucial because it will help redefine such instruments in the minds of many Americans and help them see the need to attend to identity in order to reach the kind of community that is beneficial for all of us. The necessary changes to our socioeconomic systems that are required for a fully and fairly pluralistic community will not be accepted and will likely be further opposed and dismantled unless Americans, especially white Americans, reconstruct their habits of race.

Pragmatists committed to achieving a pluralistic and democratic community should look at the interaction of race and economics in at least two ways. The first has to do with the issue of economic justice across and between different groups. This valence of an economic analysis would look at how the economic pie is sliced by group, in order to ensure as much as possible that people in different groups are being treated fairly. Affirmative action initiatives and the like were designed to address this slice-of-the-pie issue, and they should continue to do so. These sorts of legislative and policy remedies are necessary to correct the gross economic inequalities that still divided white people from people of color and make broader community impossible.

The other mode of interaction has to do with the size of the pie to which normal folk—people of all different identities who work because we have to—have access relative to the size of the pie that the rich folk who dominate the public and private sectors reserve for themselves. Rorty for one was really interested in this second issue, and we should be too. Rorty bemoaned the fact that the slice-of-the-pie issue was so much more important than the size-of-the-pie issue in the academy, that it was "as if the American Left could not handle more than one initiative at a time."[10] This size-of-the-pie issue affects racial habits for the reasons outlined by Dewey above: when a worker sees himself in competition with an immigrant he sees as belonging to another race, the fact that he is already barely getting by economically makes him much more likely to manifest race-based prejudice inside the pressure cooker of a globalized economy that is fundamentally unfair to workers.

Rorty was right to an extent to spoof the Left for being unable to, as it were, chew gum and walk at the same time: to attend to particular identity debates while not losing sight of the issue of overall economic fairness. However, he overstepped when he made the broad assertion that "Leftists in the academy have permitted cultural politics to supplant real politics, and have collaborated with the Right in making cultural issues central to public debate."[11] It makes little sense to chide queer, feminist, and race theorists for being suckered into mere "cultural politics" when they should have been focusing on the "real politics" of globalization and class if it is the case, as Rorty says in "Relativism: Finding and Making," that pragmatists "have no use for the reality-appearance distinction."[12] Rorty might reply that by real he means "more useful than" in that it is more useful to focus on issues of economics and legislation than identity and culture if you want to alleviate human suffering and promote human flourishing. However, if philosophy as he saw it comes down to telling well-considered, utopian stories that critique the present to better plot a course to the future, then why is the feminist's story about economic disparity between genders or the failure of federal and state governments to enforce laws concerning child support or domestic abuse less real or useful than the story of the "real" political reformers who focus on how globalization makes it impossible for the middle-class family to make ends meet, even with two paychecks? Furthermore, how is Rorty's economics and law-centered story more real or useful than the story about the Chicano immigrant family dying in the desert south of Yuma, or the story about the lesbian barred from her partner's hospital deathbed because she lives in a nation that has not fully or fairly understood queer identity? They all seem to be important stories for anyone who thinks that needless suffering is wrong. The sort of "real" economic and legal reforms engendered by the civil rights movement happened only after writers, teachers, and activists made the old story of white dominance untenable and new ones more viable. It seems that we *do* need to be able to do both at once.

Rorty left us the message that we should not theorize ourselves into an ineffective corner of the ivory tower by cleaving too zealously to Foucauldian suspicion or Marxist purity. Instead, we need to tell the best possible—meaning most feasible and humanizing—story of hope and possibility. He made a very strong case for the primacy of stories that talk mostly about reforming our laws and economic systems, because he thought these stories were more likely to alleviate human suffering than the identity or "multicultural" stories that he saw as being merely about "a morality of live-and-let-live, a politics of side-by-side development in which members of distinct cultures preserve and protect their own culture against incursions of other cultures."[13] He borrowed the title of one of his best utopian stories, *Achieving Our Country,* from James Baldwin's classic *The Fire Next Time.* He places Baldwin in the pantheon of American writers who not only help us imagine a reachable utopia, but remind us of the need to eschew the detached stance of the spectator in favor of the commitment of an engaged participant in the future's creation. He holds up Baldwin's famous last sentence as a testament to the importance of creative and engaged politics: "If we—and now I mean the relatively conscious whites and the relatively conscious blacks, who must, like lovers, insist on, or create, the consciousness of the others—do not falter in our duty now, we may be able, handful that we are, to end the racial nightmare, and achieve our country, and change the history of the world."[14]

I find Rorty's use of this passage not only encouraging and uplifting, but also a bit at odds with his overall dismissal of identity politics and multiculturalism. However much I agree that progressives need to sometimes engage issues of economics and globalization on their own terms apart from issues of gender, sexuality, and race, I also agree with Baldwin's work, which largely cuts against Rorty's prioritizing of economics over identity. Notice that Baldwin does *not* urge us to achieve our country as relatively conscious workers or relatively conscious people left out in the cold by globalizing plutocrats. He very clearly argues for the fact that we Americans will achieve our potential as a true and healthy democracy only when we are conscious of ourselves and others *as black and as white,* as raced people who see each other and the world through racial lenses. I can't imagine Baldwin urging us to achieve our country using a post-race, post-identity story. Instead, I think he is urging us to look at how race keeps us apart and to work through these problems for the sake of community. The reconstruction articulated here strives for the same realization of human potential that Rorty wrote about, but it takes folks like Du Bois, Anzaldúa, and Baldwin seriously when they say that we need to also attend to identity and race.

Finally, a critique of whiteness through habit enables us to answer the question asked of me by the forlorn student I described in the introduction, which is one of the main questions raised by Du Bois's work: "Where do white folk find their gift?" Our study of the history of whiteness makes it clear that white folks ought not to look for their gift within whiteness per se, or in white identity. Whiteness is so dangerous because at its root it fosters a negative pride: "I am proud to not be one of *them.*" We saw how the class solidarity between the workers of African and European descent who fought in Bacon's Rebellion was swiftly shattered when the ruling elite legalized the right of white workers to *not* be beaten as they sanctioned the increased abuse of non-white workers. We saw how murderous this pride could be when we looked at the Irish and Irish Americans who rioted in 1863 to emphasize their difference from and superiority to black people. We can use Dewey's analysis of impulses (the inchoate but propulsive feelings that demand habit formation) and habits (learned ways of organizing and making impulses meaningful) to separate, for example, the value-neutral human impulse of pride away from its current habitual form framed around the concept of whiteness toward more life-affirming and democratic forms. An impulse like pride is so basic that it cannot be eliminated and must instead be fostered through habits that are at once non-racist and also non-hierarchical.

Such a reformation is fundamental for a successful critique of whiteness from a Du Boisian perspective because pride is necessary for a group both to have something to share and to be able to appreciate the value of the other's gift. Du Bois did not want a facile multiculturalism that was merely the "live and let live" attitude criticized by Rorty and many others. We do not preserve these gifts to put them on display behind museum glass. Du Bois hoped that we could overcome the antipathy that many people feel toward people from different cultures and ethnic groups through an *exchange* of cultural gifts that would simultaneously preserve the resources of inherited memories and stories while breaking down barriers of ignorance and misunderstanding. These exchanges need to occur in a context of mutual respect and understanding and not as primarily economic transactions. Further, they are exchanges where some cultural artifacts are shared and others are not. For example, the annual Julyamsh powwow hosted by the Coeur D'Alene Tribe near Post Falls, Idaho, includes some traditional dances where all people in attendance are invited to dance, while others are reserved just for Native peoples, or just for women, or elders, or veterans. Respectful participation requires listening to the caller and either entering the circle or standing back, depending on the dance or ceremony involved. Further, by talking about the idea of a cultural gift we can hopefully leave behind the brutal and fruitless Left versus Right, progressive versus conservative, John Wayne versus John Brown dichotomies that divide people around the issue of whiteness. If we can show that race is a habit as Dewey and Du Bois describe, then we can say to Left, "Yes, there is a lot wrong with whiteness, and we need to remember and correct these wrongs," even as we say to the Right, "Yes, there is a lot in your traditions of which you should be proud, and you should share it with others."

Therefore, we need to find a way to reconstruct the habits of whiteness into new habits that reform the impulses behind the habits of whiteness. We need to guard against the tendency toward evasion that causes white folk to ignore how we did and still do benefit from white supremacist ideas and institutions. At the same time, we need to avoid making such a reformation into a kind of mass *mea culpa*. We need to find a way for white folk to be proud of themselves without falling into the trap of pride through domination and exclusion.

Habits of Shame

We can start by looking at how to better direct the *impulse of emptiness* that motivates the *habits of guilt*. The task is to find a way to sublimate the feeling of lack so that it ceases to be a part of a pointless or violent habitual response to experience. Du Bois teaches us that in order to reconstruct whiteness and solve the problems of white racism, white folk need to first remember our history as white. Of the significance of blackness for black folk, Du Bois writes, "The physical bond is least and the badge of color is relatively unimportant save as a badge; the real essence of this kinship is its social heritage of slavery."[15] These moments illustrate the sort of respectful exchange of cherished cultural gifts that DuBois saw as a vehicle of human understanding and trans-ethnic community foundation. Furthermore, if races are "generally of common blood and language, [but] always of common history" and if amnesia and nostalgia are unsatisfying substitutes for history, then what white people need, in part, is a clearer engagement with their history *as white and as not white.*[16] Rich argues that white Americans suffer from a kind of cultural emptiness that stems from a false recollection of the past. We vainly search for meaning in our commodity purchases in part because we lack the sort of deep cultural and historical connection that our predecessors relinquished in order to join the other heterogeneous people of European origin inside the unitary, homogenizing, materially privileged, and legally enforced category of whiteness. They gave up stories that explained to the individual who she was so that she could be a white American and thus be free of prejudice and free to get lots of stuff. Now her descendent has a lot of stuff, too much stuff, but no sense of who she is.

The value of race from a pragmatist point of view comes from what I term its Janus faces. Race links the individual to a cultural history and offers a future orientation that stems from this history. In the case of African Americans, the past face looks back on the history of violence and denigration shared by people who hold the badge of African features. The future face is a sense of common striving against the forces of violence, exclusion, and racism that have assailed the black community for centuries. It is common striving toward a peaceful and respected community. The impulse of lack within whiteness has to do with the absence of a rich, commonly shared historical background.

In our youth, white Americans were taught that we were effectively children of the *Mayflower*, the first Thanksgiving, and Boston Tea Party. These and other similar nostalgic tidbits become our cultural diet from a very early age. Baldwin wrote about the advantage that American blacks have over American whites in that black people never bought the myths that white folk use to brainwash themselves, like the idea that "[t]heir ancestors were all freedom-loving heroes, that they were born in the greatest country the world has ever seen, or that Americans are invincible in battle and wise in peace, that Americans have always dealt honorably with Mexicans and Indians and all other neighbors and inferiors, that American men are the world's most direct and virile, that American women are pure."[17] These myths bespeak a people of almost impossible dignity and poise, who flee into an empty wilderness to escape cruelty, deal fairly with the few backward savages in the forests, and resort to violence only when given no choice. As Rich points out, these historical recollections are designed to be as sweet as possible; they are easy to swallow but offer no real nourishment. Rich's alimentary metaphor also echoes the sort of analysis we see when we look at this historical detachment through Du Bois or Dewey.

For Du Bois, what white folk lack is a clear-eyed, past-looking Janus face. Where black Americans generally live their present and future in light of their relationship to their racial history whether they like it or not, many white folk live their present and future according to stories that encourage the feeling that white folk are the best in the world, that there is nothing at all to be ashamed of in white history, and above all, that we don't need to even think about race because racism officially ended in the 1960s. This is the stubborn rejection of the truth that he sees at work in white pathology. What he would counsel is for this past face of whiteness not to look at the pleasant tapestry we are shown, but to take a wider view that includes the disturbing and painful history of how whiteness came into being. It is a history that would cause us to strive toward different futures than the ones toward which we now reach. David Ingram summarizes the present and ongoing ill effects of this lack of historical connection on the part of white Americans:

> Because whites disingenuously deny or remain insensitive to this history—of the actual extent of present discrimination, the institutional effect of past discrimination, and of the cumulative assets that have disproportionately accrued to generations of whites through wage discrimination—what is intended as an affirmative action aimed at "leveling the playing field" appears to them as nothing more than reverse discrimination. Maintaining this deception, however, requires entering into bad faith and, even worse, caricaturing minority beneficiaries as "unqualified" on the face of it; thereby fabricating a new kind of minstrel show replete with comic stereotypes.[18]

The Deweyan response I see to the critiques by people like Rich and Du Bois would be to sublimate the *impulse of emptiness* through what I call *the habit of shame.* This sense of shame is not merely the feeling of having done something wrong, though this negative feeling is part of this habit. To have shame in the sense that I mean is to accept when you've done wrong and to take responsibility for it. In this case white folks would do well to cultivate habits of shame that would enable us to see through the glib panacea that racism ended forty years ago and come to terms with the history of how ideas and habits of whiteness separated us from other members of the American and human community, gave us unfair economic and political privileges, and caused unimaginable suffering for others. The purpose of this habit of shame is not to engage in masochistic self-hatred: it is a way of realizing what *actually* happened in our nation's past and of seeing how this shameful past lives on in a way that, once seen for what it is, very few white folks would want to continue.

"Shame" is a highly flexible term that can fairly be taken to mean many things. What I mean by shame is not self-loathing. The sense of shame to which I refer is a consciousness of impropriety or wrongdoing, in either the actual past or a possible future. One of the best instances of this sort of virtuous, responsible shame is found in the Homeric poem *The Iliad.* One of this work's greatest gifts is its juxtaposition of the Trojan hero Hector and the Achaean captain Achilles. Achilles, though beautiful, brave, and semi-divine, is selfish. When Agamemnon tells him to relinquish his war prize, he is offended and removes himself from the field. While he was well within his rights according to the strictures of the warrior code to not fight when he was denied his prize, or *geras,* that was a physical sign of his honor, or *time,* in so doing he forgot his obligations to his fellow Greeks. He left his own men, the Myrmidons, to spoil on the beaches while his fellow Greeks were butchered a spear-throw away before the walls of Troy. He forgot about the sacrifice of the last ten years that all the Greeks made, all because he had his pride wounded by a lesser man. Much of the poem's tension comes from seeing how shameless selfishness leads the greatest warrior of the age to rot in his tent for almost the entirety of the epic poem. He is jarred from his self-centered sulking only by the death of his beloved Patroclus; he learns too late the dear cost of living without shame, and descends into inhuman and grotesque brutality.

Hector, unlike his counterpart Achilles, never forgets his obligations and relationships. He does not forget because he is the shameful hero: he is, I think, the true hero of the epic because he is frequently referred to as a man driven by a sense of shame, or *aidos* in Greek. In book six, Hector has a conversation with his wife, Andromache, that is the literary archetype for the scene where the hero must leave his loved ones and face death for the greater good. We do not see a hero who swaggers off to war while his wife happily waves goodbye. We see instead real human beings who would fit as easily in our time as they do in Homer's. We see a woman who loves her husband and begs him not to face a nearly certain death at Achilles' hand, and a man rent by his competing obligations to protect his family and to protect all of Troy. This moment is made more powerful by the fact that we have a palpable sense of their genuine love for each other as well as certain knowledge that Hector will die. However, even though they both seem to know that Hector will seal his fate if he defends Troy, his sense of shame compels him to do what he must. After Andromache paints a grim portrait of the futility of standing against Achilles, Hector answers, "All these things are in my mind also, lady; yet I would feel deep shame before the Trojan women with trailing garments, if like a coward I were to shrink aside from the fighting."[19] This same sense of shame leads Hector to even be kind to Helen, someone the other Trojans find all too easy to despise as the purported cause of the Greek siege on Troy. He is kind to her because he knows that it would be shameful to shirk his duty as a host. What is most important in this example is not that shame makes him at one point go to battle and at another be kind to a stranger in a strange land. What matters is that it shows how a proper sense of shame militates against the selfishness that corrodes any social fabric by encouraging the individual to live not just in the individual moment, but as a moral agent with debts to the past, to the future, and, above all, to his or her community.

This story illustrates the distinction that I draw between the *habit of guilt* and the *habit of shame.* By guilt I mean the feeling of sickness that comes in this case from the realization of the horrors that have been wrought in the name of whiteness. It is a feeling that not only doesn't help right these wrongs, but often makes them worse. Such a response does not improve the situation or heal the wound. However, this is not the sort of exchange that Du Bois sees in the promise of race consciousness. Instead, it is simply one more act of taking. It is the dangerous habit of whiteness most frequently seen on the American Left among people who see the long trail of tears that has followed the legalized and institutionalized practices of whiteness but don't know what to do about it. It encourages the kind of forgetfulness that Rich and Du Bois associate with whiteness. It is the attempt to get away from an act of injustice by either pretending to not see race or taking someone else's traditions unjustly. I agree with Shannon Sullivan's analysis of this danger on the part of well-intentioned white folk who try to opt out of whiteness by taking on someone else's racial identity:

> Attempting to take on another race is just as problematic as attempting to shed one's whiteness, albeit in different ways. Attempting to take on another race, including the habits of lived spatiality characteristic of that race, might seem like an expression of a white person's respect for people of color and non-white lived experience. But it often is merely another example of white people's assumption that any and all spaces, whether geographical/physical or rhetorical/cultural, are open for white people to legitimately move about in. To see black and other non-white spaces as places for white people to decide they may properly inhabit is to appropriate those places in a gesture that is much closer to colonialism than one of respect.[20]

To further illustrate this distinction between guilt and shame, we can recall the words of Gloria Anzaldúa from *Borderlands/ La Frontera.* When she offers her suggestion about what white folk need to do to address the problem of white racism, she says:

> We need to say to white society: We need you to accept the fact that Chicanos are different, to acknowledge your rejection and negation of us. We need you to own the fact that you looked upon us as less than human, that you stole our lands, our personhood, our self-respect. We need you to make public restitution: to say that, to compensate for your own sense of defectiveness, you strive for power over us, you erase our history and our experience because it makes you feel guilty—you'd rather forget your brutish acts.[21]

We saw how the *habit of guilt* responds to the history of white racism by mini-mizing the person's feeling of being connected to that history. Since we can't erase the horrid history of whiteness, which we usually learn late in life after the triumphalist history has already shaped our worldview, we run from it. As Margo Thunderbird described, white folk acting through a habit of guilt re-spond to the impulse of emptiness by stealing other people's cultural traditions. People acting on guilt also take an almost masochistic attitude about their own political past. They are right to see the horrors of the past and the extent to which our nation was shaped largely through an unfair and anti-democratic notion of white supremacy. However, they take this too far by denying them-selves the opportunity to find anything salutatory in our collective history. Most importantly, they do not sufficiently recover and integrate these painful experiences into a melioristic reconstruction of the present situation.

The *impulse of emptiness* that drives the *habit of guilt* would be better chan-neled into what I call *habits of shame*. The *habit of shame* tries to fill the lack by making whole what was torn apart in the history of whiteness. The *habit of shame* is the attempt to live up to the demands of history. It does not stop at the pointless and dangerous level of guilt. It instead takes the feeling of emptiness and fills it with concrete steps to make the past whole. It is the effort to be ac-countable as Rich describes it. In Deweyan terms, it recovers past experiences that offer crucial insight into our present problems. It also leads the individual to better see the need to think and act on behalf of community. What I call the *habit of shame* is an attempt to live through history in the way described by James Baldwin's classic essay "White Man's Guilt" when he wrote:

> History, as nearly no one seems to know, is not merely something to be read. And it does not refer merely, or even principally, to the past. On the contrary, the great force of history comes from the fact that we carry it within us, are unconsciously controlled by it in many ways, and history is literally *present* in all we do. It could scarcely be otherwise, since it is to history that we owe our frames of reference, our identities and our aspirations.[22]

In *Achieving Our Country,* Rorty writes about Dewey's secular and meliorist re-imagining of the Judeo-Christian idea of sin as committing an act that nor-mally we would rather die than commit. Rorty then asks us to "suppose that one has in fact done one of the things one could not have imagined doing, and finds that one is still alive. At that point, one's choices are suicide, a life of bottomless self-disgust, and an attempt to live so as never to do such a thing again. Dewey recommends the third choice. He thinks you should remain an agent, rather than either committing suicide or becoming a horrified spectator of your own past."[23]

Now the situation with the habits of whiteness is different from particular immoral acts. I didn't orchestrate the Trail of Tears, and I can't get my head around the magnitude of the pain and suffering it wrought or the fact that my comfortable middle-class life was made possible only by access to land soaked in Native tears and blood. However, for me to figuratively flagellate myself as an expression of self-disgust would be as pointless, fruitless, and narcissistic as the medieval Christians who literally flagellated themselves over the sexual thoughts that disgusted them. The habit of guilt is to wallow in self-disgust: the habit of shame is to see this disgusting past and then "live so as never to do such a thing again."

The quote above from Anzaldúa directs us toward the *habit of shame* when she demands that we "own the fact that you looked upon us as less than human, that you stole our lands, our personhood, our self-respect." More concretely still, she demands that we "make public restitution," or restore the human bond between Chicanos and white Americans that was severed by the ideas and habits of whiteness. She is unsatisfied with the fact that some white folk feel guilty at what was done to Chicanos. What the situation calls out for is an attempt to fix the rupture that gives rise to feelings of guilt in the first place. Rather than run from the disturbing history of whiteness or try to cover over the discomfort that comes from studying it, we need to take this feeling of lack and use it to spur us on to change things here and now.

So what would be the cash value of a habit of shame? The primary value would be for white folks to have enough shame to not play the victim when we've actually received so many unwarranted privileges and to stop impeding programs designed to correct age-old inequalities separating different communities. If we had this sense of shame, we could remember for ourselves and remind others that those of us who've made it to the middle or upper class have done so in large part due to legalized white privileges enjoyed by our parents and grandparents. We could realize for ourselves and remind others that one of the main benefits of whiteness is a freedom to use one's labor and assets to improve one's economic status that has been and still is denied many people of color. We could realize for ourselves and remind others that all white immigrants enjoyed a legal status far greater than any tiebreaking benefit conferred by any affirmative action or public school integration program. It is shameless of white folk to decry modest political programs like affirmative action or diversification in the public and private sector because such acts ignore the extent to which all white folk benefit economically, politically, and socially from whiteness. Cheryl Harris describes in her groundbreaking essay "Whiteness as Property" the privileges that the habits of shame would enable us to remember and correct.

> Within the worlds of de jure and de facto segregation, whiteness has value, whiteness is valued, and whiteness is expected to be valued in law. The legal affirmation of whiteness and white privilege allowed expectations that originated in injustice to be naturalized and legitimated. The relative economic, political, and social advantages dispensed to whites under systematic white supremacy in the United States were reinforced through patterns of oppression of Blacks and Native Americans. Materially, these advantages became institutionalized privileges, and ideologically, they became part of the settled expectations of whites—a product of the unalterable original bargain.[24]

Appropriate shame would "denaturalize" the injustices suffered by native people regarding issues of land, sacred artifacts, and religious sites. The habits of whiteness led Europeans to see as justified the theft of Native lands, even lands protected by treaties between tribes and the federal government. Where I live now in eastern Washington the arrival of whites was so recent that many of these injustices come from the not-so-distant past, and could and should be remedied. For example, two historians of the Inland Northwest, Helen Boots and Guy Boudia, raised the alarm regarding the destruction of an ancient burial ground south of Cheney, Washington, that held the remains of not only Native people but also early European settlers to the region. The mounds were all leveled in 1990 as part of a logging operation, despite a 1989 law that protected Native burial grounds from desecration. Further, Boudia was able to document that the burial ground was mentioned in historical records at least as far back as 1824. If we forget all about the past and stick to the language of the free market and individual property rights, the leaser of the land, Shannon Sanderson, was well within his rights to extract the resources from lands to which he had legal access. Instead, he should be ashamed that he put his own private interests over the need to show respect for the dead. However, the state also acted without shame since "no enforcement action was taken" to stop the logging even though Helen Boots recalls that she and others living near the burial ground knew about it and respected its boundaries back when she was a girl in the 1920s.[25] Kevin Graman reports that correcting this sort of injustice seems to be a low priority for the Democratic-dominated state legislature, since, "[i]n the Washington Legislature's most recent session, Sen. Mary Margaret Haugen, D-Camano Island, introduced a bill to protect Native American and pioneer grave sites, but it died without being brought to a floor vote."[26]

The habit of shame would encourage us to see these injustices that the habits of whiteness have long rendered invisible. It would lead us to recover, accept, and integrate politically relevant experiences that stem from the history of whiteness. It would show us that this idea of an intellectually superior and morally blessed white race led to laws and economic policies that were wantonly unfair. This habit would correct our inability to see whiteness in the present by showing us not only how unfair it was in the past, but also how normative it seemed in each age. A proper sense of shame would cause white folks to want to participate in projects designed to correct these injustices and would get us wise to politicians and demagogues who would have white folks believe that immigrants or people of color, rather than the tiny few who control media, government, and commerce, are their political enemies.

Habits of Remembrance

History also plays a fundamental role in terms of how we can better integrate the *impulse of pride* into our behavior in a way that steers clear of the problem seen in the habit of entitlement. This aspect of the reconstruction of whiteness is particularly thorny, as the idea of "white pride" is still a rallying call for white supremacists in this country. As a consequence, it might seem impossible to find a way for white people to be proud of their cultural past without simultaneously fanning the flames of racism. If whiteness is an inherently violent identity that emerged at a time when Europeans found it convenient to reify themselves as a group that was different from and superior to non-Europeans, how can current white folks be proud of their race? Where can we find the gift to give to others in order to form from this exchange the sorts of bonds of friendship and kinship that must be present in any real community? To go back to the introduction, I think our failure to answer these sorts of questions motivated the defiant question asked by two of my students: "So, do they let white crackers like us come to these meetings?" Many white folks will look askance at efforts to build a community more respectful and appreciative of diversity until we envision a way for white people to be full participants in, and not just truculent observers of, these sorts of efforts.

Rorty again offers us some useful insight on the issue of pride. Writing from the issue of national pride, he argues: "Like every other country, ours has a lot to be proud of and a lot to be ashamed of. But a nation cannot reform itself unless it takes pride in itself—unless it has an identity, rejoices in it, reflects upon it and tries to live up to it. Such pride sometimes takes the form of arrogant, bellicose nationalism. But it often takes the form of a yearning to live up to the nation's professed ideals."[27] It is not hard to see the compatibility between what Rorty says about national pride and what Du Bois says about racial pride. In both cases, the individual needs to feel part of a larger whole that is worthy of pride. The trick here is to find a vehicle for this pride that is free of the arrogance and cruelty that long has manifested through the habit of entitlement.

As mentioned above, the answer again lies with history. More precisely, white people need to look for the things of which to be proud inside the cracks in the history of whiteness. Said differently, white folk need to find their source of pride in the polyvalent truth beneath the façade of uniform whiteness. Just as we need to cultivate *habits of shame* to see the ways that whiteness led to great suffering for people defined as not white and unwarranted privileges for people who were defined as white, we also need *habits of remembrance* that will connect us to a more vivid past that would offer the sort of cultural sustenance that Du Bois called the gift of race.

Recall from the brief look at the history of whiteness in the first section of this book that whiteness is an identity predicated on exclusion. According to the rules fabricated in the seventeenth century, if one drop of non-white blood mixes with white blood, the person becomes entirely not white. This is because the idea of whiteness that frames the habits of whiteness assumes superiority and purity. In turn, white pride is necessarily a negative and exclusionary pride. The same person who, while still in their home country in Europe, might have taken pride in a positive, contentful identity ("I am proud to be a Dubliner" or "I am proud to be Sicilian") was encouraged by a powerful economic and legal incentive to think of himself as white, and thus develop a pride in *not* being black, Native, Asian, or Latino. What we need to remember is that every person who is now white has, somewhere in the stretch of history, a history or set of histories that either predate the invention of whiteness or offer the sort of life-sustaining value that whiteness lacks. If we go back far enough or look carefully enough, we can find a culture and a history that is predicated on *particular memories and particular experiences,* and not on the exclusion of others.

A key task in subverting white racism is the fragmentation of whiteness itself. There is an "us" inside white people only in two regards. First, we all either adjusted, to some greater or lesser degree, to become white or descend from people who did. For Protestant, upper- and middle-class Anglo-Americans, the adjustment was minimal. For Eastern European, Italian, and Jewish immigrants, the adjustment was much greater and more difficult. However, all people now considered "white" descended from people who had to perform identity-surgery or went through it themselves if they were immigrants. The second thing that we share is that we all inherit a common legacy of benefiting from white privilege. Just as the millions of people from dozens of African civilizations were forged into one African American people by the pressures of the Middle Passage, slavery, and racist violence, an equally diverse range of European immigrants became one "white race" by the common act of historical self-censorship and social and political privilege. The only way to end our common, undemocratic social privilege is to make the idea of one white race untenable. We need to do this not only because it is the right thing morally and aesthetically, but for the sake of the sort of vibrant and flourishing human community that we individually need in order to prosper and grow. This reconstruction is in the interest of white Americans because it will help us to forge the kind of broad community we all need and give us a deeper and more meaningful connection to culture and history.

We can channel the impulse of pride away from its exceptionalist and patriarchal stories that Du Bois and Rich rightly criticize— toward new, more complex sociocultural identities. We need to recover the race gifts about which Du Bois wrote—the practices, memories, stories, and crafts that sustain a people, pass down meaning through generations, and connect the individual to a larger whole—however, we need to look for these gifts outside the pale of whiteness, per se. In order to address the problem of whiteness, we need to find a way to decolonize the minds of white Americans, by asserting the differences within whiteness. This in turn will help facilitate a greater recognition of human equality by eliminating the exclusionary dynamic within whiteness.

In "*Hablando cara a cara/* Speaking Face to Face" María Lugones offers a distinction that proves salient to our discussion. She points out that a genuine and even fierce pride in one's people or heritage need not be racist.

"Ah, how beautiful my people (or my culture, or my community, or my land), how beautiful, the most beautiful!" I think this claim is made many times non-comparatively. It is expressive of the centrality that one's people, culture, community or language have to the subject's sense of self and her web of connections. It expresses her fondness for them. In these cases, the claim does not mean "better than other people's," but "dearer to me than other people's communities, etc., are to me." [. . .] Similar claims are made many times comparatively and invidiously and I think that *only then* are they ethnocentric.[28]

Lugones's insight reiterates the need to find the best vehicle for this feeling of pride in order to remedy our current habits of whiteness. White Americans must carefully develop a responsible pride in their own cultural particularities without relying on racial exclusion. Of course, this does not need to degenerate into ethnic factionalism, whereby one tries to live out all one's different ethnicities down to the thirty-seconds and sixty-fourths. Instead, I here suggest the sort of recovery that Du Bois and Rich see as essential to selfhood: a recovery that, accepting it might be impossible to recover every moment and strand of one's cultural past, strives to recover enough that one has a rich enough sense of history that steels against the dangers of amnesia and nostalgia. Not only will these multiple, non-antagonistic identities offer more compatible alternatives than practices borrowed from other cultural traditions, but they will serve to disintegrate the racial dualities that enable white racial oppression and violence. By learning to have pride in our traditions, while engaging in a contextualization of our location within structures of class, gender, and race, white Americans can begin to decolonize our minds and participate more fairly in our democracy.

One of the works that best exemplify what I call the habit of remembrance comes from a very unusual source. The book is a cultural history of the Scots-Irish in America by the Vietnam War veteran, assistant secretary of the Navy for Ronald Reagan, and now Democratic senator for Virginia, James Webb. His work, *Born Fighting,* is motivated by many of the same insights that drive me to understand whiteness and strive to recover pre-white cultural histories that are hardly panaceas to our current problems, but are crucial tools for achieving a pluralistic racial community. While I agree with and celebrate a great many of his observations and claims in so far as they show the importance of pride and remembrance, his work also illustrates the difficulties in establishing habits of remembrance as well as the need to balance a healthy form of pride with a somber recollection of the shameful moments that led to white privilege.

Webb's work offers as clear an illustration as any of how white folk ought to manifest habits of remembrance. Even though he offers an uncharitable reading of multicultural initiatives, he does have a clear sense that he inherits not some vague Euro-mishmash, but a particular culture with a particular history: "The contributions of [Scots-Irish] culture are too great to be forgotten as America rushes forward into yet another redefinition of itself. And in a society obsessed with multicultural jealousies, those who cannot articulate their ethnic origins are doomed to a form of social and political isolation. My culture needs to rediscover itself, and in so doing to regain its power to shape the direction of America."[29] He also chafes against the idea that all white people are all part of the same WASP culture when he writes that "many of the most literate observers of American culture tend to lump the Scots-Irish in with the largely English-derivative New England Protestant groups and the original English settlers of the vast Virginia colony as 'WASPs' . . . under the rubric of 'British' ancestry. But these were, and are, distinctly separate and different peoples."[30] Most importantly, he has a pride in the Scots-Irish that is not only thoroughly genuine, but I think in line with the sort of pride that Lugones asks us to develop:

> This people gave our country great things, including its most definitive culture. Its bloodlines have flowed in the veins of at least a dozen presidents, and in many of our greatest soldiers. It created and still perpetuates the most distinctly American form of music. It is imbued with a unique and unforgiving code of personal honor, less ritualized but every bit as powerful as the samurai code. Its legacy is broad, in many ways defining the attitudes and values of the military, of working-class America, and even of the peculiarly populist form of American democracy itself. And yet its story has been lost under the weight of more recent immigrations, revisionist historians, and common ignorance.[31]

However, as keen and insightful as Webb is in many ways, he still manifests the habit of entitlement, with all its aggrieved feelings and combativeness. This is most notable whenever he turns his attention to issues of racial interaction, though it needs to be said that Webb is still laudable on this point to an extent since he clearly speaks honestly about race, which is better than most white people, and perhaps all other white politicians, can say.

Whenever he talks about race, he paints the Scots-Irish only as victims of political correctness. When talking about the issue of slavery and recent controversies over the Confederacy and the Confederate flag he writes, "This blatant use of the 'race card' in order to inflame their political and academic constituencies is a tired, seemingly endless game that is itself perhaps the greatest legacy of the Civil War's aftermath."[32] I agree with Senator Webb when he makes the case that rank-and-file Confederate soldiers were largely fighting to protect their homes against an invading army and that there were heroes and villains on both sides. I also commend his genuine desire to remember the past. However, he is committing the straw man fallacy when he says that talking about race and racism is really just playing the "race card" for political effect. This elides the fact, carefully documented by Du Bois and uncountable numbers of others, that white people, even poor, property-less people like many of the Scot-Irish, benefited—economically, socially, politically, and legally—from institutionalized white supremacism, even if they didn't actually own slaves.

Webb is also uniformly dismissive of our "obsession with multicultural jealousies" and scoffs at the idea that Scots-Irish may have benefited unjustly from white supremacist laws, ideas, or practices, even as he matter-of-factly writes, "[T]he Scots-Irish settlers were indeed restless, as if their natural makeup demanded turmoil. They showed no hesitation in pushing into Indian territory and settling on lands claimed by tribal chiefs."[33] He later falls into a fairly typical stereotype of paining Indians as dangerous savages when he cites repeatedly the need for Scots-Irish pioneers to take great steps to protect themselves from vicious native war parties: "In many mountain areas, 'blockhouse' forts were built on centrally located farms, where the settlers could gather in order to defend themselves from attack. Attacked they were, war parties sometimes carrying away women and children as prizes."[34] While it is doubtless the case that these immigrants faced challenges from Native peoples in the region, it should not surprise him or anyone else that people fought back hard when their land was invaded by people who were, as Webb himself titles his book, born fighting! It is surprising to read, however, only about Native war parties abducting European women and children and not about European violence on Native civilians, or indeed the concerted acts of genocide such as massive removal of Native peoples orchestrated by the federal government under Webb's favorite Scots-Irishman, Andrew Jackson. This sense that many white folk have, that we are the victims and that people who try to correct our nation's history of legalized and brutally enforced white supremacism are the bad guys, is palpable in Webb's work and stands as an illustration of why we need to engage the problem of whiteness at the level of habits and ideas in addition to maintaining the economic and social changes initiated in the 1960s.

Interestingly enough, Webb actually writes about the dangerous propensity of people who have been taught to think of themselves as white and are treated as white under the law to claim for themselves unfair privileges. He even uses the same terms that I use here. When he aptly decries the system of southern chattel slavery, he writes, "What had been created through the extension of the plantation system into the Deep South and Mississippi River basin was not the idyllic, Tara-like antebellum gentility that one finds in wistful novels such as *Gone with the Wind,* but instead a rapacious system based on a false sense of entitlement that looked condescendingly on whites and blacks alike."[35] I commend Webb for doing excellent work on recovering the gift of experience that Du Bois links to race and Dewey links to culture, while also urging him to more fully explore the extent to which he (like me, like almost all people raised to think of ourselves as white) is still operating according to the habits of entitlement.

Habits of Compassion

Finally, we need to redirect the impulse of antipathy behind the *habit of antipathy to the strange.* A pragmatist analysis of Bacon's Rebellion indicates that the era *after* this event witnessed a change in harnessing this impulse. Before the rebellion, the laborers showed antipathy against both the colony elites and the indigenous people. After the rebellion, the laws fostered a feeling of distrust between "Negro" and "Mullato" workers on the one hand, and those defined as "white" or "Christian" on the other. In a matter of a few years, these legal and social categories changed the direction of the antipathy felt by the European Virginian laborers. These new habits of antipathy were so well entrenched by the nineteenth century that immigrants from Ireland, many of whom were members of an oppressed class in their home country, rather than finding solidarity with African Americans who were near them at the bottom of the social hierarchy in America chose instead to adopt these habits of exclusion, and acted on them with horrific violence in 1863.

In order to correct this still-functioning habit, white folks first need to be *aware* of whatever feelings of antipathy they might feel toward other people and then find another conduit for these feelings. Instead of *habits of antipathy to the strange,* I suggest we should cultivate *habits of antipathy to suffering,* or more succinctly, *habits of compassion.* If Dewey is right to say these impulses cannot be gotten rid of, and that we must instead sublimate them, or more intelligently, incorporate them into our lives, then we need to find a way to teach white folk (and indeed all folk) to revile not each other, but each other's pain. On the one hand, this reconstruction takes hold of the impulse that is most tightly connected to the most problematic aspect of racism: the aversion that drives a wedge between people. On the other hand, it takes this impulse and seeks to harness it in a way that heals the wound that the idea of racial superiority numbed: the social and psychological wound caused by cruelty. The cruelty was rationalized in many false ways: we can kill them because they are mere savages, we can enslave them because they are animals, we can deny them equal rights and human dignity because they are not enlightened or legal citizens. Yet this wound affects both the socially dominant group and the socially dominated groups and impedes our ability to realize a healthy community.

Here I am really only suggesting that this racialized dimension of our lives follow the pragmatist re-imagining of ethics and moral philosophy of the last two decades that was well articulated by Richard Rorty and others when they asked us as philosophers and people to think less about objectivity and much more about solidarity.[36] Habits of antipathy to the strange throw up barriers between people that prevent human community. Habits of antipathy to human suffering humanize us to each other, and remind us that the human community requires that we overcome the brute animal instinct to avoid our own pain, to realize that noble human potential of enduring pain for the sake of the other. John Stuhr, in his work *Genealogical Pragmatism,* well describes our need to overcome these divisions in order to realize true community when he writes:

> As long as actual social conditions produce and reproduce selves with economic, political, religious, ethnic, racial, familial, environmental, technological, and sex-

ual interests and powers that are in fundamental conflict with one another, neither actual community nor ideal self-extension is possible. . . . It is now the task of education in the broadest sense to identify, to radically resist, and to begin to alter these continuing conditions that block community and intimacy and foster domination and opposition. Philosophers, if they are to be philosophers of community, must accept this task.[37]

The main question here is how can we habituate ourselves to not militate against people and traditions we take as strange, but instead to militate against human pain and suffering, no matter the place of origin or native language of the person in pain, in order to establish a living community? A Deweyan answer would be to cultivate what I call *habits of compassion.*

This use of habit and impulse is also compatible with many of the other approaches to questions of race we have seen so far. What unites people like Outlaw, Sullivan, Ignatiev, Zack, and Appiah? They all respond to the questions of race and the problems of racism using very different, sometimes divergent, methods. Nonetheless, they all share the belief that the history of racism was egregious and it needs to be remedied. All these theorists want to solve the problem of racism and philosophize as an attempt to imagine a solution. The solution that they seek is not primarily an "academic" one. All of them come to the problem of racism with *passion and compassion:* they want to do what they can to cease the human suffering caused by racism and assure that it will not rear up again. They all take on these issues because they have seen or experienced the negative effects of this idea and these habits, and they seek to right an injustice. By educating people to feel revulsion at injustice and cruelty, we use impulse as an aid in the attempt to reconnect that which was torn apart by the exclusionary aspect of whiteness.

To reconnect this chapter with the Deweyan framework, the engagement with the history that writers like Du Bois, Rich, Anzaldúa, and Lugones write about when they describe the problem of whiteness would change our current concept of whiteness, whiteness-as-kind in particular. Engagement with such a history would force us to see that we inherit a kind that is very different from the politically neutral kind we might like whiteness to be. Where amnesia and the wishful thinking of race-blindness leads white folk to think that we are treated just the same as everyone else and we therefore have no more or less responsibility to fight social injustice, this inquiry into the history of whiteness changes our understanding of whiteness as a kind. It enables us to see that whiteness describes not a politically inert group of people, but a group of people who have benefited economically, socially, and politically from the accident of history and morphology. It emphasizes that we *now* enjoy standards of living that are what they are due largely to these habits of whiteness. It emphasizes that white people all descend from people who received powerful, legally established, and violently defended privileges that still affect our lives. While most white folk, especially younger white folk, did not ask for these privileges and would likely wish them gone, wishing alone won't wash them away. As Rich says, we are all accountable for our action or inaction regarding existing systems of racism.

This change in whiteness-as-kind affects how we comport ourselves toward whiteness, or whiteness-as-category. In the current climate where anti-racism is more and more associated with race-blindness, whiteness-as-category has less and less meaning. That is, a colorblind response assumes that one should be disposed toward white people just the same as toward people of any race. This assumes that the best way to achieve racial justice is to minimize the significance of race. However, an inquiry into whiteness that modifies whiteness-as-kind leads us to say that whiteness *is not* the same as other races. In light of the fact that laws that targeted people of color for abuse and granted white people unfair privileges were deemed just at the time, we know that we need to treat whiteness-as-category with special scrutiny. In particular, we need to be cognizant of how the concepts and habits of whiteness can seem so natural and warranted that they can foster racist practices without our seeing it. This is why a pragmatist engagement with the problems of racism would counsel against a colorblind approach in lieu of an approach that tries to correct racism by seeing race. Shannon Sullivan says this well when she writes:

> Even though colorblindness usually is intended as a strategy for the elimination of racism and white domination, it actually tends to fuel and be fueled by white privileged habits. Colorblindness attempts to erase all race and make it invisible: "I don't see race, I just see people." Habits of white privilege support these attempts by making the invisibility of race seem like the goal that all people should aim for. Whiteness and its concomitant privileges tend to operate as invisible, and since whiteness is the standard to which all should aspire, then people of color too should aspire to give up their race and become race-free (=white). The colorblindness that results in turn fuels habits of white privilege by creating a social, political, and psychological atmosphere of racial invisibility in which white privilege can thrive. It is as if, with their style of hidden invisibility, habits of white privilege provide ready-made grooves for colorblindness to slide into, and those grooves in turn are deepened as colorblindness grows.[38]

Once we see how whiteness has been and remains so problematic in terms of its deleterious effects on community and justice, we need to treat whiteness as something that needs to be changed. This inquiry, which is reconstructing the concept of whiteness, leads us to pay particular attention to the habits of whiteness in order to address the problem of whiteness. We need to *lay claim* to whiteness as a kind (to say, "yes, I take responsibility as a white person for the fact that I inherit certain political advantages to which I am not entitled") even as we need to *reject* traditional whiteness as a category (or say, "I will not think of myself as someone who is entitled to special privileges in the way that white people did for centuries"). By accepting whiteness-as-kind we accept the historical responsibility that amnesia deadens. This is not a claim that says, "whiteness is a fixed biological category" in the ways that taxonomists thought it was. Instead, it is a way of organizing our experience that will help us achieve an end. The end is a resolution to the problem of whiteness. Claiming whiteness-as-kind is a means of countering the invisibility of whiteness that stems from its habitual aspect. By rejecting it as a category, we recognize the habitual tendency to still treat white people as better than and different from non-whites, in order to stop it from continuing. Instead, we need to establish new categories, new ways of comporting ourselves toward people now considered white. In time, these new categories would engender new kinds, and new habits. If we conduct our inquiry carefully enough, openly enough, and with a wide range of voices, the new concepts and habits that will ultimately replace the current ones will enable us to keep the positive aspects of race that Du Bois urges us to keep, while eliminating the problematic aspects of whiteness. We can overcome the idea of whiteness, and develop (or perhaps reclaim) an identity that is more authentic, biophilic, and democratic.

In the concluding section, I suggest how white Americans might reconstruct whiteness by exploring how I have been trying to reconstruct my racist habits into ones more compassionate, healthy, and democratic. As I can speak only from my experience and limited point of view, I will use the resources more available to me in my attempt to reconstruct whiteness. These resources will draw on parts of history that are of particular relevance to *my* relationship to whiteness, just as each person must draw on their own histories and resources to reconstruct their own problematic habits.

However, I want to conclude this chapter with an example of what I mean by habits of antipathy to suffering that is a bit afield from the specific issue of whiteness. Suffering is odd in that it is radically subjective in some regards (since I can never know how much pain my daughter is in when I inevitably hit a snag while brushing her hair, or how much my wife was in while she gave birth to our daughter), but also totally objective and undeniable in others (even though I can't feel the pain of childbirth, I *know* it hurts a hell of a lot). Compassionate people are people who use their own memories of their own personal and subjective pain to goad themselves out of their own potentially selfish lives to give care and support to others whose pain they cannot feel but yet know. While it is impossible and counterproductive to play the "whose suffering is the worst" game, I will venture that the people who have it the worst on planet Earth right now are the African people of Sudan living in the region of Darfur.

Black African Darfurians are being subjected to a vicious and well-coordinated genocide by their own government. Many people do nothing out of apathy or lack of resources. Others do worse than nothing: they actually continue to work with the governing regime for the sake of profit. Our government did the right thing when it took to the floor of the United Nations to decry what is happening in Sudan as genocide. Nonetheless, beyond anemic trade sanctions, our government has done very little. One reason for this has to do with the fact the government of Darfur has provided information on Al Qaeda, which may or may not be useful, in return for our inaction on the genocide in Darfur. In other words, our government thinks it wise to turn a blind eye to the suffering in Darfur in order to win Sudan's help in winning "the war on Terror."[39] They think this wise even though the Sudanese regime harbored Al Qaeda for five years and are proven liars who still deny that they are orchestrating genocide. Dwelling on our own horrid loss and pain from 9/11, we withhold help for those experiencing a 9/11 every day for years.

Not all Westerners are so hard-hearted. Particularly those who remember the pain of the Holocaust are raising the alarm now. These people of great conscience, like those who work for and with the U.S. Holocaust Memorial Museum, don't ask, "What's in this for me?" as the Bush State Department does. They ask, "How could we sit idly by while this happens *again*?" Jews and others affected by it are forced to remember the Holocaust as one of the defining experiences of their group. They draw the connection between inaction in the 1930s and inaction now. They take steps to honor the memory of those lost then by saving those in peril now.[40] They do so not just for the sake of identity or for sacred and cultural reasons. They remember to make sense of the present and to make whole the world. What is happening now in Darfur is the same as what happened in central Europe in the 1930s in terms of pain. The fact that the first tragedy involved people living in Europe and the second involves people living in Sub-Saharan Africa is completely irrelevant. As unimaginable as it would seem, the world is forgetting and ignoring. But people who remember the Holocaust use their memory of their group's pain to despise and act out against the pain of distant people in the present. It is not easy to put someone else's pain on par with your own. These people and others like them show us that it is not only possible, but essential for the realization of a sane world and true human community.

Conclusion
Gifts beyond the Pale

Those who hope to persuade a nation to exert itself need to remind
their country of what it can take pride in as well as what it should be
ashamed of. They must tell inspiring stories about episodes and figures
in the nation's past—episodes and figures to which the country should
remain true. Nations rely on artists and intellectuals to create images
of, and to tell stories about, the national past.

Richard Rorty, *Achieving Our Country*

I have been working on this scholarly project, on and off, for the last ten years,
and I have been thinking about race and whiteness ever since my return to the
States at age fourteen made being white seem awfully weird to me. Nonetheless,
I am still trying to figure out how to bring these pieces together—the history,
the gift, the need to balance pride and shame—in order to reconstruct the habits
of whiteness that I live through. Luckily, I entered philosophy late enough to
benefit from educators at Hamilton College and the University of Oregon who
impressed upon me the need to philosophize in the service of humanity with
an eye on class, race, gender, and sexuality. My run of luck brought me to Eastern Washington University, where my exchanges with students and colleagues
reinforce these early lessons daily. Nonetheless, it is sometimes difficult for me
to locate my work inside even this expanded and pluralistic canon of philosophy, what with all this stuff about gift giving, habits, and pride. Perhaps the best
way to connect this atypical work of philosophy with the larger tradition would
be to draw a comparison between it and Richard Rorty's *Achieving Our Coun-*

try, wherein one of the most notable pragmatist philosophers of the last quarter-century writes about achieving our national potential, using much the same language I use to talk about achieving a harmonious and just community across race and ethnicity. While it's obvious that this work pales compared to his, I am trying to do much the same thing that he and other pragmatist philosophers have done and still do: tell inspiring stories that critique the past, give hope for the future, and impart a proper sense of pride and shame.

It should be clear by now that the task of reconstructing a set of habits as ingrained and wide-ranging as those associated with whiteness is not an easy task and that different people will need to work this transmutation differently. One thing that has worked for me is to look at our current problems with racism in America not just through the lenses we find in pragmatist, feminist, and anti-colonialist theory, but also through the perspectives I draw from my family's past, and the histories of the different cultures in which my ancestors were raised. I, like most white Americans, descend from people who themselves came from very different cultures. On my mother's side I have ties to Italy. On my father's side I have ties to the German immigrants called the Pennsylvania Dutch. However, the tradition that was most dominant in my household as a child and in my life as an adult comes from Ireland.

My father's father and my mother's mother were Irish. My father's uncle, Fr. Charles MacMullan S.J., used to tell me in our relatively few conversations about our family's tradition in the Catholic Church, and about how the history of Christianity runs through Ireland before it gets back to Rome.[1] The last time I really talked to him was when I was taking college prep classes at Harvard during the summer between my junior and senior years of high school. Truth be told, I was not excited to spend an afternoon talking to my then frail and stooped great-uncle; I was much more interested in exploring Boston and talking up the young ladies from my classes, since, to a student at an all-male school, female classmates where quite a welcomed novelty. Nonetheless, my dad told me in no uncertain terms that I had no choice. Once I got to the cloister, I could tell this was really important to Father Charlie, and I thankfully had enough sense to pay attention. He was well into his eighties when we spoke, but he still radiated the intellectual energy that is the hallmark of his order, the compassion of a man who spent decades healing people suffering with Hansen's disease (commonly called leprosy), and the toughness of the street kid who brawled on the streets and in the gyms of South Boston. He told me a lot about my family's history: about my grandfather's youth in Belfast, about our family roots in Down Patrick, County Antrim, about relatives who fought for a free Ireland in the IRA, and about ancestors who served their communities through the Catholic Church when all of Ireland was under brutal and genocidal control of the British. My hair stood on end when he told stories about how Irish priests, poets, and singers would keep Irish culture alive by meeting at night, sometimes at ancient pagan sites of worship, to speak Gaelic, play ancient melodies that had been criminalized since the reign of Elizabeth I, and perform weddings, funerals, and baptism, all under threat of execution.

Though he passed on some years ago, the memory of my conversations with him encouraged me to study the history of Christianity in Ireland: about how Christian monks made Ireland the first country to be converted to Christianity without the sword, about how barefoot monks (who hung their precious books on their belts in the way that their warrior fathers displayed their enemy's heads) abolished a system of slavery so pervasive and dehumanizing that the very word for currency, *cumal*, literally meant "slave girl." I was struck by the extent to which Christianity of Ireland in the "Dark Ages" incorporated much of pre-Christian religion: in its calendar, its art, its prayers, and above all, its sacred places.

As I continued these studies they cast new light on experiences I had had when I was younger. For example, when I played football in high school, we would pray a special prayer that we only prayed before a game. It was called "St. Patrick's Breastplate" or "the Lorica." For some reason, we never prayed it in the church. Instead, the chaplain would lead us away from the football field silently, helmets off, into the small fen behind the chapel. There we would kneel on the damp grass as we invoked Saint Patrick's protection over us and the boys on the other team. I was surprised to learn much later this Catholic prayer was written in the much older style of a Celtic pagan prayer of protection. This hybrid prayer now speaks to me of an open and sharing love for both the old Celtic ways and the new Christian ways that was too strong to pick one over the other. It was evidence of gift sharing across two very different traditions that were synthesized into a third one that sustained a long-suffering people through countless hardships. This synthesis was an example of how the early Irish found a way to worship the Christian God through the Son that was largely free of the exclusionary and purity-obsessed concerns that would dominate later Christianity, both Catholic and Protestant. To the contrary, it was a kind of Christianity focused on the urgent need to alleviate suffering in the world, a noble mission to which my uncle and many other relatives dedicated their lives. Our family name, which means "son of the tonsured-one" or "son of the priest," links us to the early Christian clerics of Ireland, who adapted the compassion found in Christian teachings to their native practices, but little of the grief, disgust of the body, and misogyny that detracts so much from the works of early Christian theologians such as Augustine. Even more, his life embodied the motto on our family crest that reminds me of the need to put others first: it reads *Miseris Succurere Disco,* or "I learn to help those in need."

I start this section with this recollection because it is one of the most meaningful examples of the "treasures found in darkness" that Rich urges us to recover and the gift of race the Du Bois wanted us to share.[2] It is the sort of particular and complex relationship to the past that I would lose if I thought of myself as just white. It is the sort of thing that I can be proud of in the way that Lugones says: fiercely and jealously, but without any sense that my particular history is worse or better than anyone else's. Studying these and other family histories helps me direct the impulse of pride that I first felt as a child in Puerto Rico one step removed from the beauty of *lo puertorriqueño* into fruitful habits of remembrance. In fact, it is my love and affection for my family's past that makes me appreciate other people's stories and traditions all the more. They also stir in me a useful compassion for others. It is my anger and sadness over the injustices weathered by long-gone MacMullans, Callahans, Smeriglios, and Schmitts that makes me take action when I see the very same injustice inflicted on immigrants and people of color today for more or less the same narrow, selfish, and xenophobic reasons. The fact that I usually look like the people dishing it out makes me angrier, knowing that if I do nothing they would take me for one of their own.

For example, I claimed in the previous chapter that white folk, especially white liberal folk who feel guilt over being white, should harness the *impulse of emptiness* into *habits of shame* that seek to fill the void caused by whiteness by reestablishing the bonds that were severed both by the exclusionary aspect of whiteness and by the amnesia it fosters. For me, the recollection of the history of how the Irish, Germans, and Italians went from being despised immigrants to mainstream citizens and sometimes sadly to sanctimonious nativists, leads me to have shame enough to know that I should support programs of restitution and support for immigrant families. The recollection of the many nativist movements that have poisoned our communities—some with the Irish, Italians, and Germans as scapegoats, some with the same groups doing the scapegoating—gives me the necessary context to see how this nativism is often a cover for and symptom of economic pressures suffered by a dwindling and pinched middle class. It is pretty much the same trick pulled on the laborers who rebelled against the colonial elite and their lucrative drug operation. For example, in the 1870s the Irish were still despised by proper Yankees in New England as simian mongrels, just as they had been seen as sub-human "wyld Irish" by their English neighbors. Yet, just as white Americans in New England were wringing their hands about a frightful invasion of Irish maids, porters, and ditch-diggers, an Irishman named Denis Kearney was able to form and lead the Workingmen's Party of California that was dedicated to the twin goals of labor rights for white men and the violent expulsion of Chinese immigrants from California.[3] Habits of shame lead me to remember how the habits of whiteness have so easily and so often pitted working folk against each other to the detriment of all. These recollections caution me against taking the xenophobic bait dangling before us now, and encourage me to instead find common cause with my fellow human beings who now brave a gantlet as vicious as or worse than the one my ancestors faced.

The memory of these horrible moments wrought by the idea of a superior white race and its related habits, in particular the awful prejudice faced by my

Irish ancestors in Ireland and in this country, leads me to resist those who would continue to punish immigrant laborers whose entrance into this country might be undocumented but is certainly no more unjust or unethical than the immigration and colonization by waves of European immigrants over the centuries. The habits of whiteness, specifically what I call the habit of entitlement, encourage me to think that this whole country is *mine* by virtue of our manifest destiny and supposedly singular civilization. This is the sense of entitlement that leads Jared Taylor, Representative Tancredo, and the like to castigate the workers whose labor in this country feeds and houses us all. White entitlement encourages me to ignore or elide the suffering of current immigrant families because, supposedly, if my dad could make it to the middle class even though my grandfather Ted came here as an infant carried by his mother, Catherine, in 1912, then so can they. An awareness of white privilege forces me to highlight one crucial fact that is usually ignored in typical white American rags-to-middle-class narratives, namely that while my ancestors did work incredibly hard against very long odds and were indeed looked down on as dogs by other "higher" whites, they were all nonetheless *legal American citizens within a year.* As bad as the Irish (and the Italians, the Jews, the Roma, the Poles) had it, their whiteness gave them nearly automatic rights and privileges that African Americans, Asian Americans, and Latinos would not enjoy for several more decades and that are still largely denied the Native peoples who are too-gracious and long-suffering hosts of this land.

The act of recollecting the shameful history of whiteness helps me better see how economic pressures impact racial conflict. When I see the hypocrisy of a system that *requires* Latin-American labor to maintain U.S. agribusiness and construction and then makes the lives of these same laborers impossible, I see that it was much the same as the hypocrisy of the British ruling class that forced Irish tenants off their ancestral land, only to accuse them of being papist invaders in the Americas. And all this is playing out on land that should still legally belong to Native nations according to treaties with the federal government that have simply been ignored.[4] Most importantly, when I remember that I am the child of a people who faced prejudice, I realize that the only way I can heal the wound that they suffered is to help heal the wound in front of me, here and now. I cannot help my immigrant great-grandmother Catherine MacMullan as she toils in Boston while suffering mistreatment and scorn from white folk who thought themselves her betters, but I can and must be an ally of the woman who is forced to crawl and sneak and swim into this country to find a job to keep her family alive. I therefore learn that I must bite my tongue when the habits of whiteness tempt me to think that I own this country and that they are invaders. Instead, I remember with Anzaldúa and others that if anything, people like Tom Tancredo, Pat Buchanan, and me are the rude guests, and that no person has the right to deny the humanity and dignity of any other. The arrogance of whiteness, the habit of assuming that those different from us are inferior and that our traditions are the only ones that count as civilization, is what Anzaldúa calls the "doppelganger in your psyche," which white folk need to exorcize in order to achieve peace.[5]

The *habit of shame* leads me, therefore, to support programs designed to address the historical imbalance caused by whiteness. It leads me to support affirmative action, because I know that I and my father and grandfather all have or had better job opportunities because of the laws that protected white people of previous generations from competition with people of color. It makes me see that my middle-class life and my ability to not only support but enjoy leisure time with my wife and children stems not only from my work and that of my parents, but also from a system that protected my parents' and grandparents' efforts to turn labor into wealth, even as it denied the same opportunity to people of color. I agree with Rich when she writes that a great deal of the resistance to current programs designed to achieve racial equity stems from the misconception that things were fair in the past. I would add that there is another misconception that supporting these initiatives amounts to accusing all white folk of being thieves, which is obviously not the case. My forebearers did work hard and did play by the rules. But nonetheless, the rules they played by gave them, as even provisional white folk, advantages over people of color. By recognizing how and why the past was not fair, we gain a crucial perspective on present debates. The money they earned in this labor market that favored them has made my life more comfortable, and has given me advantages, even though no law bars anyone of color from competing with me. The sense of shame that I imagine ultimately leads to an engagement with the past that strives for healing. It is the sort of response that Rich describes when she says, "Historical responsibility has, after all, to do with action—where we place the weight of our existences on the line, cast our lot with others, move from an individual consciousness to a collective one. But we all need to begin with the individual consciousness: How did we come to be where we are and not elsewhere?"[6]

An appropriate sense of shame for all the horrors and injustices meted out in the name of whiteness would cause people to see things such as affirmative action and school integration as appropriate instruments for correcting a pronounced social ill. I think it would also lead us to support important symbolic measures, such as apologies by not just the government bodies that sanctioned and carried out slavery, native genocide, and the occupation of Latino lands, but also by private institutions such as the universities, banks, churches, and corporations that invested in and profited from these acts. The astounding wealth generated by the slave trade, Asian peonage, and theft of lands and property from people of color did not disappear down a big hole. It was invested and re-invested. It became the infrastructure of our great cities: Chicago's broad shoulders, Charleston's charming boulevards, the stained glass of opulent cathedrals in Boston and New York, and endowments of august institutions and benevolent charities across the country. That blood money fueled our past economic prosperity and still courses through markets that generate astounding wealth for a narrow few. In light of this fact it seems reasonable to at least consider economic reparations and certainly to allow affirmative action and similar policies to run their course until economic disparity is not so clearly cashed out on the color line.

Of course, woman and man cannot live on shame alone. While the *habit of shame* might help us sublimate the feeling of emptiness into our lives in a fruitful way, we still need to have something about which to be proud. Our failure to even address this point is a big part of why multicultural and diversification projects often feel like games played by people of color, with the white majority looking on as a passive and restive audience. As I said before, this source of pride needs to be different from the nostalgic fabrications that have justified white hegemony and whitewashed the violence of whiteness in this country. The best place to look is in the excluded and nearly forgotten aspects of our pasts, the parts that complicate and ultimately undermine the idea of whiteness.

Habits of remembrance lead us to try to recover the treasures that our ancestors were forced to bury to become white. Since the dominant history of whiteness has been dominantly patriarchal, we need to turn largely to feminist history in order to recover these lost cultural artifacts. While this means including great and influential women who were cut out of white history, Rich reminds us that we need to look deeper still: "[W]e need to be looking above all for the greatness and sanity of ordinary women, and how these women have collectively waged resistance. In searching that territory we find something better than individual heroines: the astonishing continuity of women's imagination of survival, persisting through the great and little deaths of daily life."[7]

I take pride in the Irishwomen who rejected exclusion in favor of humanity. I am proud of the fact that most of the "miscegenation" of the nineteenth century occurred between Irish women and African American men.[8] I am proud of the fact that there was a time that these people did not put themselves above fellow immigrants from other lands, even though the society around them told them they should. I reclaim the funny and human moment when two Irish women were interviewed by a reporter for the *World* in 1877 about why they married men from China. One merely laughed while the other replied that they married their husbands "[b]ecause we liked 'em, of course; why shouldn't we?"[9] To these women we can add the thousands who chose to look past the badge of color that other immigrants were being habituated to see in order to find love with African Americans and Native Americans, even though people on both sides of the color line faced violence and contempt. These moments remind us of how the exclusionary aspect of whiteness has erected walls around us that prevent us from developing bonds of love and friendship. They also remind me that if these women, who were uniformly economically destitute and little schooled, could see through the lie of racial superiority and purity, then we can do the same.

I also take pride in and recover broader moments of exchange and friendship. Tyler Anbinder writes in his excellent book *Five Points* about a saloon at 67 Orange Street run by a man named Pete Williams.[10] In the midst of the dirt and crowded squalor of this notorious Five Points neighborhood, Uncle Pete carved out a clean and warm place where people of all races could dance, laugh, and fall in love. It was largely because all of the dancers were poor folk, mostly of Irish and African descent, that they ironically escaped the racial monitoring that made such interactions impossible for "respectable people," white or black. The dynamic of this saloon run by a free black person in the 1860s and 1870s is the sort of rare and tender moment that gets lost in dominant histories. However, it also points beyond itself to a truly unique event that is a perfect representation of both Du Bois's idea of the exchange of race gifts and the sort of fierce but non-hierarchical pride that all people need to feel.

July 8, 1844, was a historic day for American art and culture. That was the day when the first uniquely American dance style—tap—started its gradual entrance into world culture. It is perhaps the single best illustration of why we need to foster these habits of remembrance not only to preserve the Du Boisian gifts of race, but also to be able to exchange them in a way that fosters true community across different groups with different histories. Tap dance was born in a fiery battle between two men. One was a free black man born in 1825 with the name William Henry Lane, though he was known then and now as Master Juba. The other was born in New York City in 1823 to Irish immigrants, and was called John "The King" Diamond. The *Herald* on July 8 proclaimed that each dancer had accumulated such worldwide fame for his virtuosity that their fans "have anxiously wished for a Public Trial between them [in order to] know which is to bear the Title of the Champion Dancer of the World."[11] They competed for a purse of five hundred dollars, an astounding sum at the time, before jam-packed audiences enthralled for *hours* by the men's jigs, reels, shuffles, and demisemis. Anbinder conveys the significance of this competition and the several that followed between Lane and Diamond:

> The "winner" of these competitions is not recorded. But we do know that such contests, as well as the friendly rivalries between native-born whites, Irish immigrants, and African Americans within Five Points' dance halls, had a profound influence on the direction of American dance. Each group incorporated favorite steps from their competitors' dance idioms into their own. In Juba's case, he adopted some of the high-stepping, foot-stomping style of the jig into his own footwork. It was from this interaction between African Americans dancing the shuffle and the Irish dancing the jig that "tap dancing" developed.[12]

This is the kind of moment that a critique of whiteness urges us to uncover, and establish as the kind of story we tell when we talk about who we are. This sort of moment is an ideal example of Du Bois's idea of the gift within race. It is what he meant when he concluded *The Souls of Black Folk* saying, "Actively we have woven ourselves with the very warp and woof of this nation. . . . Our Song, our toil, our cheer, and warning have been given to this nation in blood-brother-hood. Are not these gifts worth the giving? Is not this work and striving? Would America have been America without her Negro people?"[13]

Each dancer brought an irreplaceable, unique gift of culture. Each brought a particular idiom, developed over centuries in a particular place. They were both dancers, but their dances were distinct from each other, and particular to their cultural inheritance. It was part of the treasure that each dancer carried as African American or Irish American. What's more, we have the new, third, wonderful style—tap— only because these men and women were able to carefully cherish that which was theirs *and* value that which was cherished by another. These moments illuminate for me Dewey's statement that "the expression of difference is not only a right of the other persons but is a means of enriching one's own life-experience."[14] This competition would not be possible without the unique gifts of each artist; the fusion of styles would also be impossible were it not for the difference between them. Finally, while we can imagine each dancer throwing himself furiously into his respective steps, we can easily imagine the affection, respect, and even love between them. This is why, over the course of the competitions, each man borrowed and developed the other's style. This is the sort of moment that allows us to be proud of many different things at once. When I read about John Diamond, I know that his jigs were the same jigs my ancestors would dance at weddings and funerals. Further, I am proud of John Diamond's contribution to an American mode of expression that became a bridge across races and peoples without forcing either to give up who or what they are.

Multiculturalism is often derided as a weak show of pluralism that is a mere rainbow-wash designed to make us all seem like we are *tolerant* of people from different groups. It asks us only to clap politely for the dances and songs of different people's cultures and nod appreciatively when we eat their food. This critique of show-diversity holds to a certain extent, since what passes for multiculturalism and diversity is often just the purchasing, packaging, and consumption of commodified culture. However, this sort of polite but rootless diversity is not at all what Du Bois envisioned with his metaphor of the gift exchange.

Du Bois suggested that we learn, understand, and inhabit the cultures of the people from whom we descend because of insights gleaned from his own experience of cultural rootlessness that is all the more familiar to those of us raised after the postmodern age. Being one of only a handful of African Americans living in Great Barrington, Massachusetts, he had to go looking for these gifts of race. These gifts were so important to him that he opened each chapter of *The Souls of Black Folk* with the lyrics and melodies of traditional black American folk music. Instead of distancing himself from these artistic artifacts that were the object of rude ridicule on the minstrel stage, he embraced them and defended their uniquely American aesthetic worth:

> Little of beauty has America given the world save the rude grandeurs God himself stamped on her bosom; the human spirit in this new world has expressed itself in vigor and ingenuity rather than in beauty. And so by fateful chance the Negro folk-song—the rhythmic cry of the slave—stands to-day not simply as the sole American music, but as the most beautiful expression of human experience born this side the seas. It has been neglected, it has been, and is, half despised, and above all it has been persistently mistaken and misunderstood; but not withstanding, it still remains as the singular spiritual heritage of the nation and the greatest gift of the Negro people.[15]

It is clear that for Du Bois culture is not a commodity: it is the manifestation and preservation of cultural memories and experiences that are crucial resources for the development and prosperity of individuals, but also the realization of pluralistic communities. These songs told Du Bois not to follow Booker T. Washington, despite his moral courage and political clout, down the assimilationist road, because that would lead to the total neglect of these unique gifts and the loss of these memories. Du Bois did not want us to solve racism by all of us adopting one common aesthetic ideal or one common identity. He instead leaves us a much more complicated and challenging goal of trying to pull off a kind of Hegelian dialectic of culture. We need to preserve the individual and specific theses—the gifts of each of these race-cultures—while simultaneously striving toward a transcendent *aufhebung,* or overcoming of each particular culture through the act of mutual exchange. We learn our own gift not because it is the best or even better than another, but because it is the best way to *get* the beauty and message of the other culture's gift that would otherwise just be strange. This is not multiculturalism as smorgasbord or food-court, but as a fundamentally radical, decentering, and humanizing experience that breaks us out of our individual or cultural solipsism and opens up for us more cosmopolitan horizons.

While he used a different register, I think Dewey's *Art as Experience* hits many of the same notes as Du Bois's *The Souls of Black Folk.* Du Bois says "races" where Dewey says "civilizations" or "cultures," but their tunes harmonize easily. Dewey opens the last chapter of this work by discussing the value of art in a way that makes the identical point that Du Bois presses with his work on the gift of race:

> Art is a quality that permeates an experience; it is not, save by a figure of speech, the experience itself. Esthetic experience is always more than esthetic. . . . Esthetic experience is a manifestation, a record and celebration of the life of a civilization, a means of promoting its development, and is also the ultimate judgment upon the quality of a civilization. For while it is produced and is enjoyed by individuals, those individuals are what they are in the content of their experience because of the cultures in which they participate.[16]

Dewey, like Du Bois, sees that the work of art is always more than itself. It is not a passive field whereupon subjective judgments play. It is a refined recording of human experience and adjustment that plays a vital role in our ability to best adjust within our own current experiences. Also like Du Bois, Dewey knew that just as art can function as a bridge across time, it can also bridge the gaps between individuals from different civilizations and races.

> Just because art, speaking from the standpoint of the influence of collective culture upon creation and enjoyment of works of art, is expressive of a deep-seated attitude of adjustment, of an underlying idea and ideal of generic human attitude, the art characteristic of a civilization is the means for entering sympathetically into the deepest elements in the experience of remote and foreign civilizations. By this fact is explained also the human import of their arts for ourselves. They effect a broadening and deepening of our own experience, rendering it less local and provincial as far as we grasp, by their means, the attitudes basic in other forms of experience.[17]

The preservation of and participation in these culturally specific aesthetic practices help us see that we are a single common humanity raised and educated within different, unique cultures; most of us have ties to multiple cultures. We need to preserve these cultures as treasure chests of different experiences and different adjustments made by people who were ultimately just like us. Dewey and Du Bois see that art's power to humanize and build community is very counterintuitive; these very different vessels all hold the same water of life, yet, we can't all drink from the same cup at the same time. The fact that the gifts are different makes us struggle to understand what these different gifts are about and what they are trying to say. But it is only through the struggle to understand the thing that seemed so odd at first sight or first hearing that enables us to ultimately see and hear common human experience enshrined within it. Dewey writes that when "we install ourselves in modes of apprehending nature that at first are strange to us [. . .] we become artists ourselves as we undertake this integration."[18] This leads to a change in the individual that is absolutely essential in order for her or him to participate in the sort of pluralistic community toward which we aspire: "Barriers are dissolved, limiting prejudices melt away, when we enter into the spirit of Negro or Polynesian art. This insensible melting is far more efficacious than the change effected by reasoning, because it enters directly into attitude."[19]

I hope I've explained these first two habits—the habits of shame and remembrance—well enough that you know why I think they are preferable to their older counterparts. I hope you even agree. I will end by discussing why I think that a pragmatist reconstruction of the habits of whiteness requires us to cultivate new *habit of compassion* to replace the *habits of antipathy to the strange* that undergirds so much racial strife. This change hangs on the hope that we can take the impulse of aversion that we all have regarding some set of things, and focus on the sorts of things to which we should feel aversion. Recalling the pragmatist spirit behind Dewey and Du Bois, we recall that for them inquiry is an attempt to solve a problem. Further, the most worthwhile inquiries are the ones that are intimately tied to the needs and desires of flesh-and-blood human beings. They work best when they foster human growth, both as individuals and as communities. As a consequence, we can imagine that one thing toward which we must always cultivate a feeling of revulsion is suffering.

As we saw in the first section of this book, whiteness is like a conceptual and habitual quilt stitched together from a patchwork of older, smaller ideas and phenomena. It is part ancient ethnocentrism, part medieval Christian concerns over blood-purity, and part Enlightenment discourse about the relationship between a certain conception of reason and freedom. When pieced together, these ideas, which later became bred into the bone as habits, occluded immense human suffering. If the idea of whiteness didn't fully hide this suffering, it at least offered an excuse that was sadly believable to most people who were able to fit inside the pale of whiteness. The *habit of compassion* is in many ways, therefore, the mirror image of whiteness. Where whiteness conditioned people who defined themselves as white to not feel suffering, these new habits would sensitize white people—and all people—to feeling human suffering all the more deeply, that they might feel the need to remedy it. I'm the first to admit that this is a tall order, and I know that no law or policy can turn a person's heart. All I can do here on these pages is leave you with the best possible story that I think will guide us toward a truly fair and fruitful community, and hope that you see in it what I do.

The best story that I can think of about this sort of compassionate habit—the one to which I turn my mind when I am confused or depressed about our inability to overcome the legacy of whiteness—regards a man knows as "the Liberator," Daniel O'Connell. It has to do with his leadership of a nineteenth-century grass-roots political movement to end the English occupation of Ireland. It is worth noting that the Irish had been living under conditions of horrible oppression for centuries by the time O'Connell started his organizing. In his time, most of the oppression endured by the Irish centered on the laws passed by the British Parliament in the seventeenth century that codified Irish Catholics as non-citizens in their own country, known collectively as the Penal Laws. Noel Ignatiev, in his work *How the Irish Became White*, offers a brief summary of some of the low points of this legislation that continued unabated well into the nineteenth century.

> Catholics were not permitted to vote or serve in Parliament, . . . practice law or hold a post in the military, . . . teach in a school or serve as private tutors, attend university or educate their sons abroad, . . . own a horse worth more than five pounds, . . . buy, inherit, or receive gifts of land from Protestants. . . . By converting to Protestantism a Catholic son could dispossess his father and disinherit all his brothers. . . . In effect [the Penal Laws] established Ireland as a country in which the Irish formed an oppressed race.[20]

O'Connell organized a massive, grass-roots campaign to overturn the Penal Laws. He succeeded at ending the exclusion of the Irish Catholics from public life in 1830, and was soon after the first Irish Catholic elected to the Parliament.

O'Connell's rise to political power is salient to our situation because of the range of his solidarity and the depth of his compassion. While he fought first and hardest for the freedom of his people, he would not contribute to the enslavement of others even to win freedom for his own. While the Irish in America were angrily defending their privilege as white Americans against the perceived threat posed by African Americans, the Irish in Ireland, led by O'Connell, saw their seven-hundred-year history of oppression as point of *commonality* between them and all enslaved people, including African Americans. O'Connell took time out from his own campaign to win a free Ireland to organize sixty thousand Irish men and women and to sign an *Address from the People of Ireland to their Countrymen and Countrywomen in America* in 1841, which asked Irish Americans to *"Treat the colored people as your equals, as brethren. By your memories of Ireland, continue to love liberty—hate slavery—CLING BY THE ABOLITIONSITS—and in America you will do honor to the name of Ireland."*[21]

O'Connell didn't just make room in his heart for the suffering of men and women half a world away. He went so far as to actually stand by them when it meant increasing his own pain and the pain of his people. Ignatiev relates the famous story of O'Connell's first year in Parliament.

> In 1830, when O'Connell first entered Parliament, with one other Irish member to support him, a representative of the West India interest approached him, offering the support of their twenty-seven members on Irish issues in return for his silence on the slavery question. He replied, "Gentlemen, God knows I speak for the saddest people the sun sees; but may my right hand forget its cunning, and my tongue cleave to the roof of my mouth, if to save Ireland, even Ireland, I forget the negro one single hour!"[22]

It is important to note that O'Connell had *never been to the Americas.* He had likely *never met an African American slave.* Yet, he turned away the brass ring of freedom for which he had struggled all his life because he hated the injustice and cruelty of slavery in America. He chose to prolong his own suffering and the suffering of his fellow Irish because he held a deep hatred for all human suffering, not just his own or that of his kin. Ignatiev points out that even before his entrance into Parliament he excoriated white Americans, including Irish American immigrants, for their hypocrisy: "Let America, in the fullness of her pride wave on high her banner of freedom and its blazing stars. . . . In the midst of their laughter and their pride, I point them to the Negro children screaming for their mother from whose bosom they have been torn. . . . Let them hoist the flag of liberty, with the whip and rack on one side, and the star of freedom upon the other."[23]

O'Connell was certainly proud of his people. He was more aware of their suffering than anyone else's. Yet, his pride for his own group, and his keen awareness of their pain, is *precisely* what lead him to hate the suffering of another group, even though he had no direct contact with them. This is the virtuous metamorphosis we can work through culture: if you inhabit these cultural memories of past people just like you, you eventually come out the other end with a deeply humbling and uplifting sense of our common humanity. O'Connell's awareness of his people's pain through the centuries steeled him to fight not just for Irish humanity, but for all humanity. This cosmopolitan courage is a hopeful and healing tonic against the callous cruelty evidenced in the hearts of so many people, who view life as a competition between workers in which each one must make sure that he gets his, and to hell with the poor or those in need. We see this selfishness among a lamentable number of modern-day Irish Americans who've forgotten, or more likely never learned, O'Connell's solidarity with all who suffer, or "thole" as the Irish say. Commentators such as Bill O'Reilly and Sean Hannity fail O'Connell's test and cheapen his memory when they use their Irish heritage as a cudgel with which to bludgeon immigrants from Latin America as well as African Americans. Instead of saying, "We suffered then, so you deal with it now," O'Connell would have us say, "We suffered then, and I'll stand with you now." But then Ireland has always been equally blessed with an excess of saints and poets and cursed with a surfeit of scoundrels and fools.

To use pragmatist language, O'Connell had very good habits: his habits were conducive toward the widest possible human community and the mitigation of human suffering. They were good because they organized his impulses in a way that led him to oppose oppression and cruelty universally, rather than just oppose the oppression of the Irish. They were good because they reconciled a solvable social problem in a way that furthered human flourishing. They were good because they led him to hate pain and suffering, rather than the people who caused the pain. He channeled his impulse of aversion in a way that furthered, rather than opposed, human flourishing. As a learned European, he was more than conversant with the theories that cast people of African descent as fit for slavery. Nonetheless, he saw the danger behind these ideas, and refused to play into the idea that his suffering was odious, but theirs was warranted. Instead, he used his experiences and his impulses to strengthen him in the fight against not only Irish suffering, but *all* suffering.

Americans who love the ideals of equality and freedom and respect the plurality of cultures that bless our polity need to be more like O'Connell, or any of the hundreds of moral heroes and heroines from other cultures whose stories we should recover and retell. If we are going to realize our unique potential—to weave a strong and sumptuous communal tapestry from threads of every color that stretch back to every human experience ever felt—then we must first stop working toward our perceived short-term desires, and work instead toward the alleviation of human suffering in our midst. We need to see how our own past was in many ways like the present oppression faced by many people of color, and indeed most people in the current world. We should gather up our grandmother's and grandfather's stories of hardship and triumph that might otherwise get swept away by time and befriend people who live these same stories now. We need to realize how old ideas of white supremacism that most of us reject continue to live in the flesh, in our habits. By identifying these habits and the impulses behind them, we can finish the task of people like O'Connell and countless others. We can come to a point where we identify with something much richer and life affirming than mere whiteness. We can come to see that more for them does not mean less for us. We can discover the transformative power of art, culture, and memory as Judith Green asks: "So please bring your memories and your voices and your culture-specific instruments, and let's tune up and tell stories and dream and dance together in celebration of the power and the beauty that we have lost that binds us together in seeking the possibility of a more cosmopolitan, more deeply democratic world future."[24]

The idea of whiteness and the habits it engendered have separated us and impeded our communal growth ever since it was first written into a vicious law in 1691. If we reconstruct these habits under the guidance of people such as Dewey, Du Bois, Rich, Lugones, and Anzaldúa, we can learn to fiercely love our own people, culture, and history even as this love warms us to the needs and hopes of all our citizens and neighbors. We can then remember how to dance together as they did in Pete Williams's saloon or like I did in music class when I was a kid in Miramar.

Notes

Introduction

1. Adam Nagourney and Megan Thee, "Poll Finds Obama Isn't Closing Divide on Race," *New York Times*, July 16, 2008, A1.

2. Eddie Glaude Jr., *In a Shade of Blue* (Chicago: University of Chicago Press, 2007), 132.

3. Jennifer Cheeseman Day, *Population Projections of the United States by Age, Sex, Race, and Hispanic Origin: 1995 to 2050* (Washington, D.C.: U.S. Government Printing Office, 1996), 1.

4. Ian Haney López, "Race on the 2010 Census: Hispanics and the Shrinking White Majority," *Daedelus* 134, no. 1 (2005): 43.

5. Barack Obama, "Speech on Race," delivered Philadelphia, Pa., March 18, 2008. Reprinted in *New York Times,* March 18, 2008, http://www.nytimes.com/2008/03/18/us/politics/18text-obama.html, accessed March 24, 2008.

6. Just for the record, I voted for Barack.

7. Cornel West, "Obama and the Blues: Interview by Robert S. Boynton," *Rolling Stone,* issue 1048 (March 20, 2008): 42.

8. W. E. B. Du Bois, "The Conservation of Races," in *W. E. B. Du Bois: Writings* (New York: Library Classics of the United States, 1986), 819.

9. Shannon Sullivan, *Revealing Whiteness: The Unconscious Habits of Racial Privilege.* (Bloomington: Indiana University Press, 2005).

10. To see what EWU is doing to promote campus diversity, please visit http://www.ewu.edu/x30041.xml, accessed March 24, 2008.

11. I use the term "race traitor" in the way that it is used in *Race Traitor,* eds. Noel Ignatiev and John Garvey (New York: Routledge, 1996).

12. See Kevin Phillips, *American Theocracy* (New York: Viking, 2006) and Bart Ehrman, *Misquoting Jesus* (San Francisco: Harper Publishing, 2005).

13. Jim Wallis, *God's Politics* (San Francisco: Harper Publishing, 2005).

14. John Dewey, "The Need for a Recovery of Philosophy" in *The Middle Works, 1899–1924,* ed. Jo Ann Boydston (1917; Carbondale: Southern Illinois University Press, 1980), 10:46.

15. Lucius T. Outlaw, *On Race and Philosophy* (New York: Routledge, 1996), 26.

16. Robert Bernasconi, "Waking Up White in Memphis," in *White on White/Black on Black,* ed. George Yancy (Lanham, Md.: Rowman and Littlefield Press, 2005), 20.

17. Ibid.

18. Bill Lawson and Donald Koch, introduction, *Pragmatism and the Problem of Race,* ed. Bill Lawson and Donald Koch (Bloomington: Indiana University Press, 2004), 1.

1. Bacon's Rebellion and the Advent of Whiteness

1. While race and whiteness are concepts that have shaped world history globally, I limit the discussion in this book to their history and impact within the English-speaking colonies and the United States.

2. David Ingram, "Toward a Cleaner White(ness): New Racial Identities," *Philosophical Forum* 36, no. 3 (2005): 243.

3. Matthew Frye Jacobson, *Whiteness of a Different Color: European Immigrants and the Alchemy of Race* (Cambridge, Mass.: Harvard University Press, 1998); Theodore Allen, *The Invention of the White Race*, 2 vols. (New York: Verso, 1994); Kathleen Brown, *Good Wives, Nasty Wenches, and Anxious Patriarchs: Gender, Race, and Power in Colonial Virginia* (Chapel Hill: University of North Carolina Press, 1996).

4. Jacobson, *Whiteness of a Different Color,* 7.

5. For sources on Bacon's rebellion see Stephen Webb, *1676: The End of American Independence* (New York: Knopf, 1984); Wilcomb Washburn, *The Governor and the Rebel: A History of Bacon's Rebellion in Virginia* (Chapel Hill: University of North Carolina Press, 1957).

6. Allen, *Invention,* 2:207.

7. Howard Zinn, *A People's History of the United States* (New York: Harper Collins, 1999), 40.

8. Edmund S. Morgan, *American Slavery, American Freedom: The Ordeal of Colonial Virginia* (New York: Norton, 1975), 327.

9. Ibid.

10. "Theft of Master's Goods, 1684," *Accomack County Deeds, Wills, and Inventories, 1676–1690,* folios 389–90, reprinted in Warren Billings, ed., *The Old Dominion in the Seventeenth Century: A Documentary History of Virginia, 1606–1689* (Chapel Hill: University of North Carolina Press, 1975), 145.

11. Sometimes these men are unnamed, but on two occasions he names them: "Jack A negro" and "Jonny Negro"; Billings, *Old Dominion,* 145.

12. Of course, it is important to not beatify these African and European laborers: while their general desire to be free of an economic system that benefited only a few wealthy elite is understandable, their method for solving this problem (through the acquisition of land by attacking the people living on it) set a tragic precedent.

13. Winthrop Jordan, *White over Black: American Attitudes towards the Negro, 1550–1812* (Chapel Hill: University of North Carolina Press, 1968), 3–43.

14. *Coventry Papers Relating to Virginia, Barbados and other Colonies,* Wiltshire, UK, LXXVII, 301, as quoted in Allen, *Invention,* 2:214.

15. Allen, *Invention,* 2:215.

16. Morgan, *American Slavery,* 328.

17. William Waller Hening, ed., *The Statutes at Large; Being a Collection of All the Laws of Virginia, from the First Session of the Legislature,* 13 vols. (New York: R. & W. & G. Bartow, 1823), 3:87.

18. Ibid., 1:69.

19. Ibid., 1:146.

20. For a deeper discussion of this particular case as well as the legal history of whiteness, see Ian Haney López, *White by Law: The Legal Construction of Race* (New York: New York University Press, 1996), 23.

21. Hening, *Statutes at Large,* 1:226.

22. Ibid., 1:242.

23. For more on the impact of English gender discourses on the reproductive and productive roles of African and European women in Virginia, see Brown, *Good Wives,* 116–28.

24. Hening, *Statutes at Large,* 2:170.

25. Brown, *Good Wives,* 135.

26. Hening, *Statutes at Large,* 2:260.

27. Brown, *Good Wives,* 135.

28. Brown estimates that "free Afro-Virginians probably constituted less than 4 percent of the colony's combined African and European population," *Good Wives,* 214.

29. Hening, *Statutes at Large,* 2:283.

30. Brown, *Good Wives,* 136.

31. Hening, *Statutes at Large,* 2:273.

32. Ibid., 2:481.

33. Ibid., 2:381.

34. Ibid., 2:395.

35. Brown, *Good Wives,* 181.

36. For more on slave revolts in Virginia, see Sally Hadden, *Slave Patrols* (Cambridge, Mass.: Harvard University Press, 2001), 28–30.

37. Hening, *Statutes at Large,* 2:481.

38. Ibid.

39. Ibid., 2:491.

40. For more on this statute, see Brown, *Good Wives,* 197–201.

41. Hening, *Statutes at Large,* 3:87.

42. Brown, *Good Wives,* 201.

43. Hening, *Statutes at Large,* 3:269.

44. Ibid., 3:298.

45. Ibid., 3:276, 448.

46. Ibid., 4:133.

47. Brown, *Good Wives,* 216.

48. Allen, *Invention,* 251.

49. For a history of slave patrols, see Hadden's *Slave Patrols.*

50. W. E. B. Du Bois, *Black Reconstruction in America* (New York: Russell and Russell, 1966), 12.

51. Hening, *Statutes at Large,* 3:298.

2. The Draft Riots of 1863 and the Defense of White Privilege

1. United States Congress, *Annals of Congress: Abridgements of the Debates of Congress, 1789–1856* (New York: D. Appleton, 1857), 1:184.

2. Jacobson, *Whiteness,* 42

3. Ibid., *Whiteness,* 43.

4. Peter Fry and Fiona Somerset Fry, *A History of Ireland* (New York: Barnes and Noble, 1993), 253.

5. Jacobson, *Whiteness,* 43.

6. William Williams, *'Twas Only an Irishman's Dream* (Urbana: University of Chicago Press, 1996), 53.

7. For more on the history of anti-Catholic political movements, see Evelyn Schlatter, *Aryan Cowboys: White Supremacist Ideology and the Search for a New Frontier, 1960–1995* (Ph.D. diss., University of New Mexico, 2000), 43–48.

8. Jacobson, *Whiteness,* 41.

9. Arthur Comte de Gobineau, *Selected Political Writings* (1855; reprint New York: Harper and Row, 1970), 161, as quoted in Jacobson, *Whiteness,* 43.

10. Jacobson, *Whiteness,* 48.

11. Ibid.

12. Noel Ignatiev, *How the Irish Became White* (New York: Routledge, 1995), 41.

13. Patrick Galvin, *Irish Songs of Resistance* (New York: Oak Publications, 1962), 79; as quoted in Williams, *Irishman's Dream,* 43.

14. For more on the causes of the riots, see Iver Bernstein, *The New York City Draft Riots: Their Significance for American Society and Politics in the Age of the Civil War* (New York: Oxford University Press, 1990); James McCague, *The Second Rebellion: The Story of the New York City Draft Riots of 1863* (New York: Dial Press, 1968).

15. Bernstein, *Draft Riots,* 4.

16. Ibid., 18.

17. The description of the riots in *Harper's Weekly* states that while the "leaders . . . in the affair were boys" there was also a number of "men" and "married women"; *Harper's Weekly,* July 25, 1863, 466. A later article detailing the burning of the Colored Orphan Asylum cites an eyewitness who claimed that "hundreds, and perhaps thousands, of the rioters, the majority of whom were women and children, covered the premises"; *Harper's Weekly,* August 1, 1863, 494.

18. Bernstein, *Draft Riots,* 30.

19. Ibid., 31.

20. *Harper's Weekly,* August 1, 1863, 494; New York *Daily Tribune,* July 14, 1863.

21. Bernstein, *Draft Riots,* 23.

22. *Harper's Weekly,* August 1, 1863, 482.

23. New York *Times,* July 16, 1863.

24. New York *Daily Tribune,* July 15, 1863.

25. *Harper's Weekly,* August 1, 1863, 484.

26. Ibid., 482.

27. New York *Times,* July 16, 1863.

28. New York *Times,* July 17, 1863

29. New York *Daily Tribune,* July 20, 1863.

30. New York *Herald,* July 14, 1863.

31. New York *Irish-American,* July 18, 1863.

32. New York *Irish-American,* July 25, 1863.

33. New York *Daily Tribune,* April 14, 1863.

34. New York *Herald,* April 14, 1863.

35. For more on the struggles between the Irish and African Americans over the docks, see Bernstein, *Draft Riots,* 27–28, 118–23.

36. New York *Irish-American,* July 4, 1863.

37. Ibid.

38. Jacobson, *Whiteness,* 53.

39. Richard Slotkin, *Gunfighter Nation: The Myth of the Frontier in Twentieth-Century America* (New York: Harper Perennial, 1993), 10.

40. Ibid., 11.

41. Ibid.

42. Ibid.

43. Ibid.

44. Ibid., 19.

45. Ibid.

46. Ibid., 21.

47. Jacobson, *Whiteness,* 5.

48. W. E. B. Du Bois, *Dusk of Dawn: An Essay toward an Autobiography of a Race Concept* (1940; reprint New York: Schocken, 1968), 153.

3. John Dewey and Inquiry

1. John Dewey, *The Quest For Certainty,* in *The Later Works, 1925–1953,* ed. Jo Ann Boydston (1929; Carbondale: Southern Illinois University Press, 1984), 4:19.

2. Ibid.

3. Since this work is concerned much more with Dewey's alternative model of knowing than with the traditional view, and also since space is limited, I will omit any historical or genealogical engagement with traditional epistemologies.

4. Dewey, *Quest,* 19.

5. Ibid.

6. Ibid.

7. Ibid., 18.

8. For examples of feminist models of inquiry see Sandra Harding, *Whose Science? Whose Knowledge?* (Ithaca, N.Y.: Cornell University Press, 1986); Susan Hekman, *Gender and Knowledge* (Boston: Northeastern University Press, 1990); María Lugones, "Playfulness, 'World' Traveling, and Loving Perception," *Hypatia* 2, no. 2 (1987): 3–19; Nancy Tuana, ed., *Feminism and Science* (Bloomington: Indiana University Press, 1989). For examples of phenomenological models of inquiry, see Edmund Husserl, *Ideas: A General Introduction to Pure Phenomenology,* trans. W. R. Boyce Gibson (New York: Collier Books, 1962); Maurice Merleau-Ponty, *Phenomenology of Perception,* trans. Colin Smith (London: Routledge, 1962).

9. Dewey, *Quest,* 3.

10. Ibid., 28.

11. Ibid.

12. Ibid., 29.

13. Ibid.

14. Ibid., 86.

15. Ibid., 176.

16. Ralph Barton Perry, "The Ego-Centric Predicament," *Journal of Philosophy, Psychology and Scientific Methods* 7, no. 1 (1910): 8.

17. Dewey, *Quest,* 162.

18. Ibid.

19. Ibid., 163.

20. Ibid., 164.

21. Werner Heisenberg, *Physics and Philosophy: The Revolution in Modern Science* (New York: Harper and Brothers, 1958), 81.

22. Dewey, *Quest,* 163.

23. John Dewey, "The Postulate of Immediate Empiricism," in *The Influence of Darwin on Philosophy* (New York: Holt, 1910), 227.

24. Dewey, *Quest,* 163.

25. Ibid., 176.

26. Ibid., 106.

27. John Dewey, *Democracy and Education,* in *The Middle Works, 1899–1924,* ed. Jo Ann Boydston (1916; Carbondale: Southern Illinois University Press, 1980), 9:249.

28. John Dewey, *Logic: The Theory of Inquiry,* in *The Later Works, 1925–1953,* ed. Jo Ann Boydston (1938; Carbondale: Southern Illinois University Press, 1986), 12:109.29. Ibid., 492.

30. Dewey, *Quest,* 111.

31. Dewey, *Logic,* 493.

32. Ibid.

33. Ibid.

34. Dewey, *Logic,* 482.

4. Race as Deweyan Habit

1. Shannon Sullivan, "From the Foreign to the Familiar: Confronting Dewey Confronting Racial Prejudice," *Journal of Speculative Philosophy* 18, no. 3 (2004): 193.

2. Dewey, *Logic,* 12:259.

3. Ibid., 267.

4. Ibid., 249.

5. Ibid.

6. Ibid., 263.

7. Robert Bernasconi, *Race* (Malden, Mass.: Blackwell, 2001), Thomas Gossett, *Race: The History of an Idea in America* (New York: Schocken Books, 1965), Emmanuel Chukwudi Eze, ed., *Race and the Enlightenment: A Reader* (Malden, Mass.: Blackwell, 1997).

8. Dewey, *Logic,* 264.

9. Sullivan, *Revealing Whiteness,* 9.

10. Ibid., 96.

11. Ibid., 2.

12. Ibid., 9.

13. John Dewey, *Human Nature and Conduct* in *The Middle Works, 1899–1924,* ed. Jo Ann Boydston (1922; Carbondale: Southern Illinois University Press, 1983), 14:15.

14. Ibid., 31.

15. Ibid., 32.

16. Ibid., 65.

17. Ibid., 88.

18. Sullivan, *Revealing Whiteness,* 25.

19. As Dewey says in the footnote on page 75 of *Habit and Human Nature,* "the use of the words instinct and impulse as practical equivalents is intentional." Like Dewey, I will rely on the word "impulse" when speaking of these native activities in order to avoid the implication in "instinct" of a fully operational and innate response to the world.

20. Ibid., 65.

21. Ibid., 68.

22. Ibid., 65.

23. Ibid., 67.

24. Ibid., 75.

25. Ibid., 21.

26. Ibid., 88.

27. Ibid., 22.

28. Dewey, *Logic,* 267.

29. Ibid.

30. Dewey, *Human Nature,* 25.

31. Hening, *The Statues at Large,* 2:170.

32. Ibid., 1:242.

33. Ibid., 2:170.

34. Ibid., 2:273.

35. Ibid., 2:273.

36. Ibid., 2:481.

37. Ibid., 1:146.

38. Ibid., 3:87.

39. Brown, *Good Wives,* 80–91.

40. Dewey, *Human Nature,* 88.

41. Ibid., 77.

42. Ibid., 90.

43. Ibid., 118.

44. Ibid., 79.

45. John Dewey, "Racial Prejudice and Friction," in *The Middle Works, 1899–1924,* ed. Jo Ann Boydston (1921; Carbondale: Southern Illinois University Press, 1983), 13:243.

46. Ibid., 244.

47. Ibid., 243.

48. Ibid., 245.

49. Ibid., 253.

50. Ibid., 252.

51. Ibid., 253.

52. Associated Press, "City Sued over Immigration Ordinance," *Spokesman Review* (Spokane, Wash.), August 16, 2006, A4.

53. Ibid.

54. Sullivan, *Revealing Whiteness,* 41.

55. Michael Eldridge, "Dewey on Race and Social Change" in *Pragmatism and the Problem of Race,* ed. Bill Lawson and Donald Koch (Bloomington: Indiana University Press, 2004), 19.

56. Dewey, "Racial Prejudice," 244.

57. See Eric Avila, *Popular Culture in the Age of White Flight: Fear and Fantasy in Suburban Los Angeles* (Berkeley and Los Angeles: University of California Press, 2006) and Kevin Kruse, *White Flight: Atlanta and the Making of Modern Conservatism* (Princeton, N.J.: Princeton University Press, 2005).

58. John Dewey, *Freedom and Culture* in *The Later Works, 1925–1953,* ed. Jo Ann Boydson (1939; Carbondale: Southern Illinois University Press, 1988), 13:76.

59. Sullivan, *Revealing Whiteness,* 43.

60. For examples of Dewey's juxtaposition of the terms "civilized" and "savage" see "Interpretation of the Savage Mind," *The Middle Works, 1899–1924,* ed. Jo Ann Boydston (1916; Carbondale: Southern Illinois University Press, 1976), 2:39–52.

61. Dewey, *Human Nature,* 68.

62. John Dewey, "Address to the National Association for the Advancement of Colored People," in *The Later Works, 1925–1953,* ed. Jo Ann Boydson (1932; Carbondale: Southern Illinois University Press, 1985), 6:225.

63. Ibid., 225.

64. Ibid., 230.

65. Ibid., 225.

66. Ibid., 229.

67. Ibid., 225.

68. W. E. B Du Bois, "The Right to Work" in *Writings* (1933; New York: Library Classics of the United States, 1986), 1236.

69. Richard Rorty, *Achieving Our Country* (Cambridge, Mass.: Harvard University Press, 1998), 15.

70. Glaude, *In a Shade of Blue,* 2.

5. Du Bois and the Gift of Race

1. For a treatment of Du Bois as Marxist, see Gerald Horne, *Black and Red: W. E. B. Du Bois and the Afro-American Response to the Cold War, 1944–1963* (Albany: State University of New York Press, 1986). For Du Bois the existentialist, see Shamoon Zamir, *Dark Voices: W. E. B. Du Bois and American thought, 1888–1903* (Chicago: University of Chicago Press, 1995). For a treatment of Du Bois as Hegelian, see Ernest Allen Jr., "On Reading of Riddles: Rethinking Du Boisian 'Double Consciousness,'" in *Existence in Black: An Anthology of Black Existential Philosophy,* ed. Lewis Gordon (New York: Routledge, 1997).

2. Paul C. Taylor, "What's the Use of Calling Du Bois a Pragmatist?," *Metaphilosophy* 35, no. 1/2 (2004): 99–114.

3. Cornel West, *The American Evasion of Philosophy: A Genealogy of Pragmatism* (Madison: University of Wisconsin Press, 1989), 138.

4. Taylor, "What's the Use of Calling Du Bois a Pragmatist?," 100.

5. Edward Blum, *W. E. B. Du Bois, American Prophet: Politics and Culture in Modern America* (Philadelphia: University of Pennsylvania Press, 2007).

6. Dewey, *Quest,* 28.

7. Eddie Glaude, Jr., "Tragedy and Moral Experience: John Dewey and Toni Morrison's *Beloved,*" *Pragmatism and the Problem of Race,* eds. Bill Lawson and Donald Koch (Bloomington: Indiana University Press, 2004), 90.

8. W. E. B. Du Bois, *Dusk of Dawn: An Essay toward an Autobiography of a Race Concept* (1940; reprint New York: Schocken, 1968), 2.

9. W. E. B. Du Bois, *The Souls of Black Folk,* in *Writings* (New York: Library of America, 1986), 363.

10. Ibid., 372.

11. Dewey, *Quest,* 151.

12. Du Bois, *Dusk,* 137.

13. Ibid.

14. Du Bois, "Editorial," *Crisis* 7 (December 1913): 83.

15. Du Bois, *Dusk,* 64.

16. Dewey, *Quest,* 172.

17. Ibid., 132.

18. Du Bois, *Dusk,* 67.

19. Ibid.

20. Ibid., 26.

21. Immanuel Kant, "An Answer to the Question 'What Is Enlightenment?'" trans. Ted Humphrey, in *Perpetual Peace and Other Essays* (Indianapolis: Hackett, 1983), 41.

22. Scott Pratt, *Native Pragmatism* (Bloomington: Indiana University Press, 2002), 286.

23. Du Bois, *Dusk,* 99.

24. Ibid.

25. Ibid., 103.

26. Du Bois, "Conservation of Races," 817.

27. Wilson Jeremiah Moses, *Alexander Crummell* (New York: Oxford University Press, 1989), 264.

28. Ibid., 249.

29. Booker T. Washington, *The Future of the American Negro* (New York, 1899), 132, as quoted in Ronald White, *Liberty and Justice for All: Racial Reform and the Social Gospel* (San Francisco: Harper and Row, 1990), 93.

30. Moses, *Crummell,* 261.

31. Ibid., 259.

32. Du Bois, *Souls,* 392–404.

33. As Du Bois ultimately came to reject this idea from his early work, about which a great deal of ink has already been spilled, I will not dwell on this comparison.

34. Alexander Crummell, "The Race Problem in America," in *Africa and America: Addresses and Discourses* (Springfield, Mass.: Wiley and Son, 1891), 37, as quoted in Moses, *Crummell,* 239.

35. Glenn Loury, *The Anatomy of Racial Inequality* (Cambridge, Mass.: Harvard University Press, 2002), 157–8.

36. Prudence Jones and Nigel Pennick, *A History of Pagan Europe* (New York: Routledge, 1995), 35.

37. Du Bois, *Dusk,* 117.

38. Du Bois, "Conservation," 820.

39. Ibid.

40. This differs from Crummell's view, where African Americans were chosen by God to teach other races. See Moses, *Crummell,* 215.

41. "[W]hen, for instance, the student leader of a prayer meeting into which I had wandered casually to look local religion over, suddenly and without warning announced that 'Professor Du Bois would lead us in prayer,' I simply answered, 'No, he won't,' and as a result nearly lost my job." Du Bois, *Dusk,* 56.

42. For a source on Du Bois's relationship to the social gospel movement see Anthony Cook, *The Least of These: Race, Law, and Religion in American Culture* (New York: Routledge, 1997).

43. For a survey of the complex relationship between Christian readings of the Bible and racism, see Alan Davies, *Infected Christianity: A Study of Modern Racism* (Montreal: McGill-Queen's University Press, 1988).

44. "Accursed be Canaan/ he shall be/ his brothers' meanest slave." Genesis 9:25.

45. White, *Liberty and Justice for All,* 102.

46. Du Bois, "Credo," in *Darkwater* (1920; New York: Dover, 1999), 1.

47. I am not prioritizing the Christian Scriptures over the Hebrew Scriptures with this comparison. Instead, I am simply trying to present the relevant context behind the Christian Scripture to which Du Bois alludes.

48. Cornel West, *Prophesy Deliverance! An Afro-American Revolutionary Christianity* (Philadelphia: Westminster Press, 1982), 72.

6. Du Bois's Critique of Whiteness

1. Du Bois, *Dusk,* 137.
2. Dewey, *Logic,* 263.
3. Du Bois, *Dusk,* 129.
4. Ibid., 103.
5. Hening, *Statutes at Large,* 2:260.
6. Du Bois, "The Souls of White Folk," in *Darkwater,* 17.
7. Du Bois, "Credo," in *Darkwater,* 1.
8. Please see the beginning of the Book of Job for an almost comical dialogue between God and Satan. This example lacks the sense of polarized and apocalyptic struggle between the two so common in Christian teachings. In fact, it is on Satan's urging that God places Job through his trials.
9. Du Bois, *Dusk,* 145.
10. Ibid., 151.
11. Ibid., 152.
12. Ibid., 153.
13. Ibid.
14. Ibid., 155.
15. Ibid., 157.
16. Ibid., 160.
17. Ibid.
18. Ibid., 161.
19. Ibid., 162.
20. Ibid.
21. Ibid., 163.
22. Du Bois, *Darkwater,* 22.
23. Adam Hochschild, *King Leopold's Ghost: A Story of Greed, Terror, and Heroism in Colonial Africa* (Boston: Houghton Mifflin, 1998).
24. Du Bois, "Jacob and Esau," in *W. E. B. Du Bois Speaks: Speeches and Addresses 1920–1963,* ed. Philip Foner (New York: Pathfinder, 1970), 137–49.
25. Ibid., 139.
26. Ibid., 140.
27. Ibid., 147.
28. Ibid., 141.
29. Ibid., 147.
30. Du Bois, *Dusk,* 296.
31. Ibid., 304.
32. Ibid., 172.
33. Ibid., 304.
34. Ibid., 140.

7. Whiteness in Post–Civil Rights America

1. Cook, *Least of These,* 162.
2. Ibid.
3. National Advisory Committee on Civil Disorders, *Report of the National Advisory Commission on Civil Disorders* (New York: E.P. Dutton, 1968), 10.

4. Philip Meranto, ed., *The Kerner Report Revisited* (Chicago: Institute of Government and Public Affairs, University of Illinois, 1970), 4.

5. http://www.whitehouse.gov/news/releases/2006/07/20060727-1.html. Accessed March 25, 2008.

6. Ibid.

7. George Lipsitz, *The Possessive Investment in Whiteness: How White People Profit from Identity Politics* (Philadelphia: Temple University Press, 1998), xi.

8. Andrew Hacker, *Two Nations: Black and White, Separate, Hostile, Unequal* (New York: Scribner, 2003).

9. It is important to note that Hacker, like most theorists of race, focuses primarily on black/white relations when speaking of racism. The focus on this one facet of race in America is a troubling one, for it ignores the different dynamics between whites and other races, and those between Asians, African Americans, and Native Americans. To a certain extent, this problem must be tolerated for now: since such a preponderance of the literature is skewed in this fashion, it is almost impossible to not reproduce it to some extent here. However, I will address Native American and Latina authors who speak on whiteness in order to correct this imbalance.

10. Hacker, *Two Nations,* 94.

11. Ibid., 103.

12. Ibid., 117.

13. Ibid., 197.

14. Public Safety Performance Project, *One in 100: Behind Bars in America 2008,* (Washington, D.C.: Pew Charitable Trusts, 2008), 34.

15. Steven Holmes, "Race Analysis Cites Disparity in Sentencing for Narcotics," *New York Times,* June 8, 2000, A14.

16. Clarence Lusane, *Pipe Dream Blues: Racism and the War on Drugs* (Boston: South End Press, 1991), 45–55.

17. Randall Kennedy, "Racial Trends in the Administration of Criminal Justice," *America Becoming,* ed. Neil Smelser, William Julius Wilson, Faith Mitchell, 2 vols. (Washington, D.C.: National Academy Press, 2001), 2: 15.

18. Ibid.

19. For a general overview on racial profiling see "Patterns of Police Violence," *New York Times,* Editorial, April 18, 2001, A22; Steven Holmes, "The Stark Reality of Racial Profiling," *New York Times,* June 13, 1999, A18; and Kathryn Russell, "Racial Profiling: A Status Report of the Legal, Legislative and Empirical Literature," *Rutgers Race and Law Review* 3 (2001): 61, 68–80. For more examinations of racial profiling in the New York area, see David Kochieniewski, "Minority Drivers Tell of Troopers' Racial Profiling," *New York Times,* April 14, 1999, B1; John Kifner, "Van Shooting Revives Charges of Racial 'Profiling' by New Jersey State Police," *New York Times,* May 10, 1998, B1; Joseph P. Fried and Blaine Harden, "The Louima Case: The Overview; Officer Is Guilty in Torture of Louima" *New York Times,* June 9, 1999, A1; Dan Barry, "The Diallo Case: The Police; One Legacy of a 41-Bullet Barrage Is a Hard Look at Aggressive Tactics" *New York Times,* February27, 2000, B1; Ronald Smothers, "Rights Charges Filed in Death of a Man Wrongly Arrested," *New York Times,* June 21, 2000, A27.

20. George Yancy, "Introduction," *White on White/ Black on Black,* ed. G. Yancy (Lanham, Md.: Rowman and Littlefield, 2005), 2.

21. John Goldberg, "The Color of Suspicion," *New York Times Magazine,* June 20, 1999, 44+; Tammerlin Drummond, "It's Not Just New Jersey; Cops Across the U.S. Often Search People Just Because of Their Race, a Study Says," *Time,* June 13, 1999: 61.

22. Kennedy, "Racial Trends," 3.

23. Henry Louis Gates Jr., "Thirteen Ways of Looking at a Black Man," *New Yorker,* October 23, 1995: 56, 58–59.

24. Lipsitz, *Investment in Whiteness,* vii.

25. Ibid.

26. Cheryl Harris, "Whiteness as Property," *Harvard Law Review* 106, no. 8 (1993): 1707–93.

27. Gloria Anzaldúa, *Borderlands*/La Frontera: *The New Mestiza* (San Francisco: Aunt Lute Books, 1987), 69.

28. Adrienne Rich, "Resisting Amnesia," *Blood, Bread, and Poetry* (New York: Norton, 1985), 145.

29. Dewey, *Quest,* 172.

30. Rich, "Resisting Amnesia," 140.

31. Ibid., 141.

32. Ibid., 142.

33. Ibid.

34. Ibid., 143.

35. Ibid., 142.

36. John Salmond, *"My Mind Set on Freedom": A History of the Civil Rights Movement, 1954–1968* (Chicago: Ivan R. Dee, 1997), 153–163.

37. See Crispin Sartwell, *Act Like You Know: African-American Autobiography and White Identity* (Chicago: University of Chicago Press, 1998); Lipsitz, *Investment in Whiteness;* Peggy McIntosh, "White Privilege and Male Privilege: A Personal Account of Coming to See Correspondences through Work in Women's Studies," in *Critical White Studies: Looking Behind the Mirror,* ed. Richard Delgado and Jean Stefancic (Philadelphia: Temple University Press, 1997).

38. Charles Mills, *The Racial Contract* (Ithaca, N.Y.: Cornell University, 1997), 18.

39. Matt Wray and Annalee Newitz eds., *White Trash: Race and Class in America* (New York: Routledge, 1997), 3.

40. bell hooks, *Ain't I a Woman? Black Women and Feminism* (Boston: South End Press, 1981); *Talking Back: Thinking Feminist, Thinking Black* (Boston: South End Press, 1989).

41. bell hooks, *Killing Rage: Ending Racism* (New York: Henry Holt, 1995), 185.

42. Marilyn Frye, *Willful Virgin: Essays in Feminism* (Berkeley, Calif.: Crossing Press, 1992), 151.

43. Ibid., 153.

44. Ibid., 154.

45. Ibid., 156.

46. Allison Bailey, "Locating Traitorous Identities: Toward a View of Privilege-Cognizant White Character," *Hypatia* 13, no. 3 (1998): 34.

47. Sartwell, *Act Like You Know,* 6.

48. Ibid., 9.

49. McIntosh, "White Privilege and Male Privilege," 291.

50. Ibid., 292.

51. Ibid., 293.

52. Kennedy, "Racial Trends," 6.

53. Ruth Frankenberg, *White Women, Race Matters: The Social Construction of Whiteness* (Minneapolis: University of Minneapolis Press, 1993), 14.

8. Contemporary Debates on Whiteness

1. In addition to these defenders of whiteness (understood racially), we can add more sophisticated conservative theorists who also see themselves as defending American values against multiculturalism, but frame their argument in terms of culture rather than race. See Allan Bloom, *The Closing of the American Mind* (New York: Simon and Schuster, 1988), Arthur Schlesinger Jr., *The Disuniting of America* (New York: W. W. Norton, 1991), E. D. Hirsch, *Cultural Literacy* (Boston: Houghton Mifflin, 1987), Dinesh D'Souza, *The End of Racism* (New York: Free Press, 1995).

2. Jared Taylor, *Paved with Good Intentions: The Failure of Race Relations in Contemporary America* (New York: Carroll and Graf Publishers, 1992) as quoted in D'Souza, *The End of Racism,* 388.

3. Chip Berlet and Margaret Quigley, "Theocracy and White Supremacy: Behind the Culture War to Restore Traditional Values" in *Eyes Right!* ed. Chip Berlet (Boston: South End Press, 1995), 15–43.

4. Douglas Frantz and Michael Janofsky, "Politics: On the Move; Buchanan Drawing Extremist Support, and Problems, Too," *New York Times,* February 23, 1996, A23.

5. Paul Craig Roberts and Lawrence M. Stratton, *The New Color Line: How Quotas and Privilege Destroy Democracy* (New York: Regenery Publishing, 1995), 153.

6. For information on the political organization and funding of groups that organize to defend white supremacy and privilege, see Berlet and Quigley, "Theocracy and White Supremacy," in *Eyes Right!* and Schlatter, *Aryan Cowboys.*

7. Masatoshi Nei and Arun Roychoudhury, "Genetic Relationship and Evolution of Human Races," *Evolutionary Biology* 14 (1983): 40.

8. David Kestenbaum, "Genome Announcement," *National Public Radio: All Things Considered,* June 26, 2000, http://www.npr.org/ramfiles/atc/20000626.atc.10.ram, accessed March 25, 2008.

9. Kwame Anthony Appiah, "The Uncompleted Argument: Du Bois and the Illusion of Race," in *"Race," Writing and Difference,* ed. Henry Louis Gates Jr. (Chicago: University of Chicago Press, 1986), 23.

10. Ibid., 35.

11. Naomi Zack, *Race and Mixed Race* (Philadelphia: Temple University Press, 1993), 165.

12. Ibid., 4.

13. Ibid.

14. Naomi Zack, "Race and Philosophical Meaning," in *American Philosophical Association Newsletter on Philosophy and the Black Experience* 91, no. 1 (1994): 14–20.

15. Naomi Zack, "Race, Life, Death, Identity, Tragedy, and Good Faith," in *Existence in Black,* ed. Lewis Gordon (New York: Routledge, 1997), 105.

16. Naomi Zack, introduction, in *Women of Color in Philosophy,* ed. Naomi Zack (Malden, Mass.: Blackwell, 2000), 2.

17. Ibid., 2.

18. Kwame Anthony Appiah, *In My Father's House: Africa in the Philosophy of Culture* (New York: Oxford University Press, 1992).

19. Ibid., 37.

20. Kwame Anthony Appiah, "Race, Culture, Identity: Misunderstood Connections," in *Color Conscious: The Political Morality of Race,* ed. K. Anthony Appiah and Amy Gutmann (Princeton, N.J.: Princeton University Press, 1996), 83.

21. Zack, *Race and Mixed Race,* 2.

22. Naomi Zack, *Thinking about Race,* 2nd ed. (Belmont, Calif.: Wadsworth Publishing, 2006), 108.

23. Ibid.

24. Paul Taylor, "Pragmatism and Race," *Pragmatism and the Problem of Race,* ed. Bill Lawson and Donald Koch (Bloomington: Indiana University Press, 2004), 175.

25. Denise Bostdorff and Steven Goldzwig, "History, Collective Memory, and the Appropriation of Martin Luther King, Jr.: Reagan's Rhetorical Legacy," *Presidential Studies Quarterly* 35, no. 4 (December 2005): 661–90.

26. López, "Race on the 2010 Census," 50.

27. Loury, *Anatomy of Racial Inequality,* 113.

28. D. Micah Hester, "Situating the Self: Concerning an Ethics of Culture and Race," in *Pragmatism and the Problem of Race,* ed. Bill Lawson and Donald Koch (Bloomington: Indiana University Press, 2004), 86.

29. Noel Ignatiev and John Garvey, "Abolish the White Race by Any Means Necessary," in *Race Traitor,* ed. Noel Ignatiev and John Garvey (New York: Routledge, 1996), 10.

30. Ibid.

31. Ibid.

32. Noel Ignatiev, "Immigrants and Whites," in *Race Traitor,* ed. Noel Ignatiev and John Garvey (New York: Routledge, 1996), 21.

33. David Sears, "Symbolic Racism," in *Eliminating Racism: Profiles in Controversy,* ed. Peter Katz and David Sears (New York: Plenum Publishers, 1988), 53–84.

34. Lawrence Bobo, "Racial Attitudes and Relations at the Close of the Twentieth Century," in *America Becoming,* ed. Neil Smelser, William Julius Wilson, and Faith Mitchell, 2 vols. (Washington, D.C.: National Academy Press, 2001) 1:292.

35. Ibid.

36. Dewey, *Human Nature,* 88.

37. Wray and Newitz, introduction, in *White Trash,* 4.

38. Laura Kipnis with Jennifer Reeder, "White Trash Girl," in *White Trash: Race and Class in America,* ed. Matt Wray and Annalee Newitz (New York: Routledge, 1997), 113–30.

39. Du Bois, *Darkwater,* 22.

40. Audre Lorde, "The Master's Tools Will Never Dismantle the Master's House," in *This Bridge Called My Back: Writings by Radical Women of Color,* eds. Cherríe Moraga and Gloria Anzaldúa (New York: Kitchen Table, 1983), 99.

41. John Shuford, "Four Du Boisian Contributions to Critical Race Theory," *Transactions of the Charles S. Peirce Society* 37, no. 3 (2001): 310.

42. Outlaw, *On Race,* 13.

43. Ibid., 157.

44. Ibid., 7.

45. Ibid.

46. Ibid., 21.

47. Shannon Sullivan, *Living Across and Through Skins: Transactional Bodies, Pragmatism, and Feminism* (Bloomington: Indiana University Press, 2001), 158.

48. Ibid., 167.

49. Bailey, "Locating Traitorous Identities"; Linda Martín Alcoff, "What Should White People Do?" *Hypatia* 13, no. 3 (1998): 6–26; Linda Martín Alcoff, "Philosophy and Racial Identity," *Radical Philosophy* 75 (January/February 1996): 5–14.

50. Shuford, "Four Du Boisian Contributions," 319.

51. Du Bois, "Conservation of Races," 819.

52. Rich, "Resisting Amnesia," 144.

9. Habits of Whiteness

1. Dewey, *Human Nature,* 32.

2. Ibid., 65.

3. Ibid., 75.

4. Sullivan, *Revealing Whiteness,* 143.

5. William James, "The Moral Equivalent of War," in *Memories and Studies* (London: Longmans, Green, 1911), 265–96.

6. Dewey, *Human Nature,* 80.

7. Ibid., 90.

8. Du Bois, "The Conservation of Races," 819.

9. Dewey, "Racial Prejudice," 245.

10. Thomas Jefferson, *Notes on the State of Virginia* (1861; New York: Harper and Row, 1964), 133.

11. Noam Chomsky, "Terror and Just Response," in *Terrorism and International Justice,* ed. James Sterba (New York: Oxford University Press, 2003), 73.

12. Neela Banerjee, "Religion Journal: Muslim Staff Members on Mission to Educate Congress," *New York Times,* June 3, 2006. http://www.nytimes.com/, accessed March 12, 2008.

13. Dewey, "Racial Prejudice," 243.

14. Dewey, *Human Nature,* 108.

15. Ibid.

16. Peter Linebaugh and Marcus Rediker, *The Many-Headed Hydra: Sailors, Slaves, Commoners, and the Hidden History of the Revolutionary Atlantic* (Boston: Beacon Press, 2000), 138.

17. Tony Horowitz, "Immigration—The Curse of the Black Legend," *New York Times,* July 9, 2006. http://www.nytimes.com/, accessed February 25, 2008.

18. Ibid.

19. Center for New Community, *Shell Games: The "Minutemen" and Vigilante Anti-Immigrant Politics* (Chicago: Center for New Community, 2005), 5.

20. Nicole Colson, "Two Faces of the Anti-Immigrant Bigots," *Socialist Worker,* August 11, 2006, 5.

21. Jared Taylor, *Paved with Good Intentions,* as quoted in D'Souza, *The End of Racism,* 388.

22. Berlet and Quigley, "Theocracy & White Supremacy," 15–43.

23. Richard Schmitt, "Large Propagators: Racism and the Domination of Women," in *Revealing Male Bodies: Phenomenological and Inscriptive Accounts of Male Embodiment,* ed. Nancy Tuana, William Cowling, Maurice Hamington, Greg Johnson, and Terrance MacMullan (Bloomington: Indiana University Press, 2002), 38–54.

24. Du Bois, *Dusk of Dawn,* 151.

25. Noel Ignatiev, "Treason to Whiteness Is Loyalty to Humanity," in *Critical White Studies,* ed. Richard Delgado and Jean Stefanic (Philadelphia: Temple University Press, 1997), 609.

26. Ward Churchill, *Indians Are Us? Culture and Genocide in Native North America* (Monroe, Maine: Common Courage Press, 1994), 216.

27. Ibid., 220.

28. See Eric Lott, *Love and Theft: Blackface Minstrelsy and the American Working Class* (New York: Oxford University Press, 1993), and N. R. Kleinfiled, "Guarding the Borders of the Hip-Hop Nation," *New York Times,* June 6, 2000, http://www.nytimes.com/, accessed February 25, 2008.

29. Jason Rodriquez, "Color-Blind Ideology and the Cultural Appropriation of Hip-Hop," *Journal of Contemporary Ethnography* 35, no. 6 (2006): 646.

30. Ibid., 655.

31. Ibid.

10. Whiteness Reconstructed

1. Glaude, *In a Shade of Blue,* 130.

2. Dewey, "Racial Prejudice," 242.

3. Ibid., 250.

4. Du Bois, *Dusk of Dawn,* 129.

5. Dewey, "Racial Prejudice," 254.

6. Parents Involved in Community Schools v. Seattle School District No. 1, 551 U.S. 41 (2007)

7. Dewey, "Racial Prejudice," 254.

8. *Parents Involved in Community Schools v. Seattle School District No. 1,* 551 U.S. 68 (2007).

9. John Dewey, "Philosophies of Freedom," in *The Later Works, 1925–1953,* ed. Jo Ann Boydston (1928; Carbondale: Southern Illinois University Press, 1984), 3:101

10. Richard Rorty, *Achieving Our Country* (Cambridge, Mass.: Harvard University Press, 1998), 83.

11. Ibid., 15.

12. Richard Rorty, *Philosophy and Social Hope* (New York: Penguin, 1999), xxii.

13. Rorty, *Achieving Our Country,* 24.

14. James Baldwin, *The Fire Next Time* (1963; New York: Modern English Library, 1995), 103.

15. Du Bois, *Dusk of Dawn,* 117.

16. Du Bois, "The Conservation of Races," 817.

17. Baldwin, *The Fire Next Time,* 101.

18. Ingram, "Toward a Cleaner White(ness)," 250.

19. Homer, *The Iliad,* trans. Richmond Lattimore (Chicago: University of Chicago Press, 1951), 165.

20. Sullivan, *Revealing Whiteness,* 159–60.

21. Anzaldúa, *Borderlands*/La Frontera, 86.

22. James Baldwin, "White Man's Guilt" in *The Price of the Ticket: Collected Nonfiction, 1949–1985* (New York: St. Martin's Press, 1985), 410.

23. Rorty, *Achieving Our Country,* 33.

24. Harris, "Whiteness as Property," 1777.

25. Kevin Graman, "Burying Ground Likely Desecrated," *Spokane Spokesman Review,* June 16, 2007, http://www.spokesmanreview.com/, accessed February 25, 2008.

26. Kevin Graman, "Study Focuses on Grave Desecration," *Spokane Spokesman Review,* June 11, 2007, http://www.spokesmanreview.com/, accessed February 25, 2008.

27. Rorty, *Philosophy and Social Hope,* 253.

28. Lugones, "*Hablando cara a cara*/Speaking Face to Face," 52.

29. James Webb, *Born Fighting,* (New York: Broadway Books, 2004), 8.

30. Ibid., 14.

31. Ibid., 8.

32. Ibid., 208.

33. Ibid., 138.

34. Ibid., 159.

35. Ibid., 214.

36. Richard Rorty, "Solidarity or Objectivity?" in *Objectivity, Relativism, and Truth* (Cambridge: Cambridge University Press, 1991).

37. John Stuhr, *Genealogical Pragmatism* (Albany: State University of New York Press, 1997), 245

38. Sullivan, *Revealing Whiteness,* 191.

39. http://thehill.com/the-executive/sudan-measure-puts-administration-in-tough-spot-2006-02-16.html, accessed February 25, 2008.

40. Please visit http://www.ushmm.org/ for more on how the U.S. Holocaust Memorial Museum is working to stop the genocide in Darfur.

Conclusion

1. See Thomas Cahill, *How the Irish Saved Civilization* (New York: Anchor Books, 1996).

2. Rich, "Resisting Amnesia," 143.

3. Elmer Clarence Sandmeyer, *The Anti-Chinese Movement in California* (Urbana: University of Illinois Press, 1991); Ralph Kauer, *The Workingmen's Party of California* (Berkeley and Los Angeles: University of California Press, 1944).

4. Ward Churchill, *Since Predator Came* (Littleton, Colo.: Aigis Publications, 1995).

5. Anzaldúa, *Borderlands*/La Frontera, 85.

6. Rich, "Resisting Amnesia," 145.

7. Ibid., 148.

8. Ignatiev, *Irish Became White,* 40.

9. *New York World,* January 30, 1877.

10. Tyler Anbinder, *Five Points* (New York: Free Press, 2001), 198.

11. *New York Herald,* July 8, 1844.

12. Anbinder, *Five Points,* 175.

13. Du Bois, *Souls of Black Folk,* 544.

14. John Dewey, "Creative Democracy" in *The Later Works, 1925–1953,* ed. Jo Ann Boydston (1939; Carbondale: Southern Illinois University Press, 1988), 14:228.

15. Du Bois, *The Souls of Black Folk*, in *Writings*, 537.

16. John Dewey, *Art as Experience* in *The Later Works, 1925–1953*, ed. Jo Ann Boydson (1934; Carbondale: Southern Illinois University Press, 1987), 10:329.

17. Dewey, *Art*, 335.

18. Ibid., 337.

19. Ibid.

20. Ignatiev, *Irish Became White*, 35.

21. *The Liberator*, March 25, 1842.

22. Ignatiev, *Irish Became White*, 7.

23. Daniel O'Connell, *Daniel O'Connell upon American Slavery: With Other Irish Testimonies* (Ithaca, N.Y.: Cornell University Library Digital Collection, 1860), 6.

24. Judith Green, "Building a Cosmopolitan World Community through Mutual Hospitality," in *Pragmatism and the Problem of Race*, ed. Bill Lawson and Donald Koch (Bloomington: Indiana University Press, 2004), 204.

Biblioqraphy

Alcoff, Linda Martín. "Philosophy and Racial Identity." *Radical Philosophy* 75 (January/February 1996): 5–14.

———. "What Should White People Do?" *Hypatia* 13, no. 3 (1998): 6–26.

Alexander, Jaqui, and Chandra Talpade Mohanty, eds. *Feminist Genealogies, Colonial Legacies, Democratic Futures*. New York: Routledge, 1997.

Allen, Ernest, Jr. "On Reading of Riddles: Rethinking Du Boisian 'Double Consciousness.'" In *Existence in Black: An Anthology of Black Existential Philosophy*, ed. Lewis Gordon. New York: Routledge, 1997.

Allen, Theodore. *The Invention of the White Race*. 2 vols. New York: Verso, 1994.

Anbinder, Tyler. *Five Points*. New York: Free Press, 2001.

Anzaldúa, Gloria. *Borderlands/ La Frontera: The New Mestiza*. San Francisco: Aunt Lute Books, 1987.

Appiah, Kwame Anthony. "Identity, Authenticity, Survival: Multicultural Societies and Social Reproduction." In *Multiculturalism: Examining the Politics of Recognition*, ed. Amy Gutmann. Princeton, N.J.: Princeton University Press, 1994.

———. *In My Father's House: Africa in the Philosophy of Culture*. New York: Oxford University Press, 1992.

———. "Race, Culture, Identity: Misunderstood Connections." In *Color Conscious: The Political Morality of Race*, ed. K. Anthony Appiah and Amy Gutmann. Princeton, N.J.: Princeton University Press, 1996.

———. "The Uncompleted Argument: Du Bois and the Illusion of Race." In *"Race," Writing and Difference*, ed. Henry Louis Gates Jr. Chicago: University of Chicago Press, 1986.

Appiah, K. Anthony, and Amy Gutmann, eds. In *Color Conscious: The Political Morality of Race*. Princeton, N.J.: Princeton University Press, 1996.

Associated Press. "City Sued over Immigration Ordinance." *Spokesman Review* (Spokane, Wash.), August 16, 2006, A4.

Avila, Eric. *Popular Culture in the Age of White Flight: Fear and Fantasy in Suburban Los Angeles*. Berkeley and Los Angeles: University of California Press, 2006.

Bailey, Alison. "Locating Traitorous Identities: Toward a View of Privilege-Cognizant White Character." *Hypatia* 13, no. 3 (1998): 27–42.

Baldwin, James. *The Fire Next Time*. New York: Dial Press, 1963; reprint, New York: Modern English Library, 1995.

———. *The Price of the Ticket: Collected Nonfiction, 1949–1985*. New York: St. Martin's Press, 1985.

Banerjee, Neela. "Religion Journal: Muslim Staff Members on Mission to Educate Congress." *New York Times*, June 3, 2006; http://nytimes.com/ (accessed March 12, 2008).

Barry, Dan. "The Diallo Case: The Police; One Legacy of a 41-Bullet Barrage Is a Hard Look at Aggressive Tactics." *New York Times*, February 27, 2000, B1.

Berlet, Chip, ed. *Eyes Right!* Boston: South End Press, 1995.

Berlet, Chip, and Margaret Quigley. "Theocracy and White Supremacy: Behind the Culture War to Restore Traditional Values." In *Eyes Right!* ed. Chip Berlet. Boston: South End Press, 1995.

Bernasconi, Robert. *Race.* Malden, Mass.: Blackwell, 2001.

———. "Waking Up White in Memphis." In *White on White/Black on Black,* ed. Geroge Yancy. Lanham, Md.: Rowman and Littlefield Press, 2005.

Bernasconi, Robert, and Tommy Lott, eds. *The Idea of Race.* Indianapolis: Hackett Publishing Company, 2000.

Bernstein, Iver. *The New York City Draft Riots: Their Significance for American Society and Politics in the Age of the Civil War.* New York: Oxford University Press, 1990.

Billings, Warren, ed. *The Old Dominion in the Seventeenth Century: A Documentary History of Virginia, 1606–1689.* Chapel Hill: University of North Carolina Press, 1975.

Bloom, Allan. *The Closing of the American Mind.* New York: Simon and Schuster, 1988.

Blum, Edward. *W. E. B. Du Bois, American Prophet: Politics and Culture in Modern America.* Philadelphia: University of Pennsylvania Press, 2007.

Bobo, Lawrence. "Racial Attitudes and Relations at the Close of the Twentieth Century." In *America Becoming,* ed. Neil Smelser, William Julius Wilson, and Faith Mitchell. 2 vols. Washington, D.C.: National Academy Press, 2001.

Bostdorff, Denise, and Steven Goldzwig. "History, Collective Memory, and the Appropriation of Martin Luther King, Jr.: Reagan's Rhetorical Legacy." *Presidential Studies Quarterly* 35, no. 4 (2005): 661–90.

Brown, Kathleen. *Good Wives, Nasty Wenches, and Anxious Patriarchs: Gender, Race, and Power in Colonial Virginia.* Chapel Hill: University of North Carolina Press, 1996.

Cahill, Thomas. *How the Irish Saved Civilization.* New York: Anchor Books, 1996.

Center for New Community. *Shell Games: The "Minutemen" and Vigilante Anti-Immigrant Politics.* Chicago: Center for New Community, 2005.

Chomsky, Noam. "Terror and Just Response." In *Terrorism and International Justice,* ed. James Sterba. New York: Oxford University Press, 2003.

Churchill, Ward. *Indians Are Us? Culture and Genocide in Native North America.* Monroe, Maine: Common Courage Press, 1994.

———. *Since Predator Came.* Littleton, Colo.: Aigis Publications, 1995.

Colson, Nicole. "Two Faces of the Anti-Immigrant Bigots." *Socialist Worker.* August 11, 2006, 5.

Cook, Anthony. *The Least of These: Race, Law, and Religion in American Culture.* New York: Routledge, 1997.

Crummell, Alexander. *Africa and America: Addresses and Discourses.* Springfield, Mass.: Wiley and Son, 1891.

Davies, Alan. *Infected Christianity: A Study of Modern Racism.* Montreal: McGill-Queen's University Press, 1988.

Davis, Angela. "Masked Racism: Reflections on the Prison Industrial Complex." *Colorlines* 3 (Fall 1998): 10–19.

———. *Women, Race and Class.* New York: Vintage Books, 1983.

Day, Jennifer Cheeseman. *Population Projections of the United States by Age, Sex, Race, and Hispanic Origin: 1995 to 2050.* Washington, D.C.: U.S. Government Printing Office, 1996.

Delgado, Richard, and Stefancic, Jean, eds. *Critical White Studies: Looking behind the Mirror.* Philadelphia: Temple University Press, 1997.

Dewey, John. "Address to the National Association for the Advancement of Colored People." 1932. In *The Later Works, 1925–1953,* vol. 6, ed. Jo Ann Boydston. Carbondale: Southern Illinois University Press, 1985.

———. *Art as Experience.* 1934. In *The Later Works, 1925–1953,* vol. 10, ed. Jo Ann Boydston. Carbondale: Southern Illinois University Press, 1987.

———. "Creative Democracy." 1939. In *The Later Works, 1925–1953,* vol. 14, ed. Jo Ann Boydston. Carbondale: Southern Illinois University Press, 1988.

——. *Democracy and Education.* 1916. In *The Middle Works, 1899–1924,* vol. 9, ed. Jo Ann Boydston. Carbondale: Southern Illinois University Press, 1980.

——. *Ethics.* 1932. In *The Later Works, 1925–1953,* vol. 7, ed. Jo Ann Boydston. Carbondale: Southern Illinois University Press, 1985.

——. *Freedom and Culture.* 1939. In *The Later Works, 1925–1953,* vol. 13, ed. Jo Ann Boydston. Carbondale: Southern Illinois University Press, 1988.

——. *Human Nature and Conduct.* 1922. In *The Middle Works, 1899–1924,* vol. 14, ed. Jo Ann Boydston. Carbondale: Southern Illinois University Press, 1983.

——. *The Influence of Darwin on Philosophy.* New York: Holt, 1910.

——. "Interpretation of the Savage Mind." 1916. In *The Middle Works, 1899–1924,* vol. 2, ed. Jo Ann Boydston. Carbondale: Southern Illinois University Press, 1976.

——. *Logic: The Theory of Inquiry.* 1938. In *The Later Works, 1925–1953,* vol. 12, ed. Jo Ann Boydston. Carbondale: Southern Illinois University Press, 1986.

——. "The Need for a Recovery of Philosophy." 1917. In *The Middle Works, 1899–1924,* vol. 10, ed. Jo Ann Boydston. Carbondale: Southern Illinois University Press, 1980.

——. "Philosophies of Freedom." 1928. In *The Later Works, 1925–1953,* vol. 3, ed. Jo Ann Boydston. Carbondale: Southern Illinois University Press, 1984.

——. *The Quest for Certainty.* 1929. In *The Later Works, 1925–1953,* vol. 4, ed. Jo Ann Boydston. Carbondale: Southern Illinois University Press, 1984.

——. "Racial Prejudice and Friction." 1921. In *The Middle Works, 1899–1924,* vol. 13, ed. Jo Ann Boydston. Carbondale: Southern Illinois University Press, 1983.

Drummond, Tammerlin. "It's Not Just New Jersey; Cops across the U.S. Often Search People Just Because of Their Race, a Study Says." *Time,* June 13, 1999, 61.

D'Souza, Dinesh. *The End of Racism.* New York: Free Press, 1995.

Du Bois, W. E. B. 1897. *Black Reconstruction in America: An Essay toward a History of the Part Which Black Folk Played in the Attempt to Reconstruct Democracy in America, 1860–1880.* 1935. New York: Harcourt and Brace; reprint, New York: Russell and Russell, 1966.

——. "The Conservation of Races." In *W.E.B. Du Bois: Writings.* New York: Library Classics of the United States, 1986.

——. *Darkwater: Voices from Within the Veil.* New York: Harcourt and Brace, 1920; reprint, New York: Dover, 1999.

——. *Dusk of Dawn: An Essay toward an Autobiography of a Race Concept.* New York: Harcourt and Brace, 1940; reprint, New York: Schocken, 1968.

——. Editorial. *Crisis* 7 (1913): 83.

——. "Jacob and Esau." 1944. In *W.E.B. Du Bois Speaks: Speeches and Addresses 1920–1963,* ed. Philip Foner. New York: Pathfinder, 1970.

——. "The Right to Work." 1933. In *W.E.B. Du Bois: Writings.* New York: Library Classics of the United States, 1986.

——. *The Souls of Black Folks.* 1903. In *W.E.B. Du Bois: Writings.* New York: Library Classics of the United States, 1986.

Ehrman, Bart. *Misquoting Jesus.* San Francisco: Harper Publishing, 2005.

Eldridge, Michael. "Dewey on Race and Social Change." In *Pragmatism and the Problem of Race,* ed. Bill Lawson and Donald Koch. Bloomington: Indiana University Press, 2004.

Eze, Emmanuel Chukwudi, ed. *Race and the Enlightenment: A Reader.* Malden, Mass.: Blackwell, 1997.

Foner, Philip, ed. *W.E.B. Du Bois Speaks: Speeches and Addresses 1920–1963.* New York: Pathfinder, 1970.

Frankenberg, Ruth. *White Women, Race Matters: The Social Construction of Whiteness.* Minneapolis: University of Minnesota Press, 1993.

Frantz, Douglas, and Michael Janofsky. "Politics: On the Move; Buchanan Drawing Extremist Support, and Problems, Too." *New York Times,* February 23, 1996, A23.

Fried, Joseph P., and Blaine Harden. "The Louima Case: The Overview; Officer Is Guilty in Torture of Louima." *New York Times,* June 9, 1999, A1.

Fry, Peter, and Fiona Somerset Fry. *A History of Ireland.* New York: Barnes and Noble, 1993.

Frye, Marilyn. *Willful Virgin: Essays in Feminism.* Berkeley, Calif.: Crossing Press, 1992.

Galvin, Patrick. *Irish Songs of Resistance.* New York: Oak Publications, 1962.

Gates, Henry Lewis, Jr., ed. *"Race," Writing, and Difference.* Chicago: University of Chicago Press, 1986.

———. "Thirteen Ways of Looking at a Black Man." *New Yorker,* October 23, 1995, 56, 58–59.

Glaude, Eddie, Jr. "Tragedy and Moral Experience: John Dewey and Toni Morrison's *Beloved.*" In *Pragmatism and the Problem of Race,* ed. Bill Lawson and Donald Koch. Bloomington: Indiana University Press, 2004.

———. *In a Shade of Blue.* Chicago: University of Chicago Press, 2007.

Gobineau, Arthur Comte de. *Selected Political Writings.* 1855. New York: Harper and Row, 1970.

Goldberg, John. "The Color of Suspicion." *New York Times Magazine,* June 20, 1999, 44+.

Gordon, Lewis. *Bad Faith and Anti-Black Racism.* Atlantic Highlands, N.J.: Humanities Press, 1985.

———, ed. *Existence in Black: An Anthology of Black Existential Philosophy.* New York: Routledge, 1997.

Gossett, Thomas. *Race: The History of an Idea in America.* New York: Schocken Books, 1965.

———, ed. *Existence in Black.* New York: Routledge, 1997.

Graman, Kevin. "Burying Ground Likely Desecrated." *Spokesman Review* (Spokane, Wash.). June 16, 2007; http://www.spokesmanreview.com/, accessed February 25, 2008.

———. "Study Focuses on Grave Desecration." *Spokesman Review* (Spokane, Wash.). June 11, 2007; http://www.spokesmanreview.com/, accessed February 25, 2008.

Green, Judith. "Building a Cosmopolitan World Community through Mutual Hospitality." In *Pragmatism and the Problem of Race,* ed. Bill Lawson and Donald Koch. Bloomington: Indiana University Press, 2004.

Gutmann, Amy, ed. *Multiculturalism: Examining the Politics of Recognition.* Princeton, N.J.: Princeton University Press, 1994.

Hacker, Andrew. *Two Nations: Black and White, Separate, Hostile, Unequal.* New York: Scribner, 2003.

Hadden, Sally. *Slave Patrols.* Cambridge, Mass.: Harvard University Press, 2001.

Haney López, Ian. *White by Law: The Legal Construction of Race.* New York: New York University Press, 1996.

———. "Race on the 2010 Census: Hispanics and the Shrinking White Majority." *Daedelus* 134, no. 1 (2005): 42–52.

Harding, Sandra. *Whose Science? Whose Knowledge?* Ithaca, N.Y.: Cornell University Press, 1986.

Harris, Cheryl. "Whiteness as Property." *Harvard Law Review* 106, no. 8 (1993): 1707–93.

Harris, Leonard, ed. *Philosophy Born of Struggle.* Dubuque, Iowa: Dendall/Hunt, 1983.

Heisenberg, Werner. *Physics and Philosophy: The Revolution in Modern Science.* New York: Harper and Brothers, 1958.

Hekman, Susan. *Gender and Knowledge.* Boston: Northeastern University Press, 1990.

Hening, William Waller, ed. *The Statutes at Large; Being a Collection of All the Laws of Virginia, from the First Session of the Legislature.* 13 vols. New York: R. & W. & G. Bartow, 1823.

Hester, D. Micah. "Situating the Self: Concerning an Ethics of Culture and Race." In *Pragmatism and the Problem of Race,* ed. Bill Lawson and Donald Koch. Bloomington: Indiana University Press, 2004.

Hill, Mike, ed. *Whiteness: A Critical Reader.* New York: N. Y. U. Press, 1997.

Hirsch, E. D. *Cultural Literacy.* Boston: Houghton Mifflin, 1987.

Hochschild, Adam. *King Leopold's Ghost: A Story of Greed, Terror, and Heroism in Colonial Africa.* Boston: Houghton Mifflin, 1998.

Holmes, Steven. "The Stark Reality of Racial Profiling." *New York Times,* June 13, 1999, A18.

———. "Race Analysis Cites Disparity in Sentencing for Narcotics." *New York Times,* June 8, 2000, A14.

Homer. *The Iliad.* Trans. Richmond Lattimore. Chicago: University of Chicago Press, 1951.

hooks, bell. *Ain't I a Woman? Black Women and Feminism*. Boston: South End Press, 1981.

———. *Killing Rage: Ending Racism*. New York: Henry Holt, 1995.

———. *Outlaw Culture: Resisting Representations*. New York: Routledge, 1994.

———. *Talking Back: Thinking Feminist, Thinking Black*. Boston: South End Press, 1989.

hooks, bell, and Cornel West. *Breaking Bread: Insurgent Black Intellectual Life*. Boston: South End Press, 1991.

Horne, Gerald. *Black and Red: W.E.B. Du Bois and the Afro-American Response to the Cold War, 1944–1963*. Albany: State University of New York Press, 1986.

Horowitz, Tony. "Immigration—and the Curse of the Black Legend." *New York Times*, July 9, 2006; http://www.nytimes.com/, accessed February 25, 2008.

Husserl, Edmund. *Ideas: A General Introduction to Pure Phenomenology*. Trans. W. R. Boyce Gibson. New York: Collier Books, 1962.

Ignatiev, Noel. *How the Irish Became White*. New York: Routledge, 1995.

———. "Immigrants and Whites." In *Race Traitor*, ed. Noel Ignatiev and John Garvey. New York: Routledge, 1996.

———. "Treason to Whiteness Is Loyalty to Humanity." In *Critical White Studies*, ed. Richard Delgado and Jean Stefanic. Philadelphia: Temple University Press, 1997.

Ignatiev, Noel, and John Garvey. "Abolish the White Race by Any Means Necessary." In *Race Traitor*, ed. Noel Ignatiev and John Garvey. New York: Routledge, 1996.

———, eds. *Race Traitor*. New York: Routledge, 1996.

Ingram, David. "Toward a Cleaner White(ness): New Racial Identities." *Philosophical Forum* 36, no. 3 (2005): 243–77.

Jacobson, Matthew Frye. *Whiteness of a Different Color: European Immigrants and the Alchemy of Race*. Cambridge, Mass.: Harvard University Press, 1998.

James, William. *Memories and Studies*. London: Longmans, Green, 1911.

Jefferson, Thomas. *Notes on the State of Virginia*. 1861. New York: Harper and Row, 1964.

Jones, Prudence, and Nigel Pennick. *A History of Pagan Europe*. New York: Routledge, 1995.

Jordan, Winthrop. *White over Black: American Attitudes towards the Negro, 1550–1812*. Chapel Hill: University of North Carolina Press, 1968.

Kant, Immanuel. "An Answer to the Question 'What Is Enlightenment?'" In *Perpetual Peace and Other Essays*. Trans. Ted Humphrey. Indianapolis: Hackett, 1983.

Katz, Peter, and David Sears, eds. *Eliminating Racism: Profiles in Controversy*. New York: Plenum Publishers, 1988.

Kauer, Ralph. *The Workingmen's Party of California*. Berkeley and Los Angeles: University of California Press, 1944.

Kennedy, Randall. "Racial Trends in the Administration of Criminal Justice." *America Becoming*, ed. Neil Smelser, William Julius Wilson, and Faith Mitchell. 2 vols. Washington, D.C.: National Academy Press, 2001.

Kestenbaum, David. "Genome Announcement." *National Public Radio: All Things Considered*, June 26, 2000; http://www.npr.org/templates/story/story.php?storyId=1075911, accessed March 25, 2008.

Kifner, John. "Van Shooting Revives Charges of Racial 'Profiling' by New Jersey State Police." *New York Times*, May 10, 1998, B1.

Kipnis, Laura, with Jennifer Reeder. "White Trash Girl." In *White Trash: Race and Class in America*, ed. Matt Wray and Annalee Newitz. New York: Routledge, 1997.

Kleinfiled, N. R. "Guarding the Borders of the Hip-Hop Nation." *New York Times*, June 6, 2000; http://www.nytimes.com/, accessed February 25, 2008.

Kochieniewski, David. "Minority Drivers Tell of Troopers' Racial Profiling." *New York Times*, April 14, 1999, B1.

Kruse, Kevin. *White Flight: Atlanta and the Making of Modern Conservatism*. Princeton, N.J.: Princeton University Press, 2005.

Lawson, Bill, and Donald Koch, eds. *Pragmatism and the Problem of Race*. Bloomington: Indiana University Press, 2004.

Linebaugh, Peter, and Marcus Rediker. *The Many-Headed Hydra: Sailors, Slaves, Commoners, and the Hidden History of the Revolutionary Atlantic.* Boston: Beacon Press, 2000.

Lipsitz, George. *The Possessive Investment in Whiteness: How White People Benefit from Identity Politics.* Philadelphia: Temple University Press, 1998.

Lorde, Audre. "The Master's Tools Will Never Dismantle the Master's House." In *This Bridge Called My Back: Writings by Radical Women of Color,* ed. Cherríe Moraga and Gloria Anzaldúa. New York: Kitchen Table, 1983.

Lott, Eric. *Love and Theft: Blackface Minstrelsy and the American Working Class.* New York: Oxford University Press, 1993.

Loury, Glenn. *The Anatomy of Racial Inequality.* Cambridge, Mass.: Harvard University Press, 2002.

Lugones, María. "*Hablando cara a cara*/Speaking Face to Face." In *Making Face, Making Soul/ Haciendo Caras,* ed. Gloria Anzaldúa. San Francisco: Aunt Lute Books, 1990.

———. "Playfulness, 'World' Traveling, and Loving Perception." *Hypatia* 12, no. 2 (1987): 3–19.

Lusane, Clarence. *Pipe Dream Blues: Racism and the War on Drugs.* Boston: South End Press, 1991.

McCague, James. *The Second Rebellion: The Story of the New York City Draft Riots of 1863.* New York: Dial Press, 1968.

McClean, David. "Should We Conserve the Notion of Race?" In *Pragmatism and the Problem of Race,* ed. Bill Lawson and Donald Koch. Bloomington: Indiana University Press, 2004.

McIntosh, Peggy. "White Privilege and Male Privilege: A Personal Account of Coming to See Correspondences through Work in Women's Studies." In *Critical White Studies: Looking behind the Mirror,* ed. Richard Delgado and Jean Stefancic. Philadelphia: Temple University Press, 1997.

Meranto, Philip, ed. *The Kerner Report Revisited.* Chicago: Institute of Government and Public Affairs, University of Illinois, 1970.

Merleau-Ponty, Maurice. *Phenomenology of Perception.* Trans. Colin Smith. London: Routledge, 1962.

Mills, Charles. *The Racial Contract.* Ithaca, N.Y.: Cornell University Press, 1997.

Moraga, Cherrie, and Gloria Anzaldúa, eds. *This Bridge Called My Back: Writings by Radical Women of Color.* New York: Kitchen Table, 1981.

Morgan, Edmund S. *American Slavery, American Freedom: The Ordeal of Colonial Virginia.* New York: Norton, 1975.

Moses, Wilson Jeremiah. *Alexander Crummell.* New York: Oxford University Press, 1989.

Moya, Paula. "Postmodernism, 'Realism,' and the Politics of Identity: Cherrie Moraga and Chicana Feminism." In *Feminist Genealogies, Colonial Legacies, Democratic Futures,* ed. Jaqui Alexander and Chandra Talpade Mohanty. New York: Routledge, 1997.

Nagourney, Adam, and Thee, Megan. "Poll Finds Obama Isn't Closing Divide on Race." *New York Times,* July 16, 2008, A1.

National Advisory Committee on Civil Disorders. *Report of the National Advisory Commission on Civil Disorders.* New York: E. P. Dutton, 1968.

Nei, Masatoshi, and Arun Roychoudhury. "Genetic Relationship and Evolution of Human Races." *Evolutionary Biology* 14 (1983): 36–54.

Nelson, Lynn Hankinson. *Who Knows: From Quine to a Feminist Empiricism.* Philadelphia: Temple University Press, 1990.

New York Times. Editorial, April 18, 2001, A22.

Obama, Barack. "Speech on Race." Philadelphia, Pa. March 18. Reprinted in *New York Times,* March 18, 2008; http://www.nytimes.com/2008/03/18/us/politics/18text-obama.html, accessed March 19, 2008.

O'Connell, Daniel. *Daniel O'Connell upon American Slavery: With Other Irish Testimonies.* 1860. Ithaca, N.Y.: Cornell University Library Digital Collection.

Omi, Michael, and Howards Wynant. *Racial Formation in the United States from the 1960s to the 1980s.* New York: Routledge, 1994.

Outlaw, Lucius T. (Jr.). *On Race and Philosophy.* New York: Routledge, 1996.

Perry, Ralph Barton. "The Ego-Centric Predicament." *Journal of Philosophy, Psychology and Scientific Methods* 7, no. 1 (1910): 1–19.

Phillips, Kevin. *American Theocracy.* New York: Viking, 2006.

Pratt, Scott. *Native Pragmatism.* Bloomington: Indiana University Press, 2002.

Public Safety Performance Project. *One in 100: Behind Bars in America 2008.* Washington, D.C.: Pew Charitable Trusts, 2008.

Rich, Adrienne. *Blood, Bread, and Poetry.* New York: Norton, 1985.

Roberts, Paul Craig, and Lawrence Stratton M. *The New Color Line: How Quotas and Privilege Destroy Democracy.* New York: Regenery Publishing, 1995.

Rodriquez, Jason. "Color-Blind Ideology and the Cultural Appropriation of Hip-Hop." *Journal of Contemporary Ethnography* 35, no. 6 (2006): 645–68.

Roediger, David. *The Wages of Whiteness: Race and the Making of the American Working Class.* London: Verso, 1991.

Roosevelt, Theodore. *The Winning of the West.* 7 vols. New York: G. P. Putnam's Sons, 1907.

Rorty, Richard. *Achieving Our Country.* Cambridge, Mass.: Harvard University Press, 1998.

———. *Objectivity, Relativism, and Truth.* Cambridge: Cambridge University Press, 1991.

———. *Philosophy and Social Hope.* New York: Penguin, 1999.

Russell, Kathryn. "Racial Profiling: A Status Report of the Legal, Legislative and Empirical Literature." *Rutgers Race and Law Review* 3 (2001): 61, 68–80.

Salmond, John. *"My Mind Set on Freedom": A History of the Civil Rights Movement, 1954–1968.* Chicago: Ivan R. Dee, 1997.

Sandmeyer, Elmer Clarence. *The Anti-Chinese Movement in California.* Urbana: University of Illinois Press, 1991.

Sartwell, Crispin. *Act Like You Know: African-American Autobiography and White Identity.* Chicago: University of Chicago Press, 1998.

Schlatter, Evelyn. *Aryan Cowboys: White Supremacist Ideology and the Search for a New Frontier, 1960–1995.* Diss., University of New Mexico, 2000. Ann Arbor: UMI. 9983116.

Schlesinger, Arthur, Jr. *The Disuniting of America.* New York: W. W. Norton, 1991.

Schmitt, Richard. "Large Propagators: Racism and the Domination of Women." In *Revealing Male Bodies: Phenomenological and Inscriptive Accounts of Male Embodiment,* ed. Nancy Tuana, William Cowling, Maurice Hamington, Greg Johnson, and Terrance MacMullan. Bloomington: Indiana University Press, 2002.

Sears, David. "Symbolic Racism." In *Eliminating Racism: Profiles in Controversy,* ed. Peter Katz and David Sears. New York: Plenum Publishers, 1988.

Shuford, John. "Four Du Boisian Contributions to Critical Race Theory." *Transactions of the Charles S. Peirce Society* 37, no. 3 (2001): 301–37.

Slotkin, Richard. *Gunfighter Nation: The Myth of the Frontier in Twentieth-Century America.* New York: Harper Perennial, 1993.

———. *Regeneration through Violence: The Mythology of the American Frontier, 1600–1860.* Middletown, Conn.: Wesleyan University Press, 1973.

Smelser, Neil, William Julius Wilson, and Faith Mitchell, eds. *America Becoming.* 2 vols. Washington, D.C.: National Academy Press, 2001.

Smothers, Ronald. "Rights Charges Filed in Death of a Man Wrongly Arrested." *New York Times,* June 21, 2000, A27.

Somerset Fry, Peter, and Fiona Somerset Fry. *A History of Ireland.* New York: Barnes and Noble, 1993.

Sterba, James, ed. *Terrorism and International Justice.* New York: Oxford University Press, 2003.

Stuhr, John. *Genealogical Pragmatism.* Albany: State University of New York Press, 1997.

Sullivan, Shannon. "From the Foreign to the Familiar: Confronting Dewey Confronting Racial Prejudice." *Journal of Speculative Philosophy* 18, no. 3 (2004): 193–202.

———. *Living Across and Through Skins: Transactional Bodies, Pragmatism, and Feminism.* Bloomington: Indiana University Press, 2001.

———. *Revealing Whiteness: The Unconscious Habits of Racial Privilege.* Bloomington: Indiana University Press, 2005.

Taylor, Jared. *Paved with Good Intentions: The Failure of Race Relations in Contemporary America.* New York: Carroll and Graf Publishers, 1992.

Taylor, Paul. "Pragmatism and Race." In *Pragmatism and the Problem of Race,* ed. Bill Lawson and Donald Koch. Bloomington: Indiana University Press, 2004.

———. "What's the Use of Calling Du Bois a Pragmatist?" *Metaphilosophy* 35, no. 1/2 (2004): 99–114.

Tuana, Nancy, ed. *Feminism and Science.* Bloomington: Indiana University Press, 1989.

Tuana, Nancy, William Cowling, Maurice Hamington, Greg Johnson, and Terrance MacMullan, eds. *Revealing Male Bodies: Phenomenological and Inscriptive Accounts of Male Embodiment.* Bloomington: Indiana University Press, 2002.

United States Commission on Civil Disorders. 1968. *Report on the National Advisory Commission on Civil Disorders.* New York: E. P. Dutton.

United States Congress. *Annals of Congress: Abridgements of the Debates of Congress, 1789–1856.* 2 vols. New York: D. Appleton, 1857.

United States Supreme Court. *Parents Involved in Community Schools v. Seattle School District No. 1,* 551 U.S. 2007.

Wallis, Jim. *God's Politics.* San Francisco: Harper Publishing, 2005.

Washburn, Wilcomb. *The Governor and the Rebel: A History of Bacon's Rebellion in Virginia.* Chapel Hill: University of North Carolina Press, 1957.

Washington, Booker T. *The Future of the American Negro.* New York, 1899.

Webb, James. *Born Fighting.* New York: Broadway Books, 2004.

Webb, Stephen. *1676: The End of American Independence.* New York: Knopf, 1984.

West, Cornel. *The American Evasion of Philosophy: A Genealogy of Pragmatism.* Madison: University of Wisconsin, 1989.

———. *Keeping Faith: Philosophy and Race in America.* New York: Routledge, 1993.

———. "Obama and the Blues: Interview by Robert S. Boynton." *Rolling Stone,* issue 1048 (March 20, 2008): 42.

———. *Prophesy Deliverance! An Afro-American Revolutionary Christianity.* Philadelphia: Westminster Press, 1982.

White, Ronald. *Liberty and Justice for All: Racial Reform and the Social Gospel.* San Francisco: Harper and Row, 1990.

Williams, William. *'Twas Only an Irishman's Dream.* Urbana: University of Chicago Press, 1996.

Wray, Matt, and Annalee Newitz, eds. *White Trash: Race and Class in America.* New York: Routledge, 1997.

Yancy, George, ed. *White on White/Black on Black.* Lanham, Md.: Rowman and Littlefield, 2005.

Zack, Naomi. Introduction. In *Women of Color in Philosophy,* ed. Naomi Zack. Malden, Mass.: Blackwell, 2000.

———. *Race and Mixed Race.* Philadelphia: Temple University Press, 1993.

———. "Race and Philosophical Meaning." *American Philosophical Association Newsletter on Philosophy and the Black Experience* 91, no. 1 (1994): 14–20.

———. "Race, Life, Death, Identity, Tragedy and Good Faith." In *Existence in Black,* ed. Lewis Gordon. New York: Routledge, 1997.

———. *Thinking about Race.* 2nd ed. Belmont, Calif.: Wadsworth Publishing, 2006.

———, ed. *Women of Color in Philosophy.* Malden, Mass.: Blackwell, 2000.

Zamir, Shamoon. *Dark Voices: W.E.B. Du Bois and American Thought, 1888–1903.* Chicago: University of Chicago Press, 1995.

Zinn, Howard. *A People's History of the United States: 1492–Present.* New York: Harper Collins, 1999.

Index

TERRANCE MACMULLAN is Associate Professor of Philosophy and Honors and president of the faculty organization at Eastern Washington University. He is editor (with Nancy Tuana, William Cowling, Maurice Hamington, and Greg Johnson) of *Revealing Male Bodies* (Indiana University Press, 2002).